DATE DUE

AP 21 '03			

DEMCO 38-296

In *The Creation of a Republican Empire, 1776–1865,* Bradford Perkins traces American foreign relations from the colonial era to the end of the Civil War, paying particular attention not only to the diplomatic controversies of the era but also to the origins and development of a uniquely American approach to international relations. The primary purpose of the book is to describe and explain, in the diplomatic context, the process by which the United States was born, transformed into a republican nation, and extended into a continental empire.

The story begins with the events surrounding the American Revolution, the French alliance, and the peacemaking process that ended the Revolution and provided the United States with a "great empire" stretching to the Mississippi River. It continues with accounts of the chain of events, touched off by the French Revolution, leading to the War of 1812, as well as the American reaction to revolutions in Latin America and the promulgation of the Monroe Doctrine. Professor Perkins is also concerned with the territorial expansion of the American "empire" — the Louisiana Purchase, the treaty with Spain in 1819 that obtained Florida for the United States and drove a boundary to the Pacific, the annexation of Texas, the Oregon settlement, and the war with Mexico, which forced the southern country to cede the Southwest and Californian territory to the United States. During the Civil War, the success of the North's diplomacy, the author argues, played no small part in the preservation of a unified empire. Thus the years 1776 to 1865 saw the United States secure independence and national commercial rights and, by negotiation and pillage, build the geographic base for its future as a world power.

Exploring a theme that is carried throughout the four volumes of *The Cambridge History of American Foreign Relations,* Professor Perkins also considers constitutional aspects of the nation's diplomacy. He discusses the origins of provisions of the Constitution, the intent of its framers, and the subsequent development of, and debate over, constitutional powers, particularly those of the president.

The Cambridge History of American Foreign Relations

Volume I
The Creation of a Republican Empire, 1776–1865

THE CAMBRIDGE HISTORY OF AMERICAN FOREIGN RELATIONS

Warren I. Cohen, Editor

THE CAMBRIDGE HISTORY
OF
AMERICAN FOREIGN RELATIONS

Volume I
The Creation of a Republican Empire, 1776–1865

BRADFORD PERKINS

CAMBRIDGE
UNIVERSITY PRESS

Published by the Press Syndicate of the University of Cambridge
The Pitt Building, Trumpington Street, Cambridge CB2 1RP
40 West 20th Street, New York, NY 10011-4211, USA
10 Stamford Road, Oakleigh, Melbourne 3166, Australia

First published 1993

Printed in the United States of America

ataloging-in-Publication Data
Bradford, 1925–
can foreign relations / Bradford Perkins.
p.   cm.
hical references and index.
ican empire, 1776–1865 – v. 2. The American
. 3. The globalizing of America, 1913–1945 –
e of Soviet power, 1945–1991.
ISBN 0-521-38209-2 (vol 1). – ISBN 0-521-38185-1 (vol 2).
1. United States – Foreign relations. I. Title.
E183.7.P45   1993
327.73 – dc20   92-36165
                                       CIP

A catalog record for this book is available from the British Library

ISBN 0-521-38209-2 hardback

Contents

Maps

General Editor's Introduction

My goal for the Cambridge History of American Foreign Relations was to make the finest scholarship and the best writing in the historical profession available to the general reader. I had no ideological or methodological agenda. I wanted some of America's leading students of diplomatic history, regardless of approach, to join me and was delighted to have my invitations accepted by the first three to whom I turned. When I conceived of the project nearly ten years ago, I had no idea that the Cold War would suddenly end, that these volumes would conclude with a final epoch as well defined as the first three. The collapse of the Soviet empire, just as I finished writing Volume IV, astonished me but allowed for a sense of completion these volumes would have lacked under any other circumstances.

The first volume has been written by Bradford Perkins, the preeminent historian of late eighteenth- and early nineteenth-century American diplomacy and doyen of currently active diplomatic historians. Perkins sees foreign policy in the young Republic as a product of material interests, culture, and the prism of national values. He describes an American pattern of behavior that existed before there was an America and demonstrates how it was shaped by the experience of the Revolution and the early days of the Republic. In his discussion of the Constitution and foreign affairs, he spins a thread that can be pulled through the remaining volumes: the persistent effort of presidents, beginning with Washington, to dominate policy, contrary to the intent of the participants in the Constitutional Convention.

The inescapable theme of Perkins's volume is presaged in its title, the ideological commitment to republican values and the determination to carry those values across the North American continent and to obliterate all obstacles, human as well as geological. He sees the American empire arising out of lust for land and resources rather than for dominion over other peoples. But it was dominion over others – native Americans, Mexicans, and especially African Americans – that led to the last episode he discusses, the Civil War and its diplomacy. This is a magnificent survey of the years in which the United States emerged as a nation and created the foundations for world power that would come in the closing years of the nineteenth century.

Walter LaFeber, author of the second volume, is one of the most highly respected of the so-called Wisconsin School of diplomatic historians, men and women who studied with Fred Harvey Harrington and William Appleman Williams and their students, and were identified as "New Left" when they burst on the scene in the 1960s. LaFeber's volume covers the last third of the nineteenth century and extends into the twentieth, to 1913, through the administration of William Howard Taft. He discusses the link between the growth of American economic power and expansionism, adding the theme of racism, especially as applied to native Americans and Filipinos. Most striking is his rejection of the idea of an American quest for order. He argues that Americans sought opportunities for economic and missionary activities abroad and that they were undaunted by the disruptions they caused in other nations. A revolution in China or Mexico was a small price to pay for advantages accruing to Americans, especially when the local people paid it. His other inescapable theme is the use of foreign affairs to enhance presidential power.

The third volume, which begins on the eve of World War I and carries the story through World War II, is by Akira Iriye, past president of the American Historical Association and our generation's most innovative historian of international relations. Japanese-born, educated in American universities, Iriye has been fascinated by the cultural conflicts and accommodations that permeate power politics, particularly as the United States has confronted the nations of East Asia. Iriye opens his book with a quick sketch of the international system as it evolved and was dominated by Europe through the seventeenth, eighteenth, and nineteenth centuries. He analyzes Wilsonianism in war and peace and how it was applied in Asia and Latin America. Most striking is his discussion of what he calls the "cultural aspect" of the 1920s. Iriye sees the era about which he writes as constituting the "globalizing of America" – an age in which the United States supplanted Europe as the world's leader and provided the economic and cultural resources to define and sustain the international order. He notes the awakening of non-Western peoples and their expectations of American support and inspiration. In his conclusion he presages the troubles that would follow from the Americanization of the world.

Much of my work, like Iriye's, has focused on American–East Asian relations. My friend Michael Hunt has placed me in the "realist" school of diplomatic historians. Influenced by association with Perkins, LaFeber, Iriye, Ernest May, and younger friends such as John Lewis Gaddis, Michael Hogan, and Melvyn Leffler, I have studied the domestic roots of American policy, the role of ideas and attitudes as well as economic concerns, the role of nongovernmental organizations including missionaries, and the place of art in international relations. In the final volume of the series, *America in the Age of Soviet Power, 1945–1991,* I also rely heavily on what I have learned from political economists and political scientists.

I begin the book in the closing months of World War II and end it with the disappearance of the Soviet Union in 1991. I write of the vision American leaders had of a postwar world order and the growing sense that the Soviet Union posed a threat to that vision. The concept of the "security dilemma," the threat each side's defensive actions seemed to pose for the other, looms large in my analysis of the origins of the Cold War. I also emphasize the importance of the two political systems, the paradox of the powerful state and weak government in the United States and the secrecy and brutality of the Stalinist regime. Throughout the volume, I note the importance of the disintegration of prewar colonial empires, the appearance of scores of newly independent states in Africa, Asia, and Latin America, and the turmoil caused by American and Soviet efforts to force them into an international system designed in Washington and Moscow. Finally, I trace the reemergence of Germany and Japan as major powers, the collapse of the Soviet Union, and the drift of the United States, its course in world affairs uncertain in the absence of an adversary.

There are a number of themes that can be followed through these four volumes, however differently the authors approach their subjects. First, there was the relentless national pursuit of wealth and power, described so vividly by Perkins and LaFeber. Iriye demonstrates how Americans used their wealth and power when the United States emerged as the world's leader after World War I. I discuss America's performance as hegemon in the years immediately following World War II, and its response to perceived threats to its dominance.

A second theme of critical importance is the struggle for control of foreign policy. Each author notes tension between the president and Congress, as institutionalized by the Constitution, and the efforts of various presidents, from 1789 to the present, to circumvent constitutional restraints on their powers. The threat to democratic government is illustrated readily by the Nixon-Kissinger obsessions that led to Watergate and Reagan's Iran-Contra fiasco.

Finally, we are all concerned with what constitutes American identity on the world scene. Is there a peculiarly American foreign policy that sets the United States off from the rest of the world? We examine the evolution of American values and measure them against the nation's behavior in international affairs. And we worry about the impact of the country's global activity on its domestic order, fearful that Thomas Jefferson's vision of a virtuous republic has been forgotten, boding ill for Americans and for the world they are allegedly "bound to lead."

WARREN I. COHEN

Preface

This volume, examining as it does the foreign relations of the United States for almost the first century of its existence, necessarily cannot be comprehensive. Although I trust that I have not omitted major developments, I have felt free to neglect minor ones that, in my opinion, do not relate to the central theme.

That theme, as the title proclaims, is the creation of a republican empire stretching from the Atlantic Ocean to the Pacific. Territorial expansion is, of course, a major part of the story, but so too is the establishment of independence, the creation of an idiosyncratic view of world politics, the framing of a republican constitution and republican patterns of diplomacy, the dangers posed to a fragile young nation by the wars of the French Revolution and Napoleon, and the defeat, in the Civil War, of the great effort to destroy the empire.

The reader will quickly discern that I do not write in a hagiographic spirit. Americans and their policymakers often stumbled, they were sometimes driven by ignoble forces and ignorance as well, and at least some even of the great successes might have been attained at less cost. This is an opinionated book, although I hope my opinions are grounded on fact, and I have not hesitated to pass negative judgments when I have felt that they were called for.

Major portions of this book are based on my own researches in archives here and abroad while preparing earlier writings. In those parts of the work, however, I have incorporated findings of others, particularly those who wrote after my own books appeared, and in the other sections I rely even more heavily on my professional colleagues. If this book has merit, it is largely to their credit.

More specifically, I am grateful to my colleagues Sidney Fine and

Shaw Livermore, Jr., and to an enthusiastic "amateur," Warren E. Poitras, for their helpful readings of the manuscript. As always, for that service, but also for encouragement and support, I am especially indebted to my wife, Nancy. I also thank my youngest son, James, who frequently asked when I was going to finish my task.

1. *The Canvas and the Prism*

In One Man's Lifetime

On June 17, 1775, an eight-year-old boy, led by his mother to a height near their home, watched the distant smoke of the Battle of Bunker Hill. There was no American nation, or even claim of one, until the next year. Thirteen British colonies, with a free population of about a million and a half, straggled near the Atlantic Coast from Passamaquoddy Bay to the St. Marys River.

The sole cluster of settlement far inland was in Kentucky. Only ten towns had more than 5,000 inhabitants, although 35,000 people lived in Philadelphia. In that city, second in size only to London in the British Empire, the boy's father was serving in the Continental Congress.

Three years later, John Quincy Adams sailed to Europe. During most of the rest of the Revolution he served as secretary to his father, in diplomatic service in Paris and The Hague, and to Francis Dana, an emissary sent to the court of Catherine the Great in a futile attempt to gain Russian recognition. In 1783, he returned to Paris, making a long overland journey, shortly after his father, Benjamin Franklin, John Jay, and Henry Laurens had signed the treaty that ended the American Revolution and provided the United States with a "great empire," nearly 900,000 square miles stretching to the Mississippi River.

After a short career at Harvard (he graduated Phi Beta Kappa after two years in residence) and a few years in law, young Adams turned to politics. He endorsed the Constitution, which, for the first time, provided the U.S. government with powers essential to effective bargaining in international affairs. Like his father, when parties emerged he became a Federalist, albeit an independent one.

In 1794, President Washington sent the younger Adams to Hol-

1

land as minister, then on a brief mission to London to tidy up loose ends connected with Jay's Treaty, the first major international agreement reached by the new government. During his father's presidency, from 1797 to 1801, he remained abroad, observing from the sidelines his country's undeclared war with France, the first of two occasions when the United States was drawn into the great wars touched off by the French Revolution. With Jefferson's accession, he lost his post.

Massachusetts Federalists sent Adams to the Senate in 1803. After an arduous carriage trip of three weeks, he reached Washington one day too late to vote on the Louisiana Purchase. All other Federalist senators voted against it, essentially because they feared that western settlement would cost their party power and influence. Adams himself believed the purchase unconstitutional, a not unreasonable position since Jefferson, though the buyer, more than half agreed that nothing in the Constitution authorized the government to annex territory. However, valuing national expansion and relieved to see France deprived of a lodgement on the North American continent, the new senator voted for the appropriations – about $15 million – to complete the deal.

At about the same time, the war in Europe resumed after a short intermission. American commerce soon suffered severely at the hands both of the British and the French. Some of Adams's Federalist colleagues, particularly those from Massachusetts, let sympathies for Britain and hatred for Jefferson drive them to the verge of treason. Adams moved in an opposite direction, supporting resistance to attacks upon American interests and honor. In 1807, he served on the Senate committee that endorsed Jefferson's request for an embargo on foreign trade, though this was universally disapproved by other Federalists. "This measure," he said to a committee colleague, "will cost you and me our seats, but private interest must not be put in opposition to public good." The prediction proved accurate: Massachusetts elected a successor even before Adams's term expired. He promptly resigned from the Senate.

In 1809, after the Senate rejected his first nominee, James Madison named Adams minister to Russia. At St. Petersburg, where he became the first American minister formally recognized by the Russian government, Adams worked to secure good treatment for American commerce. He developed warm relations with Tsar Alexander I; they often strolled on the banks of the Neva together, talking all the while about every subject under the sun. Toward the end of his mission, he observed the defeat of Napoleon's invasion in 1812. "The politicians who have been dreading so long the phantom of universal monarchy may now rest their souls in peace," he wrote his father, referring to Americans who used the bogey of Napoleon to support their calls for close ties with England.

At the same time, he watched from afar, and with growing discouragement, the tangled and indeed disgraceful antics of American politicians seeking to reconcile the irreconcilable — peace, prosperity, and honor — in the face of British and French attacks upon neutral trade. When at last, in 1812, Britain relaxed assaults on American trade, Adams rejoiced. Within weeks he learned that, before this news reached Washington, Madison and the Congress had resigned themselves to war. Adams regretted the misfortune of war, believing that "its principal cause and justification was removed at precisely the moment when it occurred," but also considered it a perhaps necessary test of American republicanism.

Thus far, to his forty-seventh year, Adams had been on the fringes of diplomacy, an actor but not a major one. For the next sixteen years, he was to be the dominant figure, first as one of the negotiators of the treaty that ended the War of 1812, then as secretary of state for nearly eight years, finally as president. As secretary, among other things, he negotiated the Spanish treaty of 1819, which gained Florida for the United States and drove a western boundary through to the Pacific, and in the autumn of 1823 played a role not even second to that of the president in development of the Monroe Doctrine.

Adams's own presidency, from 1825 to 1829, was unhappy in all respects, primarily because, although he was the first chief executive to give up knee breeches for the modern dress of trousers, he was out of touch with the emerging spirit of Jacksonian America. His mismanagement of the central diplomatic issue, restrictions on American trade with Britain's Caribbean colonies, and the failure of his effort to buy Texas from Mexico, newly independent of Spain, merely conformed to the pattern of his administration.

Routed by Andrew Jackson when he sought reelection, Adams soon began a new political career in the House of Representatives, where, now a Whig, he served for seventeen years. Toward the end of this career, the expansionist surge called Manifest Destiny swept the nation. Adams had long been an expansionist, writing years before that the United States was destined to be "coextensive with the North American Continent, destined by God and by nature to be the most populous and powerful people ever combined under one social contract," but the old fire was gone. He supported the American claim to the entire Oregon country, citing the arcane legal and diplomatic record as well as the Bible to support it. On one occasion, he had the House clerk read from the Book of Psalms, "Ask of me, and I shall give thee the heathen for thine inheritance, and the uttermost parts of the earth for thy possession," a clear reference, Adams thought, to the Americans, who were God's "chosen people." When President Polk settled the matter by compromise, however, Adams did not protest. He did strongly oppose the annexation of Texas and, as much as failing health would allow, the war with Mexico. In both instances, the abolitionist emphasis of his later career was the principal reason; he saw these expansionist drives not as national but rather as slavery-driven ones.

In February 1848, Adams suffered a stroke on the floor of the House of Representatives; two days later he died in the Capitol. "Where could death have found him," asked his former foe and recent ally, Senator Thomas Hart Benton of Missouri, "but at the post of duty?" The very day that Adams collapsed, the president received word that Mexico had agreed, as the price of peace, to cede the Southwest and California. These acquisitions, and the Oregon settlement, increased the size of the United States to more than 3 million square miles, making it a continental empire with a white population of more than 20 million.[1]

Thus events from 1775 on unrolled with amazing rapidity. The United States secured independence; created a constitution, which

1 A small acquisition from Mexico, the Gadsden Purchase, rounded out the boundaries of the forty-eight states in 1853. Alaska and Hawaii, which became states much later, were acquired in 1867 and 1898 respectively.

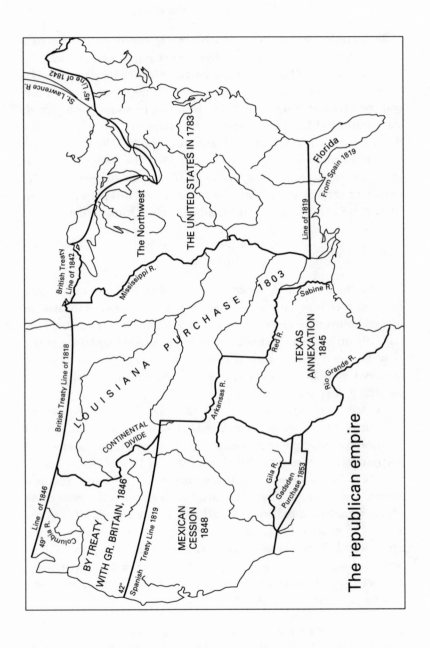

45°

Line of 1842

St. Lawrence R.

British Treaty
Line of 1842

THE UNITED STATES IN 1783

The Northwest

Florida
From Spain 1819

Line of 1819

Mississippi R.

L O U I S I A N A   P U R C H A S E   1803

British Treaty Line of 1818

Sabine R.

Red R.

TEXAS
ANNEXATION
1845

Rio Grande R.

Arkansas R.

CONTINENTAL
DIVIDE

Line of 1846

Columbia R.

49°

BY TREATY
WITH GR. BRITAIN, 1846

42°

Spanish Treaty Line 1819

MEXICAN
CESSION
1848

Gila R.

Gadsden
Purchase 1853

The republican empire

made possible the wielding of national power; survived the dangerous years of the wars of the French Revolution and Napoleon; and, by negotiation and pillage, built the geographic base for its future as a world power. As Adams had feared, however, the annexation of Texas and the Mexican cession sundered the union he so much cherished; slave states and free vied to spread their respective systems into the new territories. It required a civil war, from 1861 to 1865, to confirm the American future.[2] In the years after 1865 the nation would add the industrial strength that was to be the largest component of its twentieth-century power, but the essential base had been created in little more than the political lifetime of John Quincy Adams.

Interests

The driving forces in American foreign policy both are and are not like those of other nations. They include the same emphasis on national self-interest, the same intrusion of the larger culture, the same distortions – sometimes minor, sometimes substantial – of the view of world events seen through a prism of national but not universal values. But each of these forces, or factors, also has a peculiarly American character.

At least since publication, in 1959, of William Appleman Williams's *The Tragedy of American Diplomacy,* the most influential contribution to diplomatic history in many years, historians (and polemicists) have adopted his thesis that the United States has always been "expansionist." In at least one sense, of course, this is a truism. Every nation serves first of all its own interests, even those which, like the United States after 1776, France after 1789, and the Soviet Union after 1917, profess to represent the aspirations of the entire world. Whereas some few have acknowledged limits on their power, most have sought to expand their sway when opportunity beckoned, puissant ones showing global ambition and lesser states seeking regional influence.

2 Fittingly, one of the primary actors in wartime diplomacy was Charles Francis Adams, John Quincy's son, who served Lincoln as minister to the Court of St. James, fighting doughtily to foil Confederate efforts to gain British support.

Americans, at least many of them, certainly were expansionists, before independence and after, even before most of them thought of "America" as more than a geographical term. And they were proud of it. In 1771, a young graduate of Yale, Timothy Dwight, published the first of many patriotic effusions that, along with sermons and works of philosophy, were to flow from his pen:

> Hail land of light and glory! Thy power shall grow
> Far as the seas, which round thy regions flow;
> Through earth's wide realms thy glory shall extend,
> And savage nations at thy scepter bend.
> And the frozen shores thy sons shall sail,
> Or stretch their canvas to the ASIAN gale.

In the succeeding century, similarly chauvinistic statements echoed Dwight. More to the point, his predictions largely came true. American dominion grew "far as the seas," through to a Pacific coastline more than a thousand miles long. The Americans did force "savage nations," Mexico and the Indian tribes, to bend to their scepter. They "stretched their canvas" over the globe. Whether they achieved worldwide "glory" or influence is problematic; they were both respected and scorned – worse yet, sometimes ignored – in other lands. Still, Dwight's youthful effort laid out what would be the agenda of American diplomacy in the years before the Civil War.

In the nation's early years, foreign commerce was an extremely important factor in the economy. Although what was essentially subsistence farming remained predominant, a market economy steadily developed, and foreign markets quickly became an important part of the system. At no other time has such a high proportion of the national product been exported, and the price level of many important commodities was essentially determined by export prices. At least until John Quincy Adams's presidency, every chief executive devoted much of his attention to the fostering of trade and the vibrant merchant marine that carried it.

Even while they were colonies, and on the whole loyal ones, the Americans dissented from the mercantilism of the British Navigation Acts system, which in effect largely limited their trade to intraimperial exchange. They wanted freedom to trade with as many nations as possible, whether in or outside British domains, in whatever goods they chose. Logically enough, their policies as a nation differed from those of other countries; in general, they sought to expand commerce by unshackling rather than directing it. Still, their basic purpose differed little from that of almost all nations at many times.

Territorial expansion began when Pilgrims took the first step off Plymouth Rock and Virginians pushed up the James River. As long as the colonials were British subjects, they strongly supported imperial expansion, urging London to displace the French, in particular, from territory they wished to exploit and develop. After independence, they continued the process. By 1865, America had expanded to the Pacific Ocean, and citizens often boasted that the nation had become an empire.

Such massive expansion into contiguous areas is not common. The nearest parallel is Russian expansion under the tsars, begun in the late fifteenth century and essentially completed in the nineteenth. In that long process, the Russian people spread out from their original center around Moscow, just as Americans moved westward from the Atlantic Coast. A central purpose, however, was to establish dominion over large non-Russian populations whose efforts could be exploited by the center. The Americans, on the other hand, did not seek to reduce native Americans or, for that matter, Mexicans to the role of laborers in their vineyard. To say this is not to exalt the Americans' morality: Their purpose was no less selfish; their methods, particularly in dealing with the Indians, were often cruel. However, they sought land and its resources, not a subordinate population. They would have been happiest if the Indians had simply disappeared, and it is no accident that the half of Mexico that was seized contained only a few thousand inhabitants. This kind of expansionism was unique to the United States.

Of Dwight's catalog, there remains only the category of "glory," of expanding influence and respect. The Americans considered themselves a model society, one destined to transform the world. As John Quincy Adams's father wrote in 1765, expressing what was already a widespread view, "I always consider the settlement of America with reverence and wonder, as the opening of a grand scheme and design of Providence for the illumination and emancipation of the slavish part of mankind all over the earth." The success of the Revolution and the establishment of republican government increased such feelings, and most Americans believed, although historians still debate the degree of accuracy in their claims, that the French and Latin American revolutions, as well as the European revolts of 1848, confirmed the argument. Thus it was possible for Herman Melville to write, in his novel, *White Jacket,* published in 1850, "we bear the ark of the liberties of the world. . . . And let us always remember that with ourselves, almost for the first time in the history of earth, national selfishness is unbounded philanthropy; for we cannot do good to America, but we give alms to the world." From one end of John Quincy Adams's life to the other, Americans endlessly demanded that they be respected as a model for the world.

Before the Civil War, this thought usually was harmless arrogance; only occasionally, in happy contrast to later times, did a price have to be paid. Many other nations have phases of arrogance in their history, some of them nearly as long as the American. This last form of "expansion" is, like the others, a function of the inherent egocentrism of any nation's diplomacy. The American form differed; the central meaning did not.

Values

The form sprang, of course, from American cultural values. In all nations, those who make decisions are influenced not merely by the information at their disposal but by the values they bring to the consideration of that information. When the United States was born, and for many years thereafter, foreign policy decisions in most countries were made by and subject to the scrutiny of a relative few, at most of a legislature. George Canning, after he became foreign secretary of Great Britain in 1822, is considered the first European diplomatist who sought broader support from the political public as a whole. In the United States, things were quite different from the outset. Revolutionary leaders and, later on, government officials had to seek national concurrence in their policies; the policies had to coincide with or be justified in terms of national values. In sum, from the beginning, "the cultural setting [was] less a backdrop than a vital cog in the workings of foreign affairs."[3]

The core beliefs lasted so long – to our own time – and became so embedded in the American outlook that they seem unremarkable today. However, although drawn in part from the thinking of others, particularly in seventeenth-century England, they were radical departures from the dominant values of Europe at the time of the Revolution and for many years continued to be far more pervasive than in other countries. Moreover, they gained strength from the apparently confirming events of the years from independence to the Civil War. Indeed, it is impossible to understand American foreign policy without recognizing the profound, persistent impact of an ideology that emerged during the colonial and early national periods.

The most important belief was a commitment to republicanism, a striking departure from an otherwise nearly universal commitment to monarchy. Although Europeans might debate the proper extent of royal power, at least until the French Revolution (and in most countries the debate would continue for many more years), the stability provided by monarchical institutions was generally considered essential to political order.[4]

Largely as a consequence of lessons they rightly or wrongly drew from the pre-Revolutionary controversy, but also because their colonial experiments in local republicanism had been generally successful, the Americans rejected this concept. "By the eighteenth century," Edmund S. Morgan notes, "the sovereignty of the people was taken for granted." Of course, he adds, in practice, even in the most egalitarian colonies, elites dominated, but this was seldom discussed: "Popular sovereignty . . . became the prevailing fiction in a society whose government was traditionally the province of a relatively small elite."[5]

---

3 Morrell Heald and Lawrence S. Kaplan, *Culture and Diplomacy* (Westport, Conn., 1977), ix.

4 During the turmoil in France from 1789 to 1815, High Federalists often contrasted the stability of monarchical England with the mobocracy and then the Caesarism of England's enemy, but even this small faction never considered abandoning republicanism, as they defined it, in the United States.

5 Edmund S. Morgan, *Inventing the People* (New York, 1988), 143, 148.

For a generation or more after independence, Americans worried about the fate of their experiment in popular government. Jeremiahs at one end of the political spectrum or the other frequently bewailed the failures of republicanism as currently practiced. Some feared that republicanism would be destroyed by demagoguery; others saw the looming shape of aristocratic control or Caesarism. Still, no true American suggested that the concept itself be abandoned, only that distortions be corrected. Americans agreed that republicanism – and the United States as its preeminent practitioner – represented the hope of the present and the future.

Closely allied with republicanism, ever more so as the nation progressed, was the concept of individualism, both political and economic. The predominance of individualism was the central theme – sometimes the object of praise, often of criticism – of the great commentary, *Democracy in America,* published by Alexis de Tocqueville in 1835. Unlike French republicans after 1789, the Americans seldom talked of a "national will" transcending the views of individuals. Although government intervened in economic matters much more than is suggested by polemicists expressing reverence for the policies of the Founding Fathers, and although, too, cooperative economic efforts became increasingly important, individual free enterprise was the model form, as befitted the nation of farms and farmers that America was at its birth. As Thomas Jefferson wrote in 1815, uniting the themes of republicanism and individualism, America was a "model of government, securing to man his rights and the fruits of his labor, by an organization constantly subject to his own will."

The virtually universal endorsement of republicanism and individualism by no means translated into unanimity regarding foreign affairs. Indeed, disputatious, sometimes violent disagreements over policy began well before the celebrated clash between Hamiltonian and Jeffersonian views in the 1790s and continued beyond the Civil War. However, differences over policy should not obscure the common body of beliefs shared by virtually every American, beliefs that deeply influenced both sides in all the debates and both gave impetus to and placed limits upon the rival policies put forward.

Their credo – one could call it their ideology, were not the latter word so laden with negative implications; one could call it their ideals, were not that word so laden with favorable ones – meant that Americans and, to a very large extent, their presumably more sophisticated leaders instinctively distrusted monarchical, statist regimes. (John Quincy Adams's respect for Tsar Alexander is an exception proving the rule.) These beliefs also meant, with qualifications soon to be noted, that Americans welcomed and endorsed revolutions. In 1796, President Washington expressed a national outlook when he averred that his "best wishes were irresistibly excited whenever, in any country, he saw an oppressed nation unfurl the banners of freedom." Largely but not exclusively because noninterventionist ideas predominated, the Americans only very rarely even considered positive action in support of struggles against monarchy. But the wishes of Washington, Adams, and their countrymen were important, frequently coloring the policy of the United States.

The Prism

Every nation views others in the world through a prism shaped by its own experience. Even today, American statesmen, and those who record their actions, often overlook this simple, almost self-evident point. As Reginald Stuart observes, "Americans have historically found it difficult to step outside of themselves when judging others. And they have rarely realized how much their own values unconsciously smudged the lenses through which they viewed the world."[6] The belief system, the product of experience, conditions the way in which Americans have viewed world developments and consequently how they have responded to them.

Every nation, of course, has its own prism – the Russian view of world events, for example, is warped by memories of the series of invasions from Charles XII of Sweden early in the eighteenth century through Hitler in the twentieth – but each is, like the American, unique. America's commercial policies cannot be explained if one ignores the nations's devotion to individualism; closed systems and

6 Reginald C. Stuart, *United States Expansionism and British North America* (Chapel Hill, 1988), xiii.

statist controls were by definition condemned, and "open doors" were preferable. America's drive for territory, in large part the product of greed, derived essential strength from the prism of cultural values, which allowed Americans to see themselves as bringing progress and improvement to Louisiana or Florida or Oregon or Mexico.

Similarly, the reaction of Americans to revolutions abroad was essentially a projection of their vision of their own. They had, they firmly believed, risen against tyranny, avoided sanguinary excesses and social turmoil, created a republic — such was God's path for the world. Thus they welcomed antimonarchical risings but, in a frequently repeated "cycle of hope and disappointment,"[7] recoiled when revolutions went beyond the purely political sphere to repression, Bonapartism, and deep social change. The Terror divided Americans previously nearly unanimously in favor of the French Revolution. The "Springtime of Revolutions" in 1848, antimonarchical and nationalist explosions in half a dozen European countries triggered by a Paris rising, roused applause, but the radical violence that developed in France soon alienated many Americans. Between these dates, in 1830, still another French revolution, a move in the direction of liberalism but not even a republican one, earned praise from President Jackson because of "the heroic moderation which . . . disarmed revolution of its terrors." The contrast is instructive.

In reacting as they did, Americans too often failed to remember two special circumstances that had made their kind of revolution possible. Alexis de Tocqueville, perhaps the most perceptive foreign analyst of American society, drew attention to them 150 years ago. "Nothing," he wrote, "is more fertile in marvels than the art of being free, but nothing is harder than freedom's apprenticeship." Virtually self-governing throughout most of their history as colonies, they came to freedom with patterns of behavior and thought that made republicanism both logical and easy; they did not have to exorcise political privileges of rank or transform the economic order to create conditions in which republicanism could thrive. Others were not so lucky, and when they went past what Americans consid-

7 Michael H. Hunt, *Ideology and U.S. Foreign Policy* (New Haven, 1987), 97.

ered the proper boundaries of revolution, they lost American sympathies.

Because national egotism was strong, the inability of others to create individualist republicanism was explained in terms of their inferiority to Americans. Thus Jefferson wrote of the people in Europe in 1787, "A thousand years would not place them on that high ground on which our common people are now setting out." When revolution broke out while he was American minister in Paris, Jefferson at first considered limited monarchy rather than republicanism the appropriate solution for France, because the French were so ill-prepared for self-government. Years later, when the Latin Americans rose against Spanish rule, virtually every American welcomed the revolt but many, including Jefferson, rightly doubted that true republicanism would follow. "They have not the first elements of good or free government," John Quincy Adams asserted. "Arbitrary power, military and ecclesiastical, was stamped upon their education, upon their habits, and upon all their institutions."

These two apparently dissimilar reactions are in fact reflections of the same facet of the prism. Republicanism in the American style was the highest form of government. Those who compromised it might be inherently inferior as a result of their history, but in any event they sinned. Throughout their history, Americans have regarded foreign nations in this way.

A sentence in *Democracy in America* also encapsulates the second distortion provided by the prism. In a characteristic tone, Tocqueville wrote, "Their fathers gave them a love of equality and liberty, but it was God who, by handing a limitless continent over to them, gave them the means of long remaining equal and free." The Americans were blessed with abundant land and resources. There was of course poverty, perhaps most notably in the cities that burgeoned before the Civil War. There was slavery: One out of six Americans was a slave when the first census was taken in 1790, one out of eight – four million in all – when the Civil War began. For the great preponderance of Americans, however, conditions were much better than in other nations; in particular, the proportion of landowners was higher than elsewhere. Above all, although there were of course periodic slumps, a high rate of economic growth prevailed.

This eased the path to republicanism, contributed to national stability, and strengthened the devotion to individualism. "We supposed that our revelation was 'democracy revolutionizing the world,'" a historian has written, "but in reality it was 'abundance revolutionizing the world.'"[8] In other nations, or at least many of them, political change evoked class conflict and rivalry over economic shares, creating what from the American point of view was unrepublican turmoil. Such tensions existed in the United States, but comparatively speaking they were muted. Americans simply could not understand "the contrast between [for example] the three or four Frances that tore at each other's throats and the one America that hustled its way into the future."[9]

The prism concept suggests one other line of thought. For years it has been fashionable among scholars to distinguish between ideals and self-interest as motives of foreign policy, to see them as polar opposites. In fact, mingling is the norm; conflict between national interest and national culture is the exception. And for this the prism is largely responsible. As Max Weber wrote many years ago, "Interests (material and moral), not ideas, dominate directly the actions of men. Yet the 'images of the world' created by these ideas have very often served as switches determining the tracks on which the dynamism of interests kept action going."[10] In sum, material interests, culture, and the prism combine in a complex interplay that creates foreign policy.

There is no clearer illustration of the compatibility of the three factors than the devotion to isolationism. The Americans sought commerce with all the world, but they refused to become involved in the politics of other continents and, in particular, to align themselves with any other power. Sometimes compromised in practice, notably in the alliance with France, which was essential to the success of the Revolution, political isolation was an unvarying desire and increasingly became fixed dogma, even though the word itself

---

8 David M. Potter, *People of Plenty* (Chicago, 1954), 134.
9 Clinton Rossiter, *The American Quest* (New York, 1971), 12.
10 Quoted in Hans J. Morgenthau, *Politics Among Nations,* 4th ed. (New York, 1967), 8.

was not used to describe policy until the twentieth century. Such a policy was obviously prudent: A state with all interests save the commercial confined to its own periphery was made stronger in that area by the width of the Atlantic Ocean. A power weak by world standards could only suffer from involvement in the wars of greater ones, and an uninvolved power could hope, at a time when the rights of neutrals were taken more seriously than later, to profit greatly from wartime trade.

At the same time, involvement in the sordid politics of Europe could be and was regarded by the Americans as contaminating, a descent to the level of court intrigues and amoral national selfishness contrary to the principles of republicanism. Involvement would force compromises of principle, expose simple but honest American diplomats to the wiles of cynically tricky Europeans, and, perhaps above all, dim the "beacon of liberty," the light to the world held forth by the United States. These beliefs in turn created the prism through which Americans viewed developments across the seas, an angle of vision that conditioned interpretations of actual developments and confirmed the mind-set that had created the prism in the first place.

The concerns and ideas just discussed, as we have seen, had roots in the colonial period. In a sense, there was an American pattern of behavior and thought before there was an America. Down to at least 1763, the colonists were able to reconcile their outlook with continued devotion to the British Empire. On the whole, they were happy, reasonably prosperous, and free. During the next century, they would carry their ambitions and their culture into an ever widening theater of action.

2. The Birth of American Diplomacy

To the Declaration of Independence

Twenty-five years before the Revolution, no important person dreamed of independence. Few thought of an "American" identity in any political sense. The word itself was more often used in Britain. Even after the affrays at Lexington and Concord in April 1775, most Anglo-Americans refused to face the prospect of a breach with the mother country. As late as the spring of 1776 John Adams wrote to an impatient correspondent, "After all, my friend, I do not wonder that so much reluctance has been shown to the measure of independency. All great changes are irksome to the human mind, especially those which are attended with great and uncertain effects." Although by this time Adams and others felt independence desirable, even inevitable, they knew that many, even among Adams's colleagues in the Continental Congress, shrank from that step.

Of course, Americans were proudly aware of their burgeoning growth. From midcentury onward, Benjamin Franklin, the best-known colonial figure, spokesman in London for Pennsylvania and sometimes other colonies, frequently boasted of it. Franklin even talked of an American "empire." For him, however, this was to be but an increasingly important component of the larger empire centered in London, at least until the American population outstripped that of the metropol as a result of what he called "the American multiplication table." On the eve of the Revolution, others joined Franklin. For example, Samuel Adams, John's cousin, wrote in 1774, "It requires but a small portion of the gift of discernment for anyone to foresee, that providence will erect a mighty empire in America." Although they were soon to change, the two Adamses, like Franklin, did not grasp that the implication of power was independence.

17

The controversy with Britain had begun, after all, as an effort to maintain "the rights of Englishmen." The colonials wanted to restore a revered British constitution that, in their view, had been subverted by encroachments of government power. What could be more English than the slogan "No Taxation Without Representation"? Although history provided inexact parallels, perhaps the most apt being the Dutch rising against Spain in the sixteenth century, in modern times no empire had been blown apart from within. When the first Continental Congress met at Philadelphia in 1774, no voices called for secession from the empire. The major actions — support for Massachusetts (already on the edge of violence against a garrison of four thousand Redcoats), organization of an economic boycott, a declaration of colonial rights, a petition to George III — were radical enough and obviously unacceptable to Britain. Still, Congress claimed to seek imperial reform, not imperial disintegration.

At the second Congress, which convened in May 1775, three weeks after the musketry at Lexington and Concord, plans were made to coordinate resistance. Colonel George Washington of Virginia received command of the forces of the "United Colonies." Neither the army nor the Congress was described as "American," and, at dinner, Washington and his staff regularly toasted George III as late as January 1776. Despite repeated signs of English intransigence and the development of siege warfare around Boston, many leaders still resisted the logic of events. When Congress approved a "Declaration of the Causes and Necessity of Taking Up Arms," largely drafted by a Virginia delegate, Thomas Jefferson, the members avowed a determination "to die free men rather than to live slaves," but also asserted, "We mean not to dissolve that union which has so long and so happily subsisted between us. . . . We have not raised armies with ambitious designs of separating from Great Britain, and establishing independent States." In succeeding months, Jefferson opposed schemes to seek foreign aid because they might jeopardize reconciliation with the mother country.

Not until November 29, 1775, seven months after Lexington, did Congress create a Committee of Secret Correspondence to open communications with sympathizers across the Atlantic. Even then the cautious wording, which directed the committee to approach "our friends in Great Britain, Ireland, and other parts of the world," at least professed to emphasize the intraimperial approach. The committee, soon dominated by Franklin, the only member with extensive contacts abroad, moved cautiously, although it met with a French agent as early as December and, early in 1776, sent Silas Deane to Paris, both to arrange for the purchase of supplies (if possible, on credit) and to feel out the prospective French reaction to a decision for independence.

Both of these moves were made in deep secrecy (members of the committee approached the midnight rendezvous with the Frenchman by separate routes), partly because the full Congress was even more cautious than its agents. Although Parliament closed trade with the colonies at the end of 1775, the latter refused to pick up the challenge. As late as February 1776, Congress rejected, for the third time, Franklin's proposal to open ports to foreign ships. It did so even though this presented an obvious way to embroil other nations in the quarrel with Britain and although, too, it was becoming obvious that the rebels, lacking military necessities, could not carry on otherwise. Only in April did Congress agree to a step that so decisively challenged the imperial system.

Even this was at best a partial solution to the supply problem. Private traders, in France or wherever, could hardly be expected to satisfy America's needs; only supplies from royal arsenals could do that. Nor did the colonies have the financial resources to pay for what they required. Yet help from foreign governments, including credit, could not be expected as long as Americans professed to be fighting only for better treatment within the British Empire. "No state in Europe will either Treat or Trade with us so long as we consider ourselves Subjects of G. B.," wrote Richard Henry Lee, and he later added, "It is not choice then but necessity which calls for Independence, as the only means by which foreign Alliances can be obtained." This argument undermined and ultimately overthrew the reluctance to demand independence.

On June 7, 1776, after winning support from the Virginia legislature, Lee presented to Congress a resolution for independence. "It is expedient forthwith," the resolution declared, "to take the most effectual measures for forming foreign Alliances." After hesitating nearly a month, Congress approved Lee's resolution and an accompanying manifesto of freedom prepared by his fellow Virginian and political ally, Thomas Jefferson. At some point well before this time, no doubt, the momentum of events had made independence inevitable. Still, the crushing need for foreign assistance, rather than anything else, tipped the balance in the spring of 1776.

Nationality and Isolation

A feeble sense of nationality, as well as reluctance to break accustomed ties, had delayed the Declaration of Independence. The colonials were bound together by, and proud of, their progress since 1607 or 1620. Despite immense differences between Massachusetts and Virginia, Pennsylvania and Georgia, they believed they pursued a way of life in which the colonies had more in common with one another than with any European society. Increasingly, as intercolonial contacts developed, they began to look at many problems in a similar fashion. These things, and others, provided fertile soil for political nationalism. Still, the harvest was slow.

On the Revolution's eve, Patrick Henry, Richard Henry Lee's political mentor, declared, "The distinctions between Virginians, Pennsylvanians, New Yorkers, and New Englanders, are no more. I am not a Virginian, but an American." Henry may have meant what he said, although the parochialism of his later career suggests his remark to have been hyperbole. For his countrymen – for other "Virginians, Pennsylvanians, New Yorkers, and New Englanders" – the statement was dubious. Colonies and sections mistrusted one another, Yankees and especially Massachusetts being particularly suspect. No one proposed to substitute a centralized American government for the parliamentary domination against which the Revolution was fought.

During the pre-Revolutionary period, the colonies had agents in London to watch over their interests. Sometimes these agents were trusted Englishmen, sometimes they were colonials. Occasionally, they presented a combined front before Parliament or the Board of Trade, and a few, like Franklin just before the Revolution, had extra stature because they represented more than one colony. In the final crisis, Franklin and Arthur Lee, another agent of Massachusetts, even presumed to speak for all of the colonies, almost as if they were national representatives. Until the last crisis, however, although Britain developed a single policy toward all the colonies, the agents met this policy with only loose cooperation.

In questions of war and defense, coordination was even less developed. During King William's War, from 1689 to 1697, Connecticut declined to help New York resist a French attack, and New York understandably returned the compliment when that neighbor later came under assault. The Albany Plan of 1754, Franklin's scheme for concerted action against the French and their Indian allies, evoked absolutely no enthusiasm when referred to colonial legislatures. Those who supported integration came to believe that it would have to be imposed from London; "however necessary a Step this may be," one correspondent wrote Franklin, "for the mutual Safety and preservation of these Colonies, it is pretty certain, it will never be taken, unless we are forced to it, by the Supreme Authority of the Nation" – in other words, by Parliament.

The Seven Years' War, which began in 1756, saw an upsurge of patriotism in the colonies. They gloried in the triumphs of colonial and British arms, and they shared a desire for imperialist expansion at French expense. However, "American self-consciousness . . . was pretty well contained within the framework of local provincial loyalty, on the one side, and imperial or 'British' loyalty on the other."[1]

Each colony thought of itself as an outpost of freedom, but as an individual bastion within the defensive works of the British constitution, most liberal in the world. When, after the Seven Years' War, London moved away from the policy of "salutary neglect" so long pursued, the colonies feared for their freedoms. Even more than in the conflicts with France and its tribal allies, they felt menaced. Still, they were reluctant to unite, and when Franklin laid a plan of union before Congress in July 1775 his proposal was considered so radical it was expunged from the minutes. Eventually a common need drove the Americans together: "We must all hang together, or

---

1 Max Savelle, *Seeds of Liberty* (New York, 1948), 555.

assuredly we shall all hang separately," the old philosopher is supposed to have said when signing the Declaration of Independence.
At the same time, the struggle, cast in terms of the preservation of
freedom, reminded Americans how much they shared, how greatly
their liberties exceeded those of other people. From this was born a
republican nationalism – youthful, both ebullient and doubting,
heavily tinged with localism, but nevertheless a nationalism that
would prove enduring.

The development of an isolationist spirit was closely connected
with this new nationalism. "The Revolution itself was an act of
isolation," a leading diplomatic historian has commented, "a cutting off of the ties with the Old World, the deed of a society which
felt itself different from those which existed on the other side of the
Atlantic, and which was, indeed, unique in its composition and its
aspirations."[2] Although war's imperatives forced an American alliance with France in 1778, that alliance was effectively canceled
within five years, formally so in twenty; none followed until the
twentieth century.

Isolationism was not simply a negative policy. Americans looked
upon themselves as guides to the world. If the new republic were to
inspire others, it must preserve a pristine character, refuse to sully
itself in the sordid international politics of monarchies. By avoiding
political connections, too, the republic might speed the world toward the day of which French *philosophes* and eighteenth-century
English radicals dreamed. In that day reason would rule, not iron
and gunpowder, and mutually profitable commerce would lubricate
the machinery of peace. As Jefferson put it in 1784, when seeking a
commercial treaty with Prussia, Americans had in mind "an object
so valuable to mankind as the total emancipation of commerce and
the bringing together of all nations for a free intercommunication of
happiness." Dreams of a republican world and hope for international
peace built upon global prosperity were connected in the minds of
the Revolutionary generation and its successors to our own time,
perhaps receiving most eloquent expression in the rhetoric of Wood-

2 Dexter Perkins, *The American Approach to Foreign Policy* (Cambridge, Mass.,
  1952), 10.

row Wilson. Both themes were part of the spirit of isolationism, which paradoxically coupled global aspirations with political withdrawal.

Even more than idealism, prudence and calculation urged non-involvement. Between 1688 and 1763 – seventy-five years – the British Empire was at war almost exactly half the time; for the colonies, the cost had sometimes been heavy. As their quarrel with England developed, they began to argue that without the imperial connection – and by analogy any political connection with Europe – they need never have been involved in war at all. In one of his political writings, Franklin had "America" complain to "England," "you have quarrell'd with all Europe, and drawn me into all your Broils. . . . I have no natural Cause of Difference with France, Spain, or Holland, and yet by turns I have join'd with you in Wars against all of them." What imperial ties had done in the recent past, political connections might do in future.

This fear was heightened by an exaggerated lack of self-confidence that has never entirely disappeared. Americans saw themselves as honest, innocent men; they considered European diplomats wily knaves. Said John Adams, "The subtlety, the invention, the profound secrecy, and absolute silence of these European courts, will be too much for our hot, rash, fiery ministers, and for our indolent, inattentive ones, though as silent as they." Critics of Wilson at Versailles, of Roosevelt at Yalta, made much the same point years later. This being the case, isolation was the only safe course, the only way to avoid exploitation and perhaps even wars of no real concern to the United States but dangerous to independence and happiness.

In January 1776 Thomas Paine published a pamphlet, *Common Sense,* among the most effective pieces of propaganda in history. A failure in life (his enemies scoffed at the idea of an ex-corset-maker in politics) and marriage in England, Paine had come to America only at the end of 1774, but he soon found his métier as a propagandist of freedom and revolution, and when his American career ended he would pursue it in France, both before and after incarceration under the Terror. *Common Sense* was his first major effort, a powerfully written mobilization of all of the arguments for independence; within three months, it sold 120,000 copies.

Among Paine's themes was an explicit appeal to the isolationist spirit. Independence could be won, Paine argued, without foreign alliances. Once convinced that the Americans had crossed the political Rubicon, France and Spain would, in their own interest, grant whatever assistance was necessary to rupture the British Empire. Nor need the United States, when free, fear attack. "France and Spain never were, nor perhaps ever will be, our enemies as Americans, but as our being subjects of Great Britain." After independence, all Europe would seek only to enjoy American trade, and the interests of the United States would also flow in the direction of free commerce. "As Europe is our market for trade, we ought to form no partial connection with any part of it," Paine wrote. "It is the true interest of America to steer clear of European connections."

As noted, Lee's motion for independence included a demand for "foreign Alliances." This did not mean that Congress rejected Paine's isolationist views, for in contemporary usage the word "alliance" had a far looser meaning than it does today, encompassing mere treaties of commerce as well as political connections and military guarantees. It remained to be seen whether the Americans, following their isolationist inclinations, could avoid the latter.

The Approach to Europe

Four days after Lee offered his resolution, Congress named a five-man committee to prepare a proposed treaty with France. John Adams did the drafting. His plan, the "Model Treaty of 1776," offered no political concessions whatsoever; as the name implies, it was designed as a pattern for relations with all foreign powers, not the grant of special favors to the first state – and the greatest – approached by the rebels.

In its most radical departure from contemporary norms, the "Model Treaty" proposed that Americans trading with France should enjoy the privileges of French merchants, as should Frenchmen engaging in commerce with the United States. In commerce, in short, there would be no nationality; all the civilized world, at least all those who accepted the American scheme, would trade as equals. Recognizing that war could not be immediately abolished but seeking to minimize its impact, the "Model Treaty" also laid down an extremely liberal code of rights for neutrals in wartime. If one of the two powers, France or America, went to war with a third party, the trade of the partner remaining at peace would receive extremely tender treatment, far beyond what the eighteenth century – itself extraordinarily lenient by modern standards – usually extended. The neutral might trade, even in military supplies, with the enemy of its treaty partner. By these two groups of provisions Adams and – since Congress accepted his outlook – the new nation sought in the short run to lessen the impact of war and in the longer term to create a commercial system that would reduce international conflicts.

Such progress would of course depend upon the creation of a web of treaties binding together the world's major nations. A treaty with France was only a first step, but it would confer important immediate advantages. Any treaty opening trade would help to break down the British monopoly of American commerce. Reciprocity with France would overthrow, as far as Franco-American trade was concerned, the mercantilist rules ordinarily followed by that country. Mutual promises to deal gently with neutral commerce in time of war clearly advantaged the United States, a feeble country but one deeply interested in trade. As so often, realism and idealism coincided.

Neither Adams, no idealist but rather a cynical realist, nor his supporters in Congress expected the "Model Treaty" to be implemented *in vacuo*. The immediate need was to further the cause of independence, and the treaty sought to do this in two ways. On the one hand, any treaty with the United States would probably involve Paris in war with London; on the other, the prospect of depriving Britain of its monopoly of American trade would presumably make such a treaty irresistibly attractive to France.

Adams's cool calculation, supported with uncertain fortitude by Franklin – if Adams's characteristically ungenerous, retrospective account is to be trusted – met challenges in Congress. Like almost all members, Adams's cousin, Samuel, and Richard Henry Lee endorsed the "Model Treaty" and shared the desire to avoid political connections with Europe. But, they asked, was the prospect of commercial advantage enough to win France to America's side?

Need not political and territorial bribes be offered as well? Lee even proposed that, if France entered the war, America agree to fight until its ally regained Caribbean islands lost to Britain during the Seven Years' War.

Lee's proposal failed because he sought too much, but many members of Congress felt, albeit reluctantly, that something more than the "Model Treaty" must be offered. Consequently, instructions approved on September 24 coupled with the "Model Treaty" a political offer to France, but one so limited and suspicious as to be at most a minor incentive to that country. The instructions, which declared American opposition to the reestablishment of French power in Canada, merely promised that, if America made peace with England before the French did, the United States would not aid the former mother country while the Anglo-French war continued. A political assurance could hardly have been more modest; should France be drawn into a war because of the connection with America, the young republic would not even agree to remain by its side until that war ended!

When the war went badly and France showed no eagerness for a treaty, Congress wondered if it had not been too sanguine. In December 1776, after Adams had gone home to Massachusetts, new instructions offered to give France six months' notice prior to peace with England and even promised to support French efforts to regain Canada. Congress made these proposals reluctantly, withdrawing the latter as soon as the military picture improved. Adams's expectations were always the hopes of his colleagues.

Help from France

From the outset of the Revolution, Americans realized that France was the only nation that could give decisive aid. Ever since the Seven Years' War, French leaders had dreamed of revenge, and Count Vergennes, foreign minister since 1774, favored aid to the Americans almost as soon as the Revolution began. In his view, "the embarrassment of the British crown in America was simply an opportunity so golden that it could not possibly be squandered."[3]

3 Simon Schama, *Citizens* (New York, 1989), 48.

Following good mercantilist doctrine, he argued that disruption of the empire would deprive England of much of its American trade, an essential ingredient in its commercial health.[4] In turn, this economic blow would have important political effects, especially by crippling British prestige. Thus France would serve its own interests by helping the Revolution succeed.

In pressing these arguments, Vergennes was aided by the romantic playwright (*The Barber of Seville, The Marriage of Figaro*) and rogue, Pierre A. Caron de Beaumarchais. In 1775, Beaumarchais went to London on an unusual mission: He was to determine the sex of a French defector – a former army officer now living as a woman – and, once this was determined, employ the arts of love or the persuasion of money, whichever was appropriate, to recover documents that would embarrass Paris if they became public. Beaumarchais grumbled that "to pay court to a captain of dragoons" was not in his line, but he did his duty. While in London on this errand, Beaumarchais fell into contact with Arthur Lee, Congress's secret representative. The Frenchman's romantic nature made it inevitable that he should accept at more than face value Lee's hints that the rebels might yield to British force if they did not receive help. Encouraged by Vergennes, Beaumarchais churned out a series of reports to this effect that were passed on to Louis XVI.

The marquis de Turgot, a shrewd man in charge of French finances, took a more sophisticated view. He correctly predicted that Anglo-American trade would increase, not decrease, if separation shattered the Navigation Acts system. A conflict with Britain, he warned, would impose an unbearable burden on the financial system he was then attempting to reform. This prediction also came true; in 1789, a desire to open new sources of revenue was a major reason for convocation of the Estates General, which ushered in the French Revolution. Finally, Turgot pointed out the threat to monarchy posed by the American example; he saw nothing but danger in encouraging men to fight against their sovereign.

This cool reasoning was overborne with remarkable ease. "It is the

4 In fact, the colonies bought less than one-fifth of all British exports, and at least some of the flow was certain to continue even if the Americans won their revolution.

English, Sire," Beaumarchais instructed the hesitant king, "which it concerns you to humiliate and weaken, if you do not wish to be humiliated and weakened yourself." In May 1776, even before the Declaration of Independence, Vergennes (and his agent, Beaumarchais) won the battle. The French decided to send supplies from crown stores, although the transactions were concealed behind a commercial front, the firm of Hortalez et Cie., a firm fittingly, if not efficiently, headed by Beaumarchais. Turgot resigned.

The recklessness of those who thought themselves crafty, calculating statesmen is even more clearly shown by Spanish policy. Until Count Floridablanca came to power in 1777, leaders at Madrid were fully as eager as those at Paris to go to the aid of the enemy of their enemy, to help the Americans against Britain. Spanish authorities recognized that the revolutionary disease might spread to their own colonies; they had some concern that the United States might seek to expand at Spain's expense, particularly in the Louisiana country; and, like the French, they did not want the new nation to grow beyond client statehood. It is an instructive commentary on contemporary European statecraft that, despite all these things, Spain enthusiastically supported the French decision to send aid and even endorsed Vergennes's view that sooner or later it would have to be followed by war.

Benjamin Franklin's mission to Paris has become part of American legend. His less flamboyant, more quarrelsome colleagues, Silas Deane and Arthur Lee, were totally overshadowed, much to their distress. The philosopher-statesman played his role to the hilt, appealing to Frenchmen of all types, reformers and would-be *Realpolitikers,* courtiers and commoners alike. Exasperated by the adulation of Franklin, the king presented to one of the American's most vehement female admirers a chamber pot decorated with his portrait. The "Doctor" seemed to many to combine the almost bucolic democracy of Jean-Jacques Rousseau — Franklin's affectation of a fur cap may have helped here — and Voltaire's emphasis on reason; when the American met Voltaire at the Academy of Sciences, the two show-offs warmly embraced while observers commented on the union of the new and the old or, alternatively, the meeting of Solon and Socrates.

Franklin, Deane, and Lee were "secretly" received by Louis XVI shortly after their arrival in December 1776, and during the course of the war they procured more than $8 million in subsidies and loans. France's ally, Spain, disgorged another $650,000, and, toward the end of the war, Holland extended a loan, guaranteed by France, of $1.8 million.

Neither the Americans' reception at Versailles nor many other of their activities were kept secret for long. Seldom has an American foreign mission been so deeply penetrated by enemy agents. In addition, Franklin, at least, frequently leaked confidential information for political reasons, usually to frighten the British. Deane may have been a British agent (he shifted to their side in 1781) and was certainly a speculator who used inside information to feather his own nest. A whole series of Lee's clerks were in British pay. London's most important agent was Edward Bancroft, Deane's secretary, and Deane showed a curious disinterest in investigating rumors of Bancroft's unreliability. One of the spy's means of communication with his masters would have pleased Beaumarchais: Bancroft often left what appeared to be love letters in a hollow tree in the Tuileries; after their recovery by British agents, messages in invisible ink were developed and passed on to London. The British never entirely trusted Bancroft, and they intercepted his private correspondence, also largely concerned with speculation, learning further secrets he had chosen not to pass on.

The French Alliance

For well over a year, the three Americans failed to win their most important goal, a treaty. Sure that Congress, three thousand miles and many weeks removed from the scene, had misread European politics, they decided to disregard their instructions. They thereby initiated a pattern of behavior quite at odds with that of even the most eminent European diplomats, who, although occasionally given wide latitude in negotiations, virtually never defied instructions. Their behavior was emulated and similarly justified by other American representatives for many years, at least until 1848, when Nicholas Trist defied President Polk – and even refused to obey an

order of recall — so as to conclude peace with Mexico. Sometimes
such experiments led to triumph, as in the acquisition of Louisiana,
and sometimes to embarrassment, but they were peculiarly American.

In the case of Franklin and his colleagues, the first results were
nil. Even when they offered a pledge not to make a separate peace
with England, France could not be moved. France preferred the
cautious course of informal, nominally secret connections. For many
of the king's servants, any alliance with revolutionaries seemed a
dubious course. Trained soldiers found it hard to believe that, even
with French aid, a rabble could defeat the British army. Although
Vergennes almost certainly desired a war with England, he calculated that the French navy, in particular, would not be ready until
1778.

"We are now acting a play which pleases all the spectators," wrote
an American representative in Europe, "but none seem inclined to
pay the performers. All that we seem likely to obtain is applause."
To this observer, the attitude of the audience seemed warning for the
future. "The want of resolution in the House of Bourbon to assist us
in the hour of distress, will be an argument with our people, if
successful, to form no binding connection with them." Actually the
spectators, who had in fact been paying the actors via Hortalez et
Cie., were about to mount the stage.

In October 1777, at Saratoga, General John Burgoyne and five
thousand men surrendered to a rebel army. London began to talk
seriously of concessions, albeit concessions well short of independence; a mission headed by Lord Carlisle was sent to America to
negotiate, and agents made contact with Franklin and Deane. (London considered Lee hopelessly obdurate.) Franklin disingenuously
allowed the French to gather that, exhausted by two years of war, the
Americans might settle for imperial reform.

Vergennes made good use of the news from Saratoga, which
seemed to show that, at least if given sufficient help, the Americans
could not be beaten. He also made use of the quite unfounded
rumors that Anglo-American reconciliation was possible. That
Spain veered in the direction of caution did not deter France. With
the king's approval, Vergennes concluded a commercial treaty. More
important, he suggested and the American trio endorsed a treaty of

alliance to take effect when an Anglo-French war began, as all expected it soon to do. The agreements were secret, but, thanks to Bancroft, London learned of them in less than two days.

The treaties of February 6, 1778, demonstrated anew the tensions within American policy. The commercial treaty, which largely followed John Adams's plan of 1776, reflected the liberal, isolationist, and pacific longings of the United States. The treaty of conditional alliance, unauthorized by Congress but subsequently approved, involved the United States in world politics. In return for a French promise to assure American independence, as well as a pledge not to try to recover Canada, the envoys made two promises of their own. They committed their country not to make a separate peace: "Neither of the two Parties shall conclude either Truce or Peace with Great Britain, without the formal consent of the other first obtain'd." If observed, this pledge mortgaged America's future to French ambitions in Europe, the Caribbean, and India. The envoys also bound their country, after the war, to help defend French possessions in the Western Hemisphere; this pledge threatened to draw America into every major war involving France, since any enemy was bound to attack French islands in the West Indies. The treaties thus highlight the major theme of early American diplomacy – a hankering after isolation combined with an acceptance of political reality. And in 1778, despite Saratoga, the need for French support forced major accommodations to reality.

The courier bearing the treaties reached Boston on the third anniversary of Lexington and Concord. From there he posted to Philadelphia, where Congress approved the agreements without delay, no one choosing to raise embarrassing political questions or to rebuke the envoys for exceeding their instructions. Formal acceptance came on May 4; Congress celebrated by breaking open the wine Carlisle had sent to smooth the way to negotiations for reconciliation. When Britain and France went to war in June 1778, the conditional alliance came into effect.

Coalition Warfare, Coalition Diplomacy

Although it was to be more than three years before the allies gained a decisive victory, French military aid was vital to the success of the

American Revolution. French subsidies continued, although Vergennes doled them out on an annual basis. Supplies from abroad,
including about nine-tenths of the gunpowder used by the American
army, helped keep the revolution going, and corsairs like John Paul
Jones found haven in French (and Dutch and Spanish) ports.[5] Most
important of all, France and, after it entered the war in 1779, Spain
diverted British energies, in India and the Caribbean, at Gibraltar,
and by ostentatiously gathering forces for an attack on England
itself. On the whole, however, the North American war was almost
a sideshow as far as the European contestants were concerned. The
war ignited by France's decision to aid the American rebels became,
for all the European powers, a struggle to reorder their own continent and, indeed, the world.

Until 1781, military cooperation was ineffective. Combined operations by French naval forces and American soldiers collapsed igno-
miniously at Newport, Rhode Island, in 1778 and at Savannah in
1779. In 1780 a small army under General Rochambeau arrived,
but the larger, widely advertised "second division" never made its
appearance, and until the spring of 1781 Rochambeau declined to
stir from bivouac. Then he agreed to march, to New York and soon
to Virginia, where he and General Washington penned up a
northward-marching force under Lord Cornwallis on the Yorktown
peninsula. A fleet under Admiral de Grasse, originally sent across
the Atlantic to aid the Spaniards, not the Americans, closed the
mouth of Chesapeake Bay for a few critical weeks. On October 19,
1781, Cornwallis surrendered. The next day the usually anti-
Catholic Americans joined the more numerous French at a celebratory mass. For the rest of the war there were no major military
engagements in North America.

Despite unpleasant episodes, including seaport brawls between
French and American sailors, the alliance worked better than might
have been anticipated, granted the disparity of power between the
two nations and France's traditional role as a menace to the colonies.
As a matter of prudence, both sides kept most disagreements secret;

5 Jones's use of Holland as a haven, as well as extensive Dutch commerce with
  America, much of it in military supplies, precipitated an Anglo-Dutch war in
  1780.

historians have since ferreted out what few knew at the time. Moreover, American leaders had gone into the alliance with their eyes open. They accepted the fact that France had joined them for selfish reasons. As Washington wrote in 1778: "I am heartily disposed to entertain the most favorable sentiments of our new ally . . . ; but it is a maxim founded on the universal experience of mankind, that no nation can be trusted farther than it is bound by its own interests."

The French, who wanted only to sunder the British Empire, had no desire to prolong the war for purely American interests. By 1780 even Vergennes had tired of the war, and because spectacular successes eluded the allies, his enemies at court began to mobilize against him. The foreign minister began to seek ways to end the conflict, perhaps through mediation by Russia. To potential mediators and others, he made clear that, although France would not openly betray the Americans, Versailles did not sympathize with their ambitions. France certainly did not wish to see "the new republic mistress of the entire continent," as Vergennes phrased it. He toyed with schemes that would have left Britain in possession of bits of the colonies, and he steadily refused to support America's ambitions for Canada, not least because he hoped a continued British presence there would make the Americans feel dependent on French backing.

Nor did the foreign minister endorse the young republic's ambitions in the Mississippi valley, where France's older ally, Spain, had its own interests. Whenever France entered into the often acrimonious discussions between Spain and America over territory between the Appalachians and the Mississippi or over use of the river itself – and it often tried to avoid profitless involvement – it tended to support Madrid. Moreover, by the treaty that brought Spain into the war in 1779, France had promised to help its neighbor recover Gibraltar from Great Britain; when this proved difficult, Vergennes hoped the Spaniards would accept compensation in the American interior.

Neither Vergennes nor his agents at Philadelphia concealed their position on Canada and the West, although of course they did not expound the anti-American motives behind it. Their position angered many informed Americans, perhaps most notably and volubly

John Adams. Others, however, among them Richard Henry Lee and Robert Livingston, a New Yorker of pessimistic outlook and a francophile, agreed with the French that the war should be ended as soon as possible. Such men were unwilling to continue it to secure Canada or to confirm the right to take fish in Newfoundland waters, a prewar practice of interest almost solely to Adams's Yankee constituents. When Vergennes's representatives in the United States sought and gained congressional approval of moderate terms of peace, they did so by throwing their weight behind cautious men rather than by badgering a hostile Congress.

Maneuvering Toward Peace

In 1779, the Congress named John Adams to negotiate peace and independence with Great Britain.[6] Even after eight weeks of discussion, however, Adams's faction was unable to win its way on the fisheries, and Congress, while expressing a desire for all of Canada, authorized him to settle for only a portion of it. Adams's instructions also required him to demand a western boundary at the Mississippi River but did not seek Florida, then a British possession.

Adams reached Paris early in 1778, very impressed with his mission's importance: "The Commission to General Washington as commander-in-chief was far inferior." But the British were not yet interested in negotiations, and Adams almost immediately fell into quarrels with Vergennes, who soon told Adams that he would have nothing further to do with him, preferring to talk only with Franklin. Adams, the French minister told his representative in Philadelphia, had demonstrated "a rigidity, a pedantry, an arrogance and a self-love that render him incapable of dealing with political subjects."

Vergennes directed this representative, the chevalier de la Luzerne, to get the Americans to muzzle Adams and to retreat even from the instructions of 1779. Employing bribery and cajolery in about equal parts, Luzerne accomplished both tasks with remarkable

6 At the same time, as a counterpoise, John Jay, then pro-French, went to Spain.
  Benjamin Franklin continued as minister to France.

ease; as one historian comments, "the innocent and the corrupted together marched meekly to the slaughter."[7] New instructions were drafted in June 1781 by John Witherspoon, antiexpansionist, suspicious of Adams, on the French payroll, under Luzerne's eye. These instructions dropped the territorial ultimatums of 1779 and submerged Adams in a five-man commission.[8] They furthermore directed that quintet to subordinate itself to the wishes of the French ministers: "You are . . . to undertake nothing . . . without their knowledge and concurrence; and ultimately to govern yourselves by their advice and opinion." Only the Massachusetts and Connecticut delegations resisted this proposal, and only Virginia wanted to hold firm on the West. "Never in history," an outraged historian later wrote, "has one people voted to put its entire destiny more absolutely, more trustfully, under the control of a foreign government."[9]

These servile instructions cannot be explained merely as the work of what Gouverneur Morris later called "a set of d—d scoundrels . . . in that second Congress." The instructions reflected exhaustion after six years of inconclusive warfare (Yorktown was still four months away) and a feeling that French support must in no way be jeopardized. They also confirm the strength of factionalism and sectionalism, for Congress clearly understood itself to be hobbling Adams when it surrendered power into Vergennes's hands. Better than any other action during the Revolution, these instructions show the new nation's weakness.

Although Congress four times beat off efforts to reassert America's right to control its own destiny, the instructions fortunately became a nullity. In April 1782 Franklin began nominally informal conversations with a British representative, Richard Oswald, an old friend, a Scottish merchant, and former slaver who had lived in America for six years. The Doctor neither sought Vergennes's guidance nor informed him (nor, until later, his own colleagues or Congress, for that matter) of what passed in his talks with Oswald. Jay, who

7 Richard B. Morris, *The Peacemakers* (New York, 1965), 213.
8 One of the five, Thomas Jefferson, never went to Europe. Another, Henry Laurens, took part only in the last days of the negotiations of 1782.
9 Samuel Flagg Bemis, *The Diplomacy of the American Revolution* (New York, 1935), 190.

reached Paris in June after an extraordinarily unpleasant, unproductive mission in Spain, which obliterated his illusions about French friendship, and Adams, who returned from a mission to Holland in October, naturally preferred an independent policy; both had considered resignation when they received the instructions but instead stayed on to defy their orders. "It is glory," Adams wrote in his diary, "to have broken such infamous orders."

Franklin and Shelburne

News of Cornwallis's surrender at Yorktown, which reached Britain at the end of November 1781, was by far the most important of a series of unfavorable reports from many fronts that destroyed support for the war in Parliament and the country. As soon as the legislature returned from its Christmas recess, General John Conway offered in the Commons a resolution against "the further prosecution of offensive warfare on the Continent of North America." Although Conway and his supporters denied that they favored abject surrender to the rebellious Americans, his resolution plainly meant that military pressure would not be used to gain favorable terms. In March 1782, after Conway's Resolution passed, Lord North's ministry resigned. His successors and Franklin, the sole American then in Paris, soon opened contact with one another.

Negotiations at Paris were incredibly complex, often equally deceitful, and marked, on the American side at least, by fears of betrayal that approached paranoia. Agents from London, often responding to different superiors, frequently contradicted one another. Until the very end, misled by Franklin's bland, sanguine exterior, Jay and Adams suspected him of being in Vergennes's pocket, and Jay concealed from him one very important communication to London. Vergennes had no desire to see the Americans gain Canada — "Whatever will halt the conquest of that country accords with our views" — and let the British know so. He also had to balance the rival interests of his two allies, Spain and the United States. Although he accepted the fact of separate Anglo-American negotiations in part to pressure Spain to work for peace, on the whole he sympathized with the latter, and if he had drawn the boundaries

Spain would have received a large share of the American interior. For its part, Spain was ready to betray the Americans, and perhaps the French, if London would cede Gibraltar.

Most confusing of all was British policy, particularly as expressed by the earl of Shelburne. Shelburne was one of two ministers – this is typical of the confusion – who negotiated with Franklin for the ministry headed by North's successor, the marquis of Rockingham. On Rockingham's death in July he became head of government and sole negotiator. At first, Shelburne rather foolishly dreamed of a settlement that would leave America closely tied to England, even within the empire, and to effect reconciliation on these terms he was prepared to pay a high price. Soon he abandoned hope of a permanent tie without abandoning his desire for reconciliation. Late in July he summarized his position in a letter to his representative in Paris:

I have never made a Secret of the deep Concern I feel in the Separation of Countries united by Blood, by Principles, Habits, and every Tie short of Territorial Proximity. But you very well know that I have long since given it up *decidedly* tho' *reluctantly*: and the same motives which made me perhaps the last to give up all Hope of Re-union, make me most anxious, if it is given up, that it should be done *decidedly,* so as to avoid all future Risque of Enmity, and the Foundation of a new Connection better adapted to the present Temper and Interest of both Countries.

But Shelburne never spoke so candidly in public, and, even after reconciling himself to American independence, he was reluctant to give it formal recognition before negotiations began, not because he hoped to extort a price for it – as the Americans suspected – but rather to avoid domestic political difficulties. In addition, he tried to make abrogation of the Franco-American alliance a condition of peace. Not surprisingly, his position was misunderstood by the Americans, who thought him an enemy.

Rockingham's death allowed Shelburne to gather power into his own hands for only a few months. Because he was unable to win the backing of all those who had supported his predecessor, he controlled only a minority in the House of Commons. Barring some fortunate diplomatic success, he could not reasonably hope to stay in power very long after Parliament returned from its summer recess, particularly since he was perhaps the most hated and distrusted politician of his day. For the moment, however, he was a free agent, the only important figure on the British side.

Shortly after Shelburne became premier, Franklin read to Oswald a list of "necessary" and "advisable" terms of peace. Franklin's list of "advisable" terms, ones he said would inspire true reconciliation, included a monetary indemnity and the cession of all of Canada. Describing them merely as "advisable," of course, made their attainment much less likely. Even Oswald, usually very tender to American wishes, reported, "They will not be any way stiff on those articles he calls *advisable,* or will drop them altogether." Still, the "necessary" terms were demanding enough. Aside from the most obvious, independence, they included the right to use the traditional fishing grounds off Newfoundland and the cession of a portion of Canada. Regarding the latter, Franklin drew upon Congress's instructions of 1779: The United States demanded that Canada be limited to the territorial limits Britain had, albeit temporarily, established by royal proclamation in 1763. This boundary ran up the Ottawa River through Lake Nipissing to Lake Huron, excluding most of what later became the province of Ontario. The future of Canada would have been extremely problematic, American sovereignty over the entire Canadian west very likely, if the Nipissing line had become the boundary in 1782.

Nevertheless, Shelburne did not hesitate. He immediately told Oswald that, if Franklin would drop the "advisable" matters, Britain was prepared to settle. The exploratory conversations, Shelburne proposed, should be converted into formal negotiations. Oswald would be commissioned to undertake them. A few days later, the cabinet endorsed this position, although it also decided that Oswald should seek indemnification of Loyalists who had lost property and assurances that prewar debts to British merchants would be paid. A grand chance lay before the Americans, for unless the British reneged they could have had not only a quick peace but one that, by giving them title to the Ontario country, would have doomed Canada's future by confining it to a small enclave along the upper St. Lawrence.

The Suspicious Americans

Unfortunately, the Americans derailed negotiations before the British position was presented to them at Paris. So doing, they almost certainly delayed peace and, in the end, lost the Nipissing country. No episodes better show the Americans' combination of alarmism and guile than the events of the summer of 1782.

From the beginning of his talks with Oswald, Franklin had felt that recognition of American independence must precede negotiations on details. Jay, upon his arrival at the end of June, fully agreed with him. Otherwise, the two men feared, they might be asked to pay a price, in territory or something else, for that recognition. At the very least, they thought, when formal discussions began, Oswald would have to present credentials appointing him to negotiate with them as representatives of the United States. For his part, Shelburne simply proposed to make recognition the first article in a peace treaty.

About Oswald's commission he was unconcerned. As early as May, he agreed that "any character [will be] given to Mr. Oswald which Dr. Franklin and he may judge conducive to a final settlement of things between Great Britain and America." But things went wrong, for reasons still unclear – bureaucratic bungling is the most likely explanation. When Oswald presented his commission for American inspection early in August, Franklin and Jay instantly saw that the document avoided any mention of a nation calling itself the United States of America and spoke instead of negotiations with "any Commissioner or Commissioners named . . . by the . . . Colonies or Plantations." What did this mean, they asked themselves? How important was it?

Franklin, typically, was not inclined to make a fuss. Jay argued violently that a British doublecross was in the offing, that Shelburne was keeping open the possibility of refusing to accept American independence or at least planning to charge a high price for it. Oswald tried without success to mollify Jay by showing him that part of London's instructions which said that it was the ministry's intention to "make the Independency of the Colonies the Basis and Preliminary of the Treaty now depending." Vergennes, consulted for one of the few times during the negotiations, sided with Franklin, but the result was to make the New Yorker even more stubborn. He suspected that France intended to betray the Americans to get better terms for itself or for its Spanish ally. From Holland, John Adams wrote in support of Jay. In the end the latter dragooned Franklin into agreement: The commission would have to be changed and independence formally accepted before negotiations could proceed.

Almost immediately, London gave way. Revising the commission raised only small problems, but formal acceptance of independence was another matter, requiring, in the cabinet's view, an act of Parliament. Ministers however agreed that, if Oswald could not convince Franklin and Jay to drop this requirement, they would take the enormous political risk of seeking legislation. They also reaffirmed their willingness to accept Franklin's "necessary" terms; a minute of their meeting on August 29 reads, "We will settle the Boundaries of the Province and Contract the Limits of Canada as desir'd by Dr. Franklin." The Americans were on the brink of victory, albeit victory over obstacles largely in their imagination. All that was required was a few days' patience, until the new instructions reached Paris.

Then Jay swerved off in another direction, driven by his suspicion 44of France. When he learned that Vergennes's closest confidant, Gérard de Rayneval, had left on a secret mission to Lord Shelburne, Jay leapt to the conclusion that a sellout of American interests impended.[10] Jay talked Franklin into dropping the demand for formal recognition if a new commission authorized Oswald to negotiate with the United States. Then he went further: Behind Franklin's back, he sent a message to London broadly hinting that the United States would, despite its pledge to France, make a separate peace.

10 In fact, Rayneval had been sent to Britain to explore the chances for peace in Europe. His instructions did not direct him to raise issues involving the United States, and in his discussions with Shelburne American issues came up only in passing. No "deals" were proposed, but the Frenchman's comments did permit Shelburne to report to the king, "The Point of Independence once settled, he appears rather Jealous than partial to America upon other points." This visit was the first of three made by Reyneval, two of them after the American treaty was settled, during which Shelburne personally and very secretly worked out the terms of peace with France.

He also told the agent who carried this message that, while the United States would remain true to the alliance after the war, "yet it was a different thing to be guided by their or our construction of it." These indiscretions went far beyond anything Rayneval said to Shelburne.

They were not necessary to convince Shelburne or his lieutenants, who only a few weeks earlier had made the basic decisions, but they did ease the premier's mind. Although both Franklin and Jay had repeatedly told Oswald that favorable terms of peace would split America from France, only now was Shelburne convinced. He had new instructions sent to Oswald, who quickly discovered that the Americans would drop their demand for prior recognition, by act of Parliament or otherwise. He presented a new form that his commission might take. Jay accepted it, although it was certainly at least somewhat equivocal, authorizing Oswald to "treat with the Commissioners appointed by the Colonies [which were listed one-by-one], under the title of Thirteen United States." Approved by the cabinet, the commission reached Paris at the end of September. Formal negotiations began.

This series of events, spread over two months, certainly reflects badly on the Americans, particularly Jay. They failed to get the assurances – prior recognition, a clearly acceptable commission for Oswald – that they considered vital when the affair began, although, if Jay had not panicked, they could have had both. His betrayal of the French alliance was absolutely unnecessary and failed to be costly only because Shelburne had already made up his mind. In the largest sense, Franklin and Jay probably delayed the peace. Their major objectives were almost in hand in July, and they gained nothing (and lost the Nipissing country) by the delay they forced.

The Peace of Paris

On October 4, Jay handed Oswald a draft treaty, modeled very largely on Franklin's "necessary" proposals but omitting the "advisable" ones. He did not, for example, even ask for all of Canada. Shelburne responded with requests of his own two weeks later, and he sent a new representative, Henry Strachey, to stiffen Oswald's

spine. For their part, Jay and Franklin received reinforcement in the
disputatious person of John Adams, who came from Holland as soon
as he learned that the commission question had been settled. Often
the discussions were heated, even Franklin shedding his usual conciliatory manner. This was a surprise to Adams, who was forced to
confess – to his diary – that "He . . . has gone on with Us, in
entire Harmony and Unanimity." But soon the arguments with
Strachey petered out. On November 30 a treaty was signed at Oswald's residence, a year after the drama of Yorktown set diplomacy
in motion. This helped Shelburne to make peace with France and
Spain in January 1783.

Chief among the items sought by Britain were compensation to
Loyalists for the loss of their property, assurances that British creditors would recover monies owed them when the Revolution began,
and deletion of the article that confirmed American rights to fish in
waters off British North America. Shelburne more or less admitted
that he had little concern about these issues, save in the political
sense that he sought to disarm criticism. It is therefore not surprising that, despite the heated debates, in the end he gained little. The
treaty granted Americans the "liberty" – an ambiguous word, which
later caused trouble – to fish in accustomed areas. It also pledged
Congress to advise the states to restore confiscated Tory property and
to assure the repayment of pre-Revolutionary debts, but, as was
recognized, Congress had no power to do either of these things. The
provisions were "trifling concessions and empty formulas."[11]

The treaty fixed the line of the Great Lakes as the boundary
between Canada and the United States and the Mississippi River as
the western boundary. The Americans thus gained a handsome empire extending well beyond current areas of settlement. The negotiators have often been praised for gaining the Northwest, the area
between the Ohio River and the Great Lakes. In fact, their triumph
was imagined. Except for a brief moment when he asked for the
Northwest as a way to indemnify Loyalists, Shelburne made no effort
to hold these lands for the British Empire. Boundaries never inter-

11 James H. Hutson, *John Adams and the Diplomacy of the American Revolution*
(Lexington, Ky., 1980), 128.

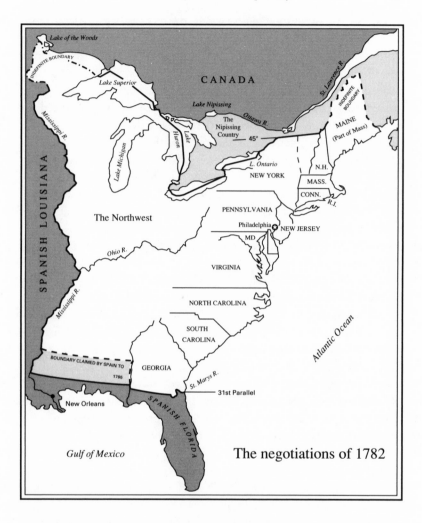

CANADA

Lake of the Woods

INDEFINITE BOUNDARY

Lake Superior

Lake Nipissing

St. Lawrence R.

Ottawa R.

The Nipissing Country

45°

INDEFINITE BOUNDARY

MAINE (Part of Mass)

Lake Huron

Lake Michigan

Mississippi R.

SPANISH LOUISIANA

L. Ontario

NEW YORK

N.H.

MASS.

CONN.

R.I.

The Northwest

PENNSYLVANIA

Ohio R.

Philadelphia NEW JERSEY

MD

VIRGINIA

Mississippi R.

NORTH CAROLINA

SOUTH CAROLINA

BOUNDARY CLAIMED BY SPAIN TO 1795

GEORGIA

St. Marys R.

SPANISH FLORIDA

31st Parallel

New Orleans

Atlantic Ocean

Gulf of Mexico

The negotiations of 1782

ested him very much; indeed, an enlarged United States, source of raw materials and market for British goods, might make even more valuable the kind of neocolonial relationship he seems to have envisioned. The Americans did not win Florida, which, as a price of peace, Britain later agreed to return to Spain, and British recognition of the Mississippi as their western boundary merely meant that they would have to contest the matter with Madrid.

In the last weeks of negotiation, the possibility of even more favorable boundaries almost silently disappeared. All of Canada had never been within their grasp. Although Franklin had asked for it and Oswald seemed sympathetic, neither Shelburne nor any of his colleagues ever considered it. However, Shelburne had repeatedly agreed to accept the Nipissing line. Strachey was authorized to accept that boundary, which was part of Jay's draft, but he was also directed to seek something better, perhaps the "French boundary," as Shelburne called it. Strachey accomplished this with remarkable ease. Failing to foresee the importance of the area — the industrial heartland of modern Canada — and gratified to receive so much other territory, the Americans retreated to the line of the Great Lakes without even being pressed to do so. It was a fateful act.

Even so, Britain gave generous terms to the new state. Its armies held the city of New York, large portions of the southern states and other areas, and in purely military terms further resistance was possible. But Britain was too weary to continue the struggle; the Conway Resolution had already demonstrated that. As was to happen again in history, suppression of a colonial rebellion proved beyond the political capacities of an immensely strong imperial state.

After signing the treaty, Strachey asked his chief, "Are we to be hanged or applauded, for thus rescuing you from an American war?" Neither hanging nor applause came, but instead much criticism and a grudging acceptance. A similar reaction greeted the treaties with Spain and France signed in January 1783, and in February Shelburne was forced to resign.

The Americans won favorable terms largely because, by violating their instructions and betraying, in spirit if not in letter, the alliance with France, they convinced Shelburne that their country would not be a satellite of England's enemy. Excuses for their behavior may be made. Europe was full of intrigue; Vergennes or the Spaniards might have betrayed them had they dallied further. Violation of instructions to follow Vergennes's advice was a matter between the commissioners and Congress, not the Frenchman and themselves. Technically, because the Americans signed only a "preliminary" peace, not a definitive one, they had not broken the terms of the alliance, although for all practical purposes they had made a separate peace.

The definitive treaty was not signed until September 1783, on the same day that the major powers formalized their own preliminary treaties at Versailles. The Americans, who precipitated the conflict thus ended, were not invited to share the society of great states on this occasion, signing instead at the British commissioners' residence. [12]

In their report to Congress after signing the preliminaries, the 48commissioners wrote, "As we had reason to imagine that the articles respecting the boundaries, the refugees, and fisheries did not correspond with the policy of this court, we did not communicate the preliminaries to the minister [Vergennes] until after they were signed. . . . We hope these considerations will excuse our having so far departed from the spirit [actually, it was the letter] of our instructions."

When they did report to Vergennes, he was astounded at what he considered British generosity. "The English," he said to Rayneval, "buy peace rather than make it. Their concessions exceed all that I could have thought possible." He told the Americans that the "abrupt signing . . . had little in it which could be agreeable to the King." And to Luzerne he wrote, "I blame nobody. I do not even blame Mr. Franklin. He yields perhaps too easily to the suggestions of his colleagues, who do not pretend to know anything of courtesy. . . . [But] if we may judge the future by what I have just seen, we shall be badly paid for all we have done for the United States of America and for securing them that title." On the other hand, the French minister was not entirely unhappy to have the Americans break the logjam blocking a general settlement, Spain's unsuccessful quest for the return of Gibraltar being the major impediment. Moreover, he could see little profit in an open quarrel with the ingrates. Consequently, he even agreed to Franklin's request for further financial assistance.

When all extenuations are offered, the fact remains that, despite

12 As of that date, of all the Continental powers only France and Holland, which became embroiled in the war in 1780 but did not grant recognition to the United States until 1782, had formal relations with the transatlantic upstarts. Even Spain, a quasi ally, had refused recognition, one of the reasons why Jay found his stay in that country so unpleasant.

the pledge in the French alliance, the Americans negotiated an end to their part of the war, thus permitting Shelburne to face his other enemies with more confidence and strength. "The peacemaking began as an encounter between innocence and guile," a prominent historian has observed, "but the Americans rapidly acquired a measure of sophistication sufficient for the task."[13] This hardly overstates the case. First Franklin, then Jay, then Adams — protesting all the while that they alone were honest men in a den of thieves — subordinated good faith to their nation's interest. They confirmed what, writing to his king, Beaumarchais had argued in 1775: "Sire, the policy of governments is not the moral law of their citizens."

Legacies

Revolutionary diplomacy — more accurately, American perceptions of it — helped to form or to harden attitudes that lasted for generations, even to the present. Thus, to take the most prominent example, exposure to European politics strengthened the desire for isolation. Americans stressed the chicanery of foreign statesmen, ignoring their own. Although France banked a modest amount of gratitude, most Americans tended as a matter of national pride to underrate their ally's contribution, and almost no one admitted that Spain had drawn off a great deal of British resources. Many argued, falsely, that Europe's ambitions lengthened the peace negotiations and might well have cost America the western country. In June 1783 James Madison introduced and Congress unanimously approved a resolution asserting that "the true interest of these states requires that they should be as little as possible entangled in the politics and controversies of European nations."

It is easy to overstress the strength of isolationism or at least to give this spirit the same form that it had a century later. Madison's resolution urged only that America be "as little as possible entangled." The league of states was too weak, security too precarious, to permit the luxury of doctrinaire isolation a stronger nation could later indulge. Thus Washington's Farewell Address of 1796, al-

13 Morris, *The Peacemakers,* 459.

though it did warn against "permanent alliances," also said, "we may safely trust to temporary alliances for extraordinary emergencies." Jefferson, who repeated Washington's warning in his first inaugural address in 1801, adapted to reality. In 1803, he ordered his representatives to seek an alliance with England if France refused to settle the Louisiana question, only to be saved by Napoleon's decision to sell. As late as 1823 he and Madison, both then in Virginia retirement, favored joint action with Britain to shelter Latin America from French intervention. President Monroe, however, decided to act unilaterally.

With Monroe's message in December 1823, what began as a dream became a reality. The Monroe Doctrine ushered in a period of about a century during which America felt so confident of its power, and so suspicious of foreigners, that it tenaciously avoided political ties, no matter what the temptation.[14] Reality and dream ossified into dogma, as they never had for the Founding Fathers. Americans tended to forget that only accidents of world politics made possible the rigid isolationism of the post-1823 period; they tended to forget that the first American diplomats, ever isolationist in spirit, dabbled deeply in European politics.

The Americans, though mostly hesitant or unknowing revolutionaries as late as 1775, correctly saw their success as the harbinger of a new political era. In Jefferson's phrase, it provided "a ralliance for the reason and freedom of the globe." Somewhat ironically, Britain and its empire escaped the full impact of the movement, although in Ireland the American success stirred nationalists into action. Britain's foes were less fortunate. Revolution struck France in 1789, and until less moderate men pushed them aside, leaders with American experience, notably the marquis de Lafayette and Thomas Paine, were in the van. "Ça Ira," predecessor of the "Marseillaise" as the revolutionary anthem, drew its title from a phrase of Franklin's, "it will pass," downplaying Washington's defeats, and the general and other Americans were honored by a gift of keys, actually spurious, to the Bastille. In 1808 a rising began in Spain, which, though

---

14 A treaty of 1846 with New Granada, later Colombia, guaranteeing the "perfect neutrality" of the Isthmus of Panama is the most important exception.

it did not lead to republicanism in that country, loosened the ties that bound Spain's empire. Fighting for their own freedom but harkening both to the American and French experiments, all Spain's mainland colonies in the New World won independence after a long struggle.

History seldom moves purposefully, single-mindedly. There occurred a spread of empires joined by the United States at the end of the nineteenth century, and decolonization did not become general until the 1960s. The world still contains many authoritarian regimes, although few authoritarian monarchies. But those who have struggled against colonialism and autocracy have often appealed to the American lesson. Leaders as diverse as Louis Kossuth and Mohandas Gandhi, Louis Thiers and Sukarno cited it. Thomas Masaryk's declaration of Czech independence in October 1918 followed the American model. Ho Chi Minh's declaration of Vietnamese independence in September 1945 began with a paraphrase of the Jeffersonian preamble of 1776, then proceeded to list colonial grievances as the American document had done. Even Lenin, bitter enemy of the capitalist republican system supported by America, declared in 1918 that the United States had "set the world an example of a revolutionary war against feudal subjection."

In 1853, ordered by Washington to abandon court uniform for plain dress, American diplomats appeared in suits at a Berlin reception. One was asked why he and his colleagues were "all dressed in black, like so many undertakers?" "We could not," the quick-witted republican replied, "be more appropriately dressed than we are, at European courts, where what we represent is the burial of monarchy." Others understood the threat. As early as 1816, a Spanish diplomat apologized for his country's "unpardonable error" in fueling "the contagious fire of rebellion and insurrection" forty years earlier. Commenting on the Monroe Doctrine a few years later, the Austrian chancellor, Prince Metternich, asked, "if this flood of evil doctrines and pernicious examples should extend over the whole of America, what would become . . . of the moral force of our governments, and of that conservative system which has saved Europe from complete dissolution?" Such fears were justified, although the "conservative system" survived far longer than Metternich expected.

Americans inevitably gave their hearts to those who attacked a system described by Jefferson as "loaded with misery, by kings, nobles and priests." He himself, while minister at Paris, extended the protection of his roof and the counsel of his mind to anti-Bourbon plotters, and he helped to draft the Declaration of the Rights of Man, the revolutionaries' major statement of principle. Moreover – though this is often forgotten because of later clashes of view between Democratic-Republicans and Federalists – almost all Americans welcomed the French Revolution in its first, moderate stage. (John Adams is an exception proving the rule.) As late as January 1793 the entire nation rejoiced at French triumphs over hostile monarchies, and in Boston two newspapers, later the bell-wethers of contending parties, joined in support of a "civic feast," featuring roast ox and rum punch, in honor of the first victory of the revolutionary armies at Valmy.

The rash of European revolutions in 1848 excited Americans. In a special message to Congress following news of the overthrow of King Louis-Philippe of France, President Polk praised those who, "imitating our example, have resolved to be free." When the movement spread to Germany, one newspaper described events there as "the revolution of 1776 extending itself across the seas." Without waiting for orders, the American minister at Paris, Richard Rush, recognized the new French republic, and President Polk applauded his conduct. Summing up opinion, at least among northern Jacksonians, the *New York Sun* declared: "Among the waving banners and the flash of uplifted sabres, . . . the finger of revolution points to us as its example, its cloud and pillar of fire! As we vowed, so are the masses of Europe vowing."

In 1848, to the distress of American observers, Louis Kossuth failed to win Hungarian independence from the Habsburg empire. In 1851, Kossuth landed in New York, where he was greeted by a band playing "Hail to the Chief." For six months, he traveled through the United States, pleading for aid to the Hungarian cause. Almost everywhere he went, the Hungarian exile was greeted enthusiastically. At one banquet, Secretary of State Daniel Webster declaimed, "We shall rejoice to see our American model upon the Lower Danube and on the mountains of Hungary." This and other

Websterian excesses led the Austrian minister to withdraw from Washington.

Because the American Revolution had been a colonial uprising as well as an antimonarchical one, later generations almost inevitably endorsed resistance to colonial rule. For example, enthusiasm for the Latin American risings nearly swamped President Monroe's cautious wish to delay recognition of the new states, and the pressures of that enthusiasm played a part in his decision to announce his famous doctrine in December 1823. At exceptional times – the Boer revolution against British control, which began in 1899, was perhaps the first, and the Vietnamese and Algerian risings against France are more recent examples – opinion has been divided and, at least at the governmental level, predominantly hostile. Moreover, America has been much more interested in ending political than economic subordination, and the United States itself took a fling at colonialism in 1898. Still, although cynics correctly point out that, by breaking down imperial trade fences, decolonization may serve American economic interests, the anticolonial strain – an ideological one – in policy and attitudes has been about as consistent as the antimonarchical one. Both clearly find their roots in the American Revolution.

Sympathy did not mean help. Even at the height of enthusiasm in 1789, few seriously proposed more than moral support for the French cause. In 1823 Albert Gallatin's suggestion, the more striking since it came from an unusually judicious Jeffersonian elder, that the navy be loaned to the Greeks to help them in their struggle for freedom from the Turkish empire, was not so much rejected as ignored by Monroe's administration. Only rarely, as when, just after the Civil War, Union armies were maneuvered to give support to Washington's opposition to monarchicocolonial enterprise in Mexico, has even the shadow of force been at the service of revolutionary causes. Only in 1898, when America threw its weight behind a Cuban revolution against Spain, has force actually been employed.

Americans preferred to see themselves as torchbearers or guardians of the flame, not crusaders in arms. In his Fourth of July oration of 1821, disguised in a professor's gown so as to avoid seeming to speak officially, Secretary of State John Quincy Adams denounced monarchy and described America as "a beacon on the summit of the mountains, to which all the inhabitants of the earth may turn their eyes for a genial and saving light." When Louis Kossuth announced that he came to America to seek, not "an asylum for exiles, . . . but an avenger . . . against the oppression of a holy cause," he simply made certain that President Fillmore and every other politician who greeted him would add a *caveat* about nonintervention and the cherished policy of isolation. Not only was effective action impossible – at a time when Kossuth had been driven into exile and indeed, given America's minuscule armed forces, for many years thereafter – but, Americans believed, others would be more likely to steer toward Adams's beacon if the nation remained separate from and thus morally superior to the old order. Better to await, said Senator Lewis Cass during the Kossuth season, the spread of "the contagion of liberty . . . to the established systems of oppressions."

A further qualification, the fruit this time of arrogance rather than prudence, remains to be noted. Americans have often considered themselves a special people, favored by Providence with virtues denied to others. They have often doubted that these unfortunates, conditioned by an absolutist or colonial past, perhaps racially "inferior," could maintain their balance in the midst of a violent rush for freedom.

In the twentieth century, Woodrow Wilson worked to establish the mandate system, essentially an effort to make rulers serve the ruled, not to obliterate that rule, at least in part because he did not consider Africans and Asians ready for self-government. Only one of the mandates, Iraq, gained independence before World War II. Later, fulminations about British imperialism by Franklin D. Roosevelt and more noisily by some of his subordinates angered even anticolonialists like the Labour leader, Clement Attlee. Still, Roosevelt confessed that "he did not think that India [the chief focus of discussion] was ready . . . for complete independence." He aimed, a recent writer comments, "at stabilizing, not undermining, the colonial world. He wanted a peaceful [and gradual] transition to independence."[15]

15 Wm. Roger Louis, *Imperialism at Bay* (New York, 1978), 9.

The historical record leaves the clear impression that, because they consider others to lack their own natural virtues, Americans have been more certain of their antiimperialism and antimonarchism than confident of the success of republicanism in the world at large. At the same time, however, they have felt free to criticize emerging peoples for straying from the path, have sought, usually ineffectively, to prod them in that direction, or, contrariwise, have accepted authoritarian regimes that served their global purposes.

Americans sometimes lament that they have lost the radical, revolutionary image they had in Metternich's time. Leaders as disparate as John Foster Dulles and John F. Kennedy have appealed to the world to remember that theirs, in the latter's words, is "the greatest revolutionary country on earth." This misses the point. No one would consider radical, by today's standards, the views of the barons who forced King John to accept Magna Charta or Abraham Lincoln's attitudes toward blacks. Similarly, the movement of the 1770s, truly radical and certainly risky when it occurred, seems less far-reaching when wrenched into today's context. Unlike the French a few years later or the Russians as late as 1917, the Americans did not confront a pervasive legacy of feudalism. To break with the king was a dramatic act, nearly unprecedented, but it did not require new patterns of internal political behavior.

Moreover, the social revolution that accompanied the break with England was, at most, moderate by today's standards. Established churches disappeared, several northern states abolished slavery, perhaps as many as one hundred thousand Tories left the country, but the social structure was not markedly transformed. Neither guillotines nor firing squads were necessary to carry out the few reforms demanded by the American consensus. Nor were economic institutions transformed. Most white Americans saw no need for that, in marked contrast to later revolutionaries who considered political liberation only a first step on the road to broader justice and equality. Especially in later years, leaders as different as Thomas Jefferson and John Adams worried that a polarization of wealth might threaten republicanism, but they believed that this polarization could be controlled within existing institutions.

The special characteristics of the American Revolution help to explain why many of today's new nations, socially and economically as well as politically oppressed, find the American experience an inadequate guide. They help to explain why Americans, sincerely believing themselves to favor revolutions, at least when progressive and republican, have looked askance upon those accompanied by internal turmoil and the disruption of societies. Thus Americans often ask if new regimes, raised to power by revolution, intend to follow the path of republicanism and capitalism. Only in such instances – and they are rare – do Americans feel really comfortable with them.

But this is to look ahead. When news of the peace of Paris reached America in February 1783 – it was first published in a Tory newspaper in British-occupied New York – Americans could not foresee this legacy. If they had, it would not have troubled them. They took justifiable pride in the success of the bold crusade upon which they had embarked in 1775 and 1776. They knew they had altered the flow of history.

3. The Constitution

Peoples who emerge from colonialism usually find their triumph exhilarating, but almost all soon discover that independence is only the beginning of a process of nation building. Despite advantages – relative prosperity, experience in self-government – the Americans learned this lesson in the 1780s. Historians still debate the truth of the matter – was or was not the decade a time of economic growth? a period of political maturation? – but contemporaries had little doubt they were in a "critical period," critical not only for their country but for the fate of republican government as well. John Quincy Adams, indeed, used the phrase in a commencement oration in 1787. Several years later, his father wrote, "I suspect that our posterity will view the history of our last few years with regret." When the elder Adams wrote these words, he was vice-president under the new Constitution, an instrument of government produced both by the political philosophy undergirding the Revolution and by the frustrations of the 1780s.

The Articles of Confederation

The Continental Congress, legitimized only by the willingness of states to send delegates, had no power of coercion over them. Seeking to improve things, Congress proposed, and in 1781 the states approved, Articles of Confederation, but the remedy failed to create an effective national government. The approved text failed to capitalize "united states," thus emphasizing the continued sovereignty of the parts. Almost all decisions, even in areas where Congress nominally had power, required the concurrence of nine of the thirteen states. Amendments, several times proposed in an effort to improve the system, could be – and were – blocked by a single state's negative. A man as suspicious of government power as Jefferson might believe that comparing the Articles with European constitutions "is like a comparison of heaven and hell. . . . With all the imperfections of our present government, it is without comparison the best existing or that ever did exist." Those who wanted a true nation came to disagree.

The state-oriented thrust of the Articles of Confederation was underlined by the absence of an executive branch. Congress, working sometimes through committees, did all the governing in what was "in effect parliamentary government without a prime minister."[1] The committee system worked badly because there were so many that no congressman could give adequate attention to any one of them, because they competed for influence and because the steady turnover of membership prevented continuity. The Committee of Secret Correspondence and its successor, the Committee for Foreign Affairs, never gained full control of diplomacy, had no staff to manage correspondence and records, and met only intermittently. One member wrote in disgust, "There is really no such thing as a Committee for Foreign Affairs existing – no secretary or clerk further than I presume to be one or the other."

In 1781 Congress established a Department of Foreign Affairs, made up of a secretary and four employees, but it kept the department on a very short leash. Initially, the secretary, while allowed to attend sessions of Congress, could ask no questions and propose no actions. Even after this changed, he remained little more than a none-too-glorified clerk, receiving correspondence and preparing responses at Congress's direction. Robert Livingston, the first incumbent, understandably resigned after a year. Congress then left the position vacant for more than a year before appointing John Jay. Jay did direct the negotiation of a consular convention with France made necessary by Franklin's carelessness in the matter, but this was hardly an earth-shattering accomplishment. If remembered at all, it is because in time it became the first agreement to be ratified under the new Constitution. During Jay's tenure, commercial treaties were concluded with three European countries, all of them small markets for American goods, and with Morocco, more of a problem because

1 Arthur M. Schlesinger, Jr., *The Imperial Presidency* (Boston, 1973), 2.

Morocco, like others of the Barbary states, tended to pillage American trade once British protection was lost. Jay's efforts to negotiate with Spain over commerce, the western country, and the use of the Mississippi River involved him in deep controversy with the Congress, which watched him suspiciously throughout his tenure.

Flaws in the diplomatic machinery reflected the central weakness of the Articles of Confederation. The nation did not command respect abroad and had little ability to develop any. As Jefferson, Franklin's successor at Paris, observed in 1784, Americans were "the lowest and most obscure of the diplomatic tribe." Because the states retained so much power, the government at Philadelphia could not raise revenue, could not bargain effectively, could not assure other nations that any agreements it made would actually be observed by the states, could not develop a unified commercial policy to extort concessions from other countries, could not maintain an effective military or naval force.

The effects of this weakness were pervasive. Leaders in Vermont went so far as to weigh the comparative advantages of a Canadian connection against an American one. Spanish authorities in Louisiana intrigued with Indian tribes and American settlers in territory disputed by Spain and the United States. Canadian officials maintained as much influence as they could over tribes south of the Great Lakes, although, contrary to American belief, they did not urge the Indians to make war on the United States. British garrisons remained in a string of posts stretching from Lake Champlain to Lake Superior, London using as justification the fact that the Congress had been unable to induce the states to carry out promises made in the Treaty of Paris regarding Tory property and the payment of prewar debts. "If we are now to pay the debts due to British merchants," Virginians were alleged to ask, "what have we been fighting for all this time?"

Most important of all was commerce. Looking back, James Madison wrote in 1789, "our trade . . . entirely contradicted the advantages expected from the Revolution, no new channels being opened with other European nations, and the British channels being narrowed by a refusal of the most natural and valuable one to the U.S." Various envoys, most notably Jefferson in France, sought to negotiate the lowering of trade barriers, but they had little to bargain with – Congress could not threaten to close trade, or tax it – and accomplished little.

Particularly galling was the loss of trade with the British West Indies. As colonies, the Americans had carried on a highly profitable triangular trade, of benefit to their goods and their ships alike, with the Caribbean and Europe. Jay's draft of a peace treaty, presented to the British in October 1782, called for commercial reciprocity, the opening of all ports on each side to the shipping and goods of the other, but this was one of the articles that disappeared in the closing weeks of negotiations. As far as the record shows, the Americans scarcely exerted themselves in this area, a lapse as astonishing as their failure to press for the Nipissing line. Not for half a century would their country regain the commerce that had been a mainstay of colonial prosperity.[2]

American powerlessness meant that London had a free hand. Lord Sheffield, an influential advocate of sternness toward the ex-colonies' commerce, justified it in part on the ground that "America cannot retaliate. It will not be an easy matter to bring the American States to act as a nation. They are not to be feared as such by us." An Order in Council issued in 1783 to regulate the direct trade across the Atlantic was not illiberal, and, as the British hoped, that trade soon regained prewar levels. But another Order in Council closed the British West Indies to American vessels, depriving shipowners, exporters, and farmers of traditional business. John Adams, the first American minister to Britain, totally failed in his efforts to improve matters. Although Americans read all of this as a sign of British malevolence, it really reflected nothing more than an understanding of American weakness.

The Constitutional Movement

Within only a few years of the euphoric confirmation of independence, these problems came to cloud the skies. So, too, did internal

2 During its wars with France, from 1793 to 1815, Britain frequently suspended controls on trade between various islands and the United States, but the trade was firmly cut off in 1815.

problems, varying from state to state, often centering around the broad issues of liberty and order, property and persons, liberalism and conservatism. At least since 1913, when Charles A. Beard published *An Economic Interpretation of the Constitution,* scholars have emphasized and debated the internal issues. Indeed, these evoked most discussion at the convention that drafted a new constitution and provided the principal battlefield during debates over ratification in each of the states.

Nevertheless, a good case can be made for the primacy of concerns over American weakness in the world. "Nothing contributed more directly to the calling of the 1787 Constitutional Convention," Walter LaFeber writes, "than did the spreading belief that under the Articles of Confederation Congress could not effectively and safely conduct foreign policy."[3] The Annapolis Convention of 1786, which itself failed to accomplish anything but issued the call for the successful meeting of the next year, was convened specifically to consider the sad condition of American trade. If there was comparatively little discussion at Philadelphia of diplomatic and even military matters, it was because almost everyone agreed that the mechanisms of foreign policy had to be changed. They agreed, too, that American diplomacy had to be further armed for controversies with other nations. Differences were almost always over detail, and far-reaching changes were not so much debated as assumed.

Essentially, no matter how devoted to the rights of states, the delegates at Philadelphia believed that the central government must be made strong enough to command the respect of foreign nations. From Paris, Jefferson pithily summarized the opinion of those who opposed centralized government: "I wish to see our states made one as to all foreign, and several as to all domestic matters." Despite deep concern about standing armies, seen as potential instruments of tyranny, there was general agreement that the national government must be given war powers, both to deter possible enemies and to fight wars effectively.[4]

3 Walter LaFeber, "The Constitution and United States Foreign Policy," *Journal of American History* 74 (1987–8): 697.
4 Fewer than one thousand men were in the armed forces of the United States at the

Similarly, it was recognized that the thirteen states could not, acting individually, extort commercial concessions from other nations. Thus, despite fears that the interests of some states might be sacrificed by a national legislature, Congress was given the power to create policies that might compel Great Britain and others to relax some of their restrictions on American trade.[5] Finally, it was agreed that, if the United States were to bargain effectively, the national government must not only have the power to conclude treaties but to compel states to observe them.

This by no means suggests that the framers of the Constitution wanted or expected the United States to plunge deeply into traditional diplomacy. Even strong nationalists like Madison and Alexander Hamilton thought that the United States should never have more than five or six missions abroad. Others wanted fewer. Some even suggested that none would be needed; other nations should be required to send envoys to America whenever there was anything to negotiate.[6] Such attitudes showed that "the delegates assumed that diplomatic negotiations *per se* would be rare, that foreign relations would be commercial in nature, and that treaties would be few."[7] The creation of a nation with power to defend itself and to bargain commercially, primarily by legislation, would, the delegates thought, be sufficient to transform the scene.

The Constitution and Foreign Affairs

The Philadelphia convention opened in May 1787, two weeks behind schedule because many delegates were tardy. Rhode Island, the

time of the Philadelphia convention. Within ten years the figure rose to about seven thousand. Deployment was primarily directed against Indians in the West.

5 Having agreed on this, the convention had to give the federal government control of interstate commerce. Otherwise, individual states could have sabotaged national policy by placing restrictions on imports, foreign in origin, that came to them from other states. The enormous implications of this grant of power were, like so much else, not seen in 1787, but the "commerce clause" became the chief engine that advanced federal power at the expense of the states.

6 In 1784, the United States had two ministers abroad, as well as one commission to negotiate commercial treaties with twenty-two European states.

7 Frederick W. Marks III, *Independence on Trial* (Baton Rouge, 1973), 155.

most reluctant to expand national power, especially over commerce, declined to send representatives. The other states sent, at one time or another, fifty-five men. Usually, no more than thirty were present, and discussion was dominated by an even smaller group of men who remained in Philadelphia from start to finish. This inner group, in particular, included many of America's most distinguished political minds, and the mere presence of Franklin and Washington sanctified the convention for many people, although in fact Franklin was too old and ill to contribute much and Washington presided rather than participated. Jefferson called it an "assembly of demigods."

But there were nonentities present, and obstructionists, too. There were also important absentees. Patrick Henry and Richard Henry Lee declined to serve, which meant that the Virginia delegation was dominated by nationalists, most notably Madison. John Jay was busy with his work as secretary of foreign affairs, and John Adams and Thomas Jefferson were serving abroad.

The delegates were remarkably young (the average age was about forty-two), but three-quarters had had firsthand experience with the shortcomings of the Articles of Confederation from service in Congress. Virtually all were determined, if they did nothing else, to strengthen the nation in the field of foreign affairs.

Provisions attempting to accomplish this end are spread throughout the Constitution. Many were drafted in committees, about whose activities we know very little, and none evoked extensive debate in the full convention, in contrast, for example, to repeated discussions of the composition of Congress and election of the president. The framers, a recent study concludes, "intended Congress to control the making and conduct of war, the Senate to control foreign policy, and the President to control the ceremonial functions of representing the nation in its foreign relations, personally or through diplomats."[8] This brisk summary is not so much wrong as oversimplified.

In fact, although many of the Constitution's provisions seem clear-cut, "in foreign affairs, it was often cryptic, ambiguous and

8 Leonard W. Levy, *Original Intent and the Framers' Constitution* (New York, 1988), 30–1.

incomplete."⁹ This was so partly because members of the convention could not foresee the future, partly because they shrank from giving power to the president but knew the details of foreign affairs and war making could not be managed by Congress. Because these provisions were so important, and so often debated, in the future, it is imperative to try to discern the intentions of the Founding Fathers.

Article VI declares that "This Constitution, and the Laws of the United States and all Treaties, . . . shall be the supreme Law of the Land, . . . any Thing in the Constitution or Laws of any State to the contrary notwithstanding." This provision, the core of the Constitution in that it establishes a sovereign national government, had profound implications in areas other than diplomacy. Even in our own time its proper meaning in these areas is debated. But the clause, vital to the practice of foreign policy, was much less challenged in that area in the future.

Everyone recognized that, if treaties were to be national bargains, state action must not negate them. If commercial legislation were to have its intended effect, states could not be allowed to levy duties of their own. Nor could they engage in diplomacy or carry on wars (with, for example, Indian tribes) for their own parochial interests, if the nation were to mean anything.¹⁰ These principles seem blindingly obvious, but under the Articles of Confederation one or more states had contradicted every one of them. These violations were, indeed, a major reason the reform movement became so strong. Few if any members of the convention questioned the need to give the federal government absolute authority in foreign relations.

It was therefore fitting that the "supremacy clause" was first used by the Supreme Court to overthrow a state law in a case involving the treaty power. During the Revolution, the Commonwealth of Virginia arrogated to itself debts owed to Englishmen by its citizens. Although the Treaty of Paris provided that "Creditors . . . shall meet with no lawful Impediment to the Recovery of . . . all bona fide Debts heretofore contracted," after the war Virginia courts ig-

---

9 Schlesinger, *Imperial Presidency*, 2.

10 Prohibitions against such actions, which in effect further develop the "supremacy clause," are in Article I, Section 10.

nored this pledge. In 1796 a creditor's suit, *Ware v. Hylton,* reached
the Supreme Court, which ordered debtors to pay — even if they had
already paid the commonwealth![11] The decision stimulated a great
deal of protest but clearly reflected the intent of the Constitutional
Convention.

An early draft presented to the convention gave Congress the
power to "make" war, a proposition on which there was universal
agreement. But an enemy might not be so kind as to attack when
Congress was sitting. Must the nation wait until legislators returned
from their homes before it "made" war? To meet this problem, "Mr
MADISON and Mr [Elbridge] GERRY moved to insert '*declare,*' striking out '*make*' war; leaving to the Executive the power to repel
sudden attacks." The motion passed, and "declare" rather than
"make" was the word finally used in Article I, Section 8, of the
Constitution.[12]

Although the implications of the change fathered by Madison and
Gerry are still debated, it seems reasonable to take them at their
word: They did not want, and their colleagues did not want, either
to deny the president the power to resist surprise attacks or to give
him a means to initiate military action. James Wilson of Pennsylvania, a leading figure in the convention, assured his colleagues, "It
will not be in the power of a single man, or a single body of men, to
involve us in such distress" as war.[13]

During the nation's first undeclared war, with France in the late
1790s, congressional legislation authorized what action was taken.
At the time, even Alexander Hamilton, who usually took an expansive view of presidential powers, held that, while a president could

11 The justices did agree that Virginia had a moral obligation to see that debtors
    did not pay twice.
12 The same article gave Congress the power to maintain an army and a navy, but
    the fear of standing armies led the convention to add, regarding the former, that
    "no Appropriation of Money to that Use shall be for a longer Term than two
    Years."
13 Although once again the available evidence is incomplete, the convention
    apparently wished to make Congress an integral part of any decision for
    undeclared or limited wars. In Article I, Section 8, Congress also was
    empowered to issue "Letters of Marque and Reprisal," in other words to initiate
    military operations short of full-scale war.

repel attack, he could not order reprisals on his own authority. In 1801, in an opinion upholding the legality of action during the undeclared war, Chief Justice John Marshall declared, "The whole powers of war . . . are vested in Congress." Future presidents who "made" war — defending Korea, invading Grenada — without the prior approval of Congress would have to find such justification as they could in other provisions of the Constitution.

Usually they relied upon Article I, Section 2, of the Constitution, a list of several disparate powers of the president, one of which is that he "shall be Commander in Chief of the Army and Navy of the United States." This article was one of those drafted in committee, in this instance the Committee on Detail, and the full convention barely discussed it. However, the purport of this clause clearly was less than chief executives later claimed for it. Members of the convention recognized that, as Alexander Hamilton wrote in the *Federalist,* "Of all cares or concerns of government, the direction of war most peculiarly demands those qualities which distinguish the exercise of power by a single hand." However, they appear to have expected the president to act as commander only, carrying out policies determined by Congress. When, during the ratifying debates, opponents of the Constitution expressed fears that the president was being given too much power, Hamilton responded, in another of the *Federalist* essays, "his authority would be nominally the same with that of the king of Great Britain, but in substance much inferior to it. It would amount to nothing more than the supreme command and direction of the military forces, as first general and admiral of the Confederacy; while that of the British king extends to the *declaring* of war and to the *raising* . . . of fleets and armies — all of which, under the Constitution being considered, would appertain to the legislature."

Almost from the beginning of the republic, presidents or their subordinates did use military force beyond the boundaries of the United States, usually to protect the lives or property of American citizens. With a few exceptions like Andrew Jackson's invasion of Spanish Florida in 1818, these operations were small-scale and short-lived, rarely challenging the sovereignty of another nation. None, certainly, were confessed to be "war" in the constitutional sense, and justification for most was not even framed in terms of the commander-in-chief clause. Until 1950, two scholars have written, "no judge, no President, no legislator, no commentator ever suggested that the President had legal authority to initiate war."[14]

Predictably, given the concern over commerce, members of the convention took it almost as a given that the national government should be clothed with authority in this field. As Hamilton was to put it in the *Federalist,* "The importance of the Union, in a commercial light, is one of those points about which there is the least room to entertain a difference of opinion, and which has, in fact, commanded the most general assent of men who have any acquaintance with the subject." Something had to be done to foil European efforts to strangle the United States, to "make them bid against each other for the privileges of our markets." So universally accepted was this line of reasoning that both the Virginia and New Jersey plans, outlines of the Constitution put forward by nationalists and limited-government men respectively, granted commercial power to Congress.

Southern delegates, however, feared that, if some limitations were not placed on Congress, their interests might be sacrificed to those of the middle states and New England. When the Committee on Detail met, they managed to have three safeguards approved: There could be no ban on the importation of slaves, no duties on exports were to be permitted, and all "navigation acts" must pass by two-thirds majorities in Congress.

The prohibition of export duties relieved the South from fear that its rice and tobacco exports would be burdened with taxes, but it deprived the nation of a weapon of economic diplomacy widely used by other countries, especially Great Britain. Such duties allowed a nation, in effect, to raise the foreign price of its goods, or such of them as were specified, and could be used as a bargaining tool in commercial negotiations.

The two-thirds requirement, Southerners felt, was needed to protect them against other sections. Otherwise, states with large maritime interests might, to protect and stimulate shipping, impose

14 Francis D. Wormuth and Edwin Firmage, *To Chain the Dogs of War* (Dallas, 1986), 28.

heavy charges upon or even prohibit the entry of foreign merchant-men, forcing the South to absorb huge increases in freight rates. As the event was to prove, gaining simple majorities for commercial legislation was challenging enough. If this provision had gone into effect the United States would have found it difficult, sometimes impossible, to carry on commercial diplomacy.

Most Northerners, as well as a few Southern nationalists like Madison, objected to the proposals of the Committee on Detail. They were unable to get the full convention to disapprove the ban on export taxes, but, in one of the convention's major compromises, they otherwise got most of what they wanted. At Gouverneur Morris's suggestion, a special committee was created, as the Pennsylvanian said, to "form a bargain among the northern and southern states." In this committee it was agreed that at least until 1808 no legislation closing the slave trade could be enacted, but – and this was far more important to the nationalists and Northerners – "navigation acts" could be passed by ordinary majorities. Over some Southern protests – Madison could not convert his own delegation – the compromise passed.

The decision was far-reaching. Had the two-thirds proposal gone through, there would in all probability have been no legislation to protect American shipping, to create protective tariffs, to authorize reciprocal trade agreements with foreign countries. Nor, for that matter, would it have been easy to find the funds to make the new government a success. Until 1814 customs duties generated about nine-tenths of federal revenue, and they remained the largest single source in all but a few years until the twentieth century.

The matters so far discussed, although critically important for foreign relations, do not include what are traditionally called diplomatic powers – negotiation, recognition of other governments, appointment of diplomats, and, above all, treaty making. Regarding the first two of these, the Constitution is silent, and the proper distribution of power between Senate and president had to be worked out in the first years after it came into effect. On the other hand, the convention fairly easily agreed that diplomatic appointments, like those to other important federal offices, should be made by the president with the Senate's approval.

Discussions of the treaty-making power were sporadic, mostly at the tail end of the convention. Whenever the subject came up, delegates showed that their thoughts were distorted by an anticipation that conflicts in the future would be between large and small states. Moreover, they utterly failed to foresee, and would have deplored, the rise of parties. They also made it clear that they neither wanted nor expected many treaties to be made. Finally, they shrank from giving the president powers like those of European sovereigns, and the ultimate decision to give him a role in treaty making by no means meant that they intended him to dominate the process.

In early sessions of the convention, delegates assumed that the Senate alone would make treaties.[15] The report of the Committee on Detail included a provision to this effect. But since that report, embodying another of the convention's important compromises, also recommended that all states, large and small, should have two Senate seats, the proposal regarding treaties ran into opposition. As far as we can tell, this, not a desire to increase presidential power or even to make negotiations more efficient, led the convention to adopt the system we still have.

If states were equal in the Senate, small ones would have disproportionate weight. How could this be corrected? Gouverneur Morris suggested that the House of Representatives be given a coequal role. This proposal was rejected, largely because the House, members thought, would be too large and too indiscreet to perform well. Madison suggested that the proper remedy was to involve the president, who would be chosen in a process that gave each state a weight roughly proportional to population. "The Senate represented the States alone," he said, "and . . . for this as well as other obvious reasons," by which he meant the difficulty of carrying on detailed negotiations by committee, "it was proper that the President should be an agent in Treaties." He was able to get the recommendation for

---

15 One might have expected that the experience of diplomacy-by-committee under the Articles of Confederation would have led them in another direction, but such was not the case. On the other hand, in fairness to the delegates, it must be remembered that they expected the Senate to be, at least for a long time, essentially a medium-sized committee, not a large body.

Senate control referred to another committee, one on which he gained membership. This committee, called by various names, all suggesting that it was tidying up leftover matters, produced the formula that became part of Article II, Section 2: the president "shall have power, by and with the Advice and Consent of the Senate, to make Treaties." The convention approved it unanimously.

The decision to include the president, it must again be emphasized, did not originate in a desire to enhance his powers. "The Convention," a historian has recently written, "appears to have been more aware of the defects of the Senate and the limitations of the House than of any of the inherent virtues of a vigorous presidency."[16]

Certainly the framers did not expect the Senate merely to pass upon treaties the president negotiated. Madison suggested that it be empowered to make treaties of peace without his approval. In the *Federalist,* Jay asserted that the Senate would have the power to "form and introduce" treaties. Arthur Bestor, one among many scholars who has explored this issue, concludes that "The treaty clause . . . was designed to make the President a joint participant in the treatymaking process, not to transfer the process to him. . . . Treatymaking was to be a cooperative venture from the beginning to the end of the entire process."[17] Here, too, history was to stray from the intentions of the framers of the Constitution.

The Constitution requires that not only the Senate but two-thirds of the Senate vote to approve treaties. Although alternatives were proposed, most requiring lesser majorities, for varying reasons delegates found the two-thirds rule comfortable. Representatives of states with interests in the West remembered that a majority had been ready, during the Confederation, to surrender claims to use of the Mississippi River; they also feared that a majority might vote to approve Indian treaties unfavorable to their (avaricious) interests. Yankees worried that the fisheries might be surrendered. Perhaps most important, none of the delegates wanted it to be easy to

16 Jack N. Rakove, "Solving a Constitutional Puzzle: The Treatymaking Clause as a Case Study," *Perspectives in American History,* n.s., 1 (1984): 249.

17 Arthur Bestor, "Respective Roles of Senate and President in the Making and Abrogation of Treaties – the Original Intent of the Framers Historically Reviewed," *Washington Law Review* 55 (1979): 118, 135.

conclude treaties, unless they were treaties of peace: "The prospect of having one more than one-third of the members of the Senate defeat a treaty was not one to excite apprehensions in the minds of the framers of the Constitution."[18] Commercial diplomacy, not treaties – this is what they expected and wanted.

The effect of the two-thirds rule has been largely indirect. Only a handful of treaties commanding a majority have fallen short of the required two-thirds. The only truly important one was the Treaty of Versailles, and if it had gained the necessary support President Wilson almost certainly would have killed it because of conditions upon which the Senate insisted. And there is another way of looking at the ability of one more than one-third of the Senate to defeat a treaty. Although the Federalists briefly commanded a two-thirds majority in the 1790s and their opponents, the Republicans, did so for a longer time ending in 1820, since that date one party has almost never (there are three exceptions) been that strong in the Senate. Successful treaties, that is to say, are by necessity truly national and not merely partisan agreements.

The two-thirds rule has often colored negotiations, since those who make treaties have to be aware, as Wilson really was not, of the danger of losing the needed support. Thus, for example, the nature of the American pledge in the North Atlantic Treaty of 1949 was less definite than the negotiators would have preferred, and the Carter administration had to include unwanted provisions in the Panama Canal agreements of 1977. Moreover, to win the support of two-thirds of the Senate, treaty supporters have often found it necessary to amend them or to attach reservations to the resolution of approval. Federalists invented this tactic in 1795 to save Jay's Treaty with England. It has been widely used ever since, sometimes without jeopardizing the agreement, sometimes with the result that either the president or the foreign government involved backed away from it.

The Achievements of the Convention

By mid-September, the work was done. The Pennsylvania legislature, waiting to convene, could at last reclaim its hall. The conven-

18 W. Stull Holt, *Treaties Defeated by the Senate* (Baltimore, 1933), 10.

tion had lasted nearly four months, and tempers were frayed. Franklin, in a speech read for him by Wilson, appealed for unity:

when you assemble a number of men to have the advantage of their joint wisdom, you inevitably assemble with those men all their prejudices, their passions, . . . their local interests. . . . From such an assembly can a perfect production be expected? It therefore astonishes me, Sir, to find this system approaching so near to perfection as it does. . . . I cannot help expressing a wish that every member of the Convention who may still have objections to it would, with me, on this occasion doubt a little of his infallibility, and, to make manifest our unity, put his name to this instrument.

Three individuals, including a future secretary of state, rejected Franklin's invitation, but the compromising had been so well done that all twelve state delegations, Rhode Island still being absent, approved the final product. The delegates held a celebratory dinner, then dispersed to their homes, where most of them would play leading parts in the struggle for ratification.

They had accomplished great and permanent things. Their greatest achievement was simply that they succeeded at all, transforming a fragile, fractious coalition of states into a nation. By itself, this accomplishment transformed the United States's position in the world. Urging his countrymen to ratify the Constitution, Hamilton wrote, "Let Americans disdain to be the instruments of European questions. Let the thirteen States, bound together in a strict and indissoluble Union, concur in erecting one great American system superior to the control of all transatlantic force or influence and able to dictate the terms of the connection between the old and the new world!" So wished they all.

The specific provisions important for the diplomatic future had often been worked out, like the rest of the document, by a process of give and take. Consideration often disappeared from the agenda for weeks at a time, only to pop up and be settled almost without debate. In particular, introduction of the president into the treaty-making process came at the very end of the convention, and only an act of collective will – a desire to finish the job – can explain its easy acceptance. Except for the supremacy clause and the commerce clause, which clearly determined that "navigation acts" would be enacted like any other legislation, the provisions bearing on international affairs were often marked by ambiguity, perhaps to paper over disagreements but also because the delegates understandably did not foresee what might develop in the future.

Whatever the intent of the convention, the Constitution left unsettled the division of responsibility between the president and Congress. The eminent constitutional historian Edward S. Corwin made this point in a passage often quoted:

Where does the Constitution lodge the power to determine the foreign relations of the United States? . . . Many persons are inclined to answer offhand "in the President"; but they would be hard put to it, if challenged, to point out any definite statement to this effect in the Constitution itself. What the Constitution does, *and all that it does,* is to confer on the President certain powers capable of affecting our foreign relations, and certain other powers of the same general kind on the Senate, and still other such powers on Congress; but which of these organs shall have the decisive and final voice in determining the course of the American nation is left for events to resolve.

The Constitution, Corwin concluded, "is an invitation to struggle for the privilege of directing American foreign policy."[19] In that struggle, the president had important advantages, notably the possession of superior information and the ability to act with dispatch. Using these, presidents from George Washington onward expanded the executive power far beyond the intent of the Philadelphia convention and the understanding of those who debated ratification.

Ratification of the Constitution

Nine states had to approve the Constitution, the delegates decided, before it could go into effect. In fact, had a single important state – New York or Virginia, for example – refused to go along, the accomplishments of the convention would have been nullified.

19 Edward S. Corwin, *The President: Office and Powers,* 4th ed. (New York, 1957), 170–1.

In those two states, and in others, the contest for approval was bitter.

During the struggle, Federalists stressed what they knew was an appealing, almost unchallengeable argument: The Constitution would strengthen the nation's ability to survive and prosper in a hostile world. Twenty-five of the first thirty-six *Federalist* essays made this point in one way or another. While no single argument can explain ratification in every state, this one played a vital role.

Almost all Antifederalists professed to wish to strengthen the national government in foreign affairs, but many of them complained that the provisions proposed to meet this desirable end actually jeopardized liberty. They objected to the supremacy clause, particularly as it applied to treaties. "If anything should be left us," Patrick Henry complained, "it would [only] be because the President and senators were pleased to admit it." They objected to the mechanics of the treaty power, which, they argued, meant that a president-Senate cabal could sell out state interests. Some proposed that the popularly elected House of Representatives be brought into the process, others that an even greater majority of senators be required to approve treaties. On the whole, however, Antifederalists were wise enough not to challenge the Federalists where they were on strong popular ground.

Their criticisms did, however, cause the authors of the *Federalist* to rebut their opponents in later essays in the series. Madison stressed that "this class of powers forms an obvious and essential branch of the federal administration. If we are to be one nation in any respect, it clearly ought to be in respect to other nations." Jay, who had not been at the convention, and Hamilton, who had, each devoted an essay to the treaty power. The latter asserted, "I scruple not to declare my firm persuasion that it is one of the best digested and most unexceptionable parts of the plan." Mixed responsibility for treaties meant that a possibly corruptible president could not act alone, but on the other hand experience under the Articles of Confederation had shown that detailed negotiations could not easily be managed by committee. Jay justified exclusion of the House, saying that it was too large to act with secrecy and dispatch, whereas the

Senate, a smaller body of more experienced men serving for longer terms, could be expected to show these qualities.[20]

Making effective use of their most advantageous argument, the Federalists were able to carry every ratification convention, although sometimes, as in the important states of Massachusetts, New York, and Virginia, by narrow margins. In June 1788, New Hampshire became the ninth state to approve the Constitution. Two others soon followed, but North Carolina and Rhode Island held out until 1789. Presidential electors were chosen in the fall, and in April 1789, to absolutely no one's surprise, they unanimously chose George Washington as first president of the United States. Because the new Congress was already in session, in New York, government could begin.

The New Government

The new government was dominated, predictably, by supporters of the Constitution. George Washington had been both participant in and symbol of the movement toward union. His first cabinet, when completed in 1790, contained two fellow Virginians, Thomas Jefferson and Edmund Randolph, who had misgivings, but also Alexander Hamilton, more nationalist than most framers of the Constitution, and into Hamilton's hands as secretary of the treasury fell chief responsibility for making the new government effective. Two-thirds of the twenty-six senators and fifty-five representatives in the first Congress had served either in the Philadelphia convention or in state ratifying conventions, and only seven had opposed the Constitution. Madison, the most important figure at Philadelphia, became in effect leader of the House of Representatives. Together, Congress and the president set out to implement in practical terms the shared ideas they had brought to the constitutional movement, but they also soon collided with ambiguities and lacunae in the new charter of government.

20 In the event, of course, the Senate became notable for neither. Some treaties were acted upon almost without discussion, but others provoked extended debate. Although all treaties were considered in executive session until 1888, and the Senate opened its doors only twice before the great debate on the Treaty of Versailles in 1919 and 1920, from the very beginning "leaks" were common.

Fittingly, the first important legislation was a tariff act with protectionist overtones, although the desire to establish a revenue base was more important. As originally proposed by Madison, the tariff bill discriminated against ships and goods of countries that had no commercial treaty with the United States; Britain, so frequently denounced at Philadelphia and in the *Federalist* essays, was the obvious target. "Her interests can be wounded almost mortally," Madison said, "while ours are invulnerable." The Senate, reluctant to start a commercial war that might jeopardize the revenue upon which the new government was to depend, rejected Madison's proposal, and the disagreement foreshadowed similar differences in the future.

But both Madison and his opponents wanted to use commercial legislation for nationalistic purposes. As finally passed, the bill gave protection to some domestic products by levying high charges on competitive imports. It also required foreign-owned ships to pay tonnage duties, the port charges levied on ships no matter what their cargo, eight times as high as those levied on American-owned ships. In sum, the Americans, sentimentally and in principle in favor of unrestricted trade, felt that they had to do commercial battle with others in traditional mercantilist ways.

Washington chose to sign the tariff act of 1789 on the Fourth of July. The law's results were not as dramatic as many of its framers hoped, although it doubtless contributed to the growth of the merchant marine which soon followed. It was five years before Great Britain reached a commercial agreement with the United States, in Jay's Treaty, and for many more years guaranteed access to British West Indian ports eluded the Americans. Still, the law of 1789 began a process that fulfilled the hope of the Constitution's framers, that a united nation could accomplish things beyond the reach of thirteen separate states.

The Machinery of Diplomacy

At about the same time that the tariff became law, so also did an act establishing a Department of Foreign Affairs, and this too was introduced by Madison. Debate was far less contentious, no doubt because legislators, like members of the convention, expected foreign relations, in the modern sense of the term, to be a minor part of government activity. In contrast to the law establishing the Treasury, which made the secretary directly responsible to Congress on important matters, Madison's bill declared that the secretary for foreign affairs should act "in such a manner as the President of the United States shall, from time to time, order and direct,"[21] and the legislation several times reiterated that diplomatic business belonged to the executive. Presumably this emphasis merely reflected the conviction that only the executive branch could efficiently manage the nuts and bolts of diplomacy; there certainly is no indication that Madison or anyone else in Congress expected the president to embark on major policy departures without their concurrence.

A few months later, in September, Congress decided that the secretary for foreign affairs would not have enough to do to keep himself occupied. A new law changed the name of the office and charged the secretary of state with a potpourri of nondiplomatic functions: handling correspondence between the federal government and the states, guarding the Great Seal, publishing the public laws, taking the census, and so forth. A bit later, the secretary was also made responsible for the mint.

Thomas Jefferson, who would have preferred to continue as minister to France and disliked the chores recently added to the secretary's charge, agreed to accept appointment as secretary of state only when Washington appealed to his sense of duty. In March 1790, he took over from Jay, who had served ad interim. Jefferson received a salary of $3,500 and had a staff of five, copyists and translators. The War and Treasury Departments began with much larger staffs and grew much more rapidly.[22] In New York, State made do with a small house on Broadway, and its quarters in Philadelphia, to which the

---

21 On the other hand, only the vote of Vice-President John Adams defeated a proposal, in the Senate, to withhold from the president the authority to remove a secretary who displeased him.

22 The Department of State still had a staff of only fourteen in 1820, and until 1853, when the office of assistant secretary was created, a "chief clerk" was second in command.

federal government moved in 1790, and Washington, where it settled down in 1800, were scarcely larger.

The secretary, perforce, did almost all of the work himself. At
least until the 1830s he personally drafted almost all correspondence
to ministers abroad, clerks then transcribing a fair copy in a bound
volume and preparing multiple copies for the mails.[23] For the secretaries, this was not too burdensome a task: All of the instructions
from the beginning of the federal government until the War of 1812
fill only eight moderate-sized volumes. Incoming correspondence
was more voluminous but still did not tax the recipient. Sometimes,
tacitly using distance or the absence of important events to report as
an excuse, representatives abroad simply lapsed into silence. In
March 1791, Jefferson rebuked the American chargé d'affaires at
Madrid, writing, "Your letter of May. 6 1789. is still the last we
have received, and that is now near two years old." But even when
business was heavy, American envoys often spared the pen: During
four and a half months of important, intricate negotiations at London in 1806, the American representatives sent home only six reports.

On the whole, the two dozen men who served as secretary of state
through Lincoln's administration were distinguished men. Six later
became president, although only one of those, James Buchanan,
held the secretaryship after 1830. Henry Clay, Daniel Webster,
John C. Calhoun, and William H. Seward – all towering figures and
presidential aspirants – also held the office. Two of the less distinguished secretaries, Timothy Pickering, under John Adams, and
Robert Smith, under Madison, were fired for insubordination, compounded in Smith's case by incapacity. Most, even such strong individuals as James Madison and John Quincy Adams, deferred to the
chief executive. All consulted frequently with the president, even on
unimportant matters, and Washington, for one, reviewed all outgo-
ing correspondence before it was sent. Sometimes – perhaps the
most notable instance being Jefferson's secretary of the treasury,
Albert Gallatin – a particularly trusted outsider was asked to com-

23 Sometimes the president himself drafted important papers, most notably when
Madison lost confidence in his first secretary of state, Robert Smith.

ment on almost every important matter before the Department of State. Under a few presidents – Washington, Monroe, and Polk, for example – major issues were discussed by the entire cabinet. Usually but not always, the secretary of state had his way, but some, notably Polk's subordinate, James Buchanan, were frequently humiliated by their superior. Few had any doubt where the final authority lay. Presidential control of foreign policy was a fact from the beginning of the Republic, just as it was a fact that the Department of State was essentially one individual.

The size of the diplomatic service, like the size of Jefferson's staff, reflected prevailing views of the nature of American relations with the rest of the world. A substantial minority of Congress was reluctant to station diplomats permanently at even the most important foreign capitals, including London. Congress cut Washington's initial request for funds to support diplomatic representation from $49,000 to $40,000. In 1791, when the structure was complete, the United States had only four ministers and one chargé at European courts. (In addition, Washington, who worked with cautious determination to strengthen his office, had, without seeking Senate approval, sent at least two personal representatives to Europe.) Soon, the problems created for American commerce by war in Europe and, somewhat later, the successful Latin American revolts against Spain led to expansion, but as late as 1838 the United States had only thirty-one permanent legations.[24] Embassies, more prestigious establishments, were shunned until the 1890s because they were considered unrepublican.

Thus, even though they found themselves drawn into conventional diplomacy by European wars, by their own drive for expansion, by commercial aspirations, and by the international ramifications of the Civil War, Americans never entirely shed the attitudes of 1787. The United States was a great nation, but it was so partly because it was not like all others. A diplomatic establishment on the European

---

24 In addition, of course, there was a steadily increasing number of consuls and consular agents. Remunerated, until 1855, largely by fees paid to them for their services, they were a rather shabby lot, often engaging in dubious business on the side.

scale was anathema. Happily, Americans believed, it was also unnecessary.

Defining the Constitutional Partnership

The Founding Fathers, as we have seen, neither wanted nor expected the new government to make many treaties. Five or six commercial agreements with major powers, some thought, should be about the limit. During the first generation of the new government, this ceiling was exceeded. Still, from 1789 to 1815 the Senate passed judgment on only thirteen agreements with foreign countries, about one every other year, and only five can be said to have been important. Not one was defeated by the Senate, although a minor agreement with Great Britain died because London would not accept a condition insisted upon by the Senate. In the next quarter century, in sheer statistical terms the pace sharply accelerated, but almost all agreements did no more than establish formal relations with another country; only three or four were important settlements. Contrary to the Founding Fathers' expectations, in discussing treaties senators acted neither as a group of sages nor as spokesmen for their respective states, but rather as politicians often influenced by partisan considerations.

Nor were expectations of true partnership between president and Senate long fulfilled. A few months after the new government began to function, Washington informed the Senate that he intended to "advise with them on the terms of the treaty to be negotiated with the southern Indians." The meeting was not a success. Senators resented the president's apparent attitude of "take it or leave it." Washington found the Senate's nit-picking and refusal to act at once intolerable. At last, after an interval of tense silence, the president withdrew. "He did so with a discontented air," one of the participants, Senator William Maclay of Pennsylvania, wrote in his journal. "Had it been any other man than the man whom I wish to regard as the first character in the world, I would have said, with sullen dignity. I can not now be mistaken. The President wishes to tread on the necks of the Senate." Washington returned a few days later, apparently "placid and serene," and agreement was reached.

He did not, however, repeat the experiment, nor have his successors.[25]

On the other hand, when he asked the Senate to approve appointments to foreign posts, Washington at first submitted the instructions he proposed to give those envoys, and the Senate in effect considered them along with the nomination. This practice ended in 1794, when John Jay was sent to London to negotiate a vast panoply of issues. Many were too explosive to make possible a consensus in a Senate filled with partisan tempers, so Washington merely submitted Jay's name. Thus it has been, with rare exceptions, down to the present. "Advice," a word intended by the Philadelphia convention to mean consultation before and during negotiations, has come to mean nothing more than "consent," post hoc approval of what the executive branch has decided.

In other ways, too, the powers of the president have developed in ways unforeseen at Philadelphia. Since 1792, when the Washington administration concluded a postal agreement with Canadian authorities, presidents have made literally thousands of "executive agreements" for which they did not seek Senate approval. Most but not all of these have been noncontroversial, essentially administrative actions. But even in the early period presidents sometimes used executive agreements in ways that went far beyond this. In 1817, Acting Secretary of State Richard Rush and the British minister, Charles Bagot, signed an agreement for the demilitarization of the Great Lakes. President Monroe merely reported this to Congress in his annual message that December. In 1818, prodded by Bagot, he asked the Senate "whether this is such an arrangement as the executive is competent to enter into by the powers vested in it by the Constitution, or is such a one as requires the advice and consent of the Senate." Carefully avoiding a direct answer, the Senate approved "the agreement," but it never became a treaty and formal ratifications were never exchanged.

25 In 1846, President Polk sent a British proposal regarding the Oregon boundary dispute to the Senate, asking its advice before signing a formal treaty, but he did not appear before the Senate in person.

Very early, too, presidents began to make dubious use of their power as commander in chief. In 1810 and 1811, convinced that the panhandle of Florida belonged to the United States as a result of the Louisiana Purchase, a claim that Spain denied, Madison "plotted in secret, used agents and troops, threatened force, and eventually proclaimed and effectuated the occupation of an area ruled by Spain."[26] Even the president privately admitted, during this rather *opéra bouffe* affair, that there were "serious questions, as to the authority of the Executive." Far more important was the action of President James K. Polk in 1845, following the annexation of Texas. He sent troops commanded by General Zachary Taylor into territory south of Texas's limits while a province of Mexico, and in 1846 this resulted, as Polk may have hoped, in war. In any event, in making the president commander in chief, the authors of the Constitution, although recognizing the need for central direction of armies in the field, in wars declared by Congress, had never expected that authority to be used to control policy.

Executive agreements and expansive use of command powers are but two developments that were not foreseen in 1787. For example, in agreeing to give the president authority to "receive Ambassadors and all other public Ministers," the Philadelphia convention meant nothing substantial. Members apparently did not anticipate that this seemingly innocuous phrase would give the executive power to determine which governments should be recognized and which should not. But such has been the case since 1793, when, without consulting Congress, the Washington administration decided to "receive" Citizen Edmond Genet, in effect agreeing that the House of Bourbon, which still claimed the French throne, was defunct.

The purpose of these illustrations is not to denigrate presidents as usurpers, although some have been. Without at least some greater presidential power than the framers anticipated, the United States could hardly have pursued consistent, to say nothing of effective, policies in foreign affairs. The framers combined hardheaded realism

26 Abraham D. Sofaer, *War, Foreign Affairs and Constitutional Power: The Origins* (Cambridge, Mass., 1976), 303.

and a vision of a world as it never was to be, of an international role that was utopian. What deserves emphasis, however, is that the "original intents" of the Founding Fathers succumbed to political realities in a process that began even before the presidency of George Washington was well under way.

Whether or not the machinery functioned as they anticipated, the fifty-five authors of the Constitution succeeded in their central task: They created a nation out of a league of states. And it endured to expand across a continent and play an increasing role in the world. Of course, as Tocqueville observed in 1835, "The Constitution of the United States is like one of those beautiful creations of human diligence which give their inventors glory and riches but remain sterile in other hands." The Constitution served the people, and the people served the Constitution.

4. Federalist Diplomacy: Realism and Anglophilia

For the future of the nation, the dozen years from Washington's inauguration in 1789 to Jefferson's in 1801 were fully as "critical" as the preceding era. The Americans had to establish both new policies and new machinery of government. They had to meet challenging problems of foreign policy, some inherited from the Confederation period and others generated by the outbreak of a new European war. Perhaps most important, they had to prove that the new structure had a chance to become permanent. Here, they accomplished things that today seem foreordained but ones that distinguished the United States from most other postcolonial nations. In 1796 they showed both that power could be shifted into new hands from the hero of their revolution and that it could be done by election. In 1801 they proved it possible to change political direction without a coup d'état, a striking accomplishment, "the first election in modern history which, by popular decision, resulted in the quiet and peaceful transition of national power from the hands of one of two embattled parties to another."[1]

Central in these developments was the emergence of political parties. The Federalist and Antifederalist groupings of the fight over the Constitution were essentially coalitions for the occasion. True parties emerged only after the new government was well under way. To a large degree, the Federalist and Republican parties were, in terms of leaders and support, heirs of the earlier coalitions, but there were sufficient exceptions so that a direct line of descent cannot be assumed. For example, Madison, a leading Federalist in the 1780s, became a founder of the Republican party in the 1790s. The so-called first party system lasted until the 1820s, when Federalism died an overdue death.

1 Richard Hofstadter, *The Idea of a Party System* (Berkeley, 1969), 128.

Americans came to independence with a highly useful tradition of participatory politics, but not one of organized parties. Indeed, like many newly freed people, they considered parties almost illegitimate threats to national unity. Still, parties did develop, although many congressmen and even (in 1796) at least some presidential electors declined to identify with one or the other, and party discipline remained pitiful for a long time. In his Farewell Address of 1796 George Washington warned "in the most solemn manner against the baneful effects of a Spirit of Party," a pious sentiment that ignored his administration's increasingly partisan character or at least suggested, as many in fact believed, that the "Spirit of Party" was the disloyal monopoly of opponents. The Federalists' Sedition Act of 1798 and President Jefferson's prosecution of opposition newspapers reflected the same sentiment. Still, by the end of the 1790s party conflict had come to be accepted if not embraced. Most important of all, despite conflicts and bitterness, the nation had agreed to accept arbitrament by the ballot box.

These accomplishments, which have eluded most emerging nations, were clearly essential to success in foreign relations. They gave the nation a structure and a process that, whatever the rhetoric and even physical violence, produced both stability and flexibility. But they were not easy, and only the passage of time gave them sanctity. In 1808, twenty years after ratification of the Constitution, an English journal sneered that the American machinery had "the appearance . . . rather of an experiment in politics, than a steady, permanent system." This skepticism, widely held abroad, encouraged European governments to treat the United States with limited respect, only slightly more than that they had offered the Confederation. But the perspective of time clearly shows us, if not all contemporaries, that the years after 1789 were years of success and progress.

Federalists, Republicans, and the European Conflict

Rival attitudes toward the wars set off by the French Revolution of 1789 played a major part in party development. From 1792 to 1815, with only two pauses for breath, the Old World was wracked by the longest sustained combat in modern history, involving all

Europe but with England and France as chief antagonists. What began as a struggle between republicanism and monarchy brought on by the toppling of France's ancien régime became something quite different with the rise of Napoleon Bonaparte, who dominated the French state by 1798 and crowned himself emperor in 1804. The young general once hailed as the savior of republicanism revealed himself a cold-eyed autocrat aiming at European and perhaps world hegemony. Pro-French Americans ceased to name new towns after Bonaparte's victories, and in far more substantial ways, too, Americans had to adjust to the *bouleversement*.

Similarly, shifting British and French policies toward the United States affected American attitudes. The French revolutionaries at first counted on republican America to support them for reasons of ideology and gratitude. Disappointment — in their view, American betrayal — turned France to a harsh policy that escalated into undeclared war between 1798 and 1800. Although Bonaparte liquidated that conflict, he had little respect for a land peopled, in his view, "by greedy merchants with a weak government and an impotent army."[2] His attitudes — they lacked the continuity to be called policy — shifted according to the interests of the moment, particularly his estimate as to whether the stick or the carrot would prove more effective.

At first, largely because they also expected America to support France, the British struck heavily at Yankee commerce. A treaty negotiated in 1794 liquidated this policy, initiating a decade of fairly smooth relations. However, like American cold warriors later on, Englishmen considered their nation "the last stay of the liberties of the world." They demanded that others tolerate any measures they believed necessary to defeat Napoleon. After 1805 this attitude meant greater harshness toward the United States, producing in turn American hostility toward Britain. When the Americans declared war in 1812, the British premier complained that America ought instead "to have looked to this country as the guardian power to which she was indebted . . . for her very existence."

Looking back many years later, a Massachusetts Federalist recalled

2 Clifford L. Egan, *Neither Peace Nor War* (Baton Rouge, 1983), 25.

that "the French Revolution drew a red hot ploughshare through the history of America." The metaphor is both apt and slightly misleading. Soon after the new government began to function, Congress fiercely debated a series of financial proposals presented by Secretary of the Treasury Hamilton, but coalitions were shifting and the struggles at Philadelphia appear not to have excited the country. The French Revolution changed the nature of the contest, but only after several years in which Americans of all political persuasions, proud that their republican example had spread across the ocean, watched it with "widespread enthusiasm and . . . little alarm."[3] Especially after the Anglo-French war began in 1793, the American parties solidified and extended their appeal to the electorate.

In effect, Federalists and Republicans both came to view the European contest as an extension of their own struggle. Federalists already felt that democracy could go too far; they believed that events in France so proved, and they could not respect those who differed with them. "Republicans had already identified the domestic conflict as an effort to defend America against corrupting English ways, and it was easy now to see administration policy as an attempt to ally the country with England and the league of despots against liberty and the French."[4] Thus Federalists called their opponents "democrats" or, even worse, "Jacobins." Republicans disavowed both labels and characterized their foes as "monocrats" or "Anglomen." And each party came to believe its own propaganda: Republicans were pro-French, Federalists pro-British.

The truth was rather more complex and shifting. Federalists, virtually all of whom had welcomed the first stages of French protest against the ancien régime, deplored its turn to violence, especially the use of the guillotine against real and presumed opponents during the "Reign of Terror" in 1793 and 1794. They denied, in Hamilton's words, that there was any "resemblance between what was the cause of America and what is the cause of France . . . the difference is no less great than that between Liberty and Licentiousness." They mistrusted the republicanism of Americans who did not turn against the

3 David B. Davis, *Revolutions* (Cambridge, Mass., 1990), 32.
4 Lance Banning, *The Jeffersonian Persuasion* (Ithaca, 1978), 211.

land of the Terror, confiscations, and unstable governments. They blamed these troubles on an excess of democracy, and later they explained Napoleon's tyranny in Aristotelian terms as an inevitable product of populistic license. Years later, after resuming a friendship sundered by the passions of the 1790s, John Adams, one of the handful who had misgivings from the start, wrote to the Sage of Monticello, "The French Revolution I dreaded; because I was sure it would, not only arrest the progress of Improvement, but give it a retrograde course."

Particularly when they contrasted it with France, some Federalists described Britain – its political and social order – as nearly perfect or at least "the abode . . . of all that distinguishes Man from the Brute and the Daemon." Such talk was by no means universal, and particularly while in power Federalists were by no means supine friends of England. Even Alexander Hamilton at least professed to believe that "it is the true policy of our government, to act with spirit and energy as well toward Great Britain as France." He often criticized England's policies, particularly commercial ones, although, both because of his basic sympathies and because of his conviction that the new nation could not survive the loss of trade with England, he steadily worked for accommodation, even to the extent of passing inside information to British representatives.

John Adams, Hamilton's bête noire within the party, hated and distrusted Britain. The British minister welcomed Adams's election to the presidency in 1796, "not because," he reported, "I perceive in Mr. Adams any partiality of sentiment towards Great Britain, but because he detests our enemies." Adams abhorred French radicalism, and like most Federalists, he believed that Britain shielded the United States from France. "The wind of the cannon ball that smashes John Bull's brains out," argued Congressman Fisher Ames, an Adams supporter, "will lay us on our backs." But until his death in 1826 Adams remained convinced of John Bull's "jealousy, envy, hatred and revenge, covered under pretended contempt." Although Adams, among the best haters in American history, used strong language, his views, not those of Anglophiles, were representative of rank-and-file Federalism.

If Adams thought the French Revolution would "arrest the

progress of Improvement," Republicans considered it an extension of a world movement begun in 1775. "The French cause is the cause of man," one newspaper declared. Moreover, Republicans feared that a French defeat would encourage reaction everywhere; in Jefferson's words, "The liberty of the whole earth was depending on the issue of the contest." If France's enemies triumphed, he believed, "it is far from being certain that they might not choose to finish their job completely by obliging us to a change in the form of our government at least." Despite misgivings of varying intensity about the Terror ("and was ever such a prize won with so little blood?" Jefferson mused), Republicans remained uncompromisingly pro-French for several years. They held the Federalists exclusively responsible for rising tension between the two countries.

Then things changed. In 1798, publication of reports from American envoys in Paris revealed that French agents – Messieurs X, Y, and Z – had demanded bribes as the price of negotiations to settle differences. Republicans sought to prevent the resulting brouhaha from escalating into war, but they never again took France on faith. Their alienation was completed when, a few months later, Bonaparte overthrew the existing government. By 1799, French republicanism was dead.

In 1801, just after becoming president, Jefferson told the British chargé that, while "for *republican* France he might have felt some interest, there was assuredly nothing in the present Government of that country, which could naturally incline him to show the smallest undue partiality to it at the expense of Great Britain." Federalist charges to the contrary, his presidential career bore out this statement. Learning of Napoleon's abdication in 1814, Jefferson's comment mingled surprise and pleasure: "The Attila of the age [is] dethroned, the ruthless destroyer of millions of the human race, . . . the great oppressor of the rights and liberties of the world, [is] shut up within the circle of a little island in the Mediterranean."

After 1798 neither Jefferson nor his followers hoped for British collapse. "The complete subjugation of England would be a general calamity," he wrote in that year, adding, "But happily it is impossible." In 1803 he said that the United States would "be seriously afflicted were any disaster to deprive mankind of the benefit of such a Bulwark against the torrent which has for some time been bearing down all before it." Republicans wished to see Britain chastened; they did not wish to see its enemy free to terrorize the globe. Like Fisher Ames and many others on the opposite side of the political fence, they saw the advantages of a European balance of power.

Neutrality, 1793

Although members of each party often accused the other of wanting to enter the European war in support of that nation to which it was allegedly subservient, the truth was otherwise. "Peace is our interest," Jefferson once wrote, "and peace has saved to the world this only plant of free and rational government now existing in it." In his Farewell Address, the first president expressed much the same thought: "With me, a predominant motive has been to endeavor to gain time to our country to settle and mature its yet recent institutions and to progress without interruption to that degree of strength and constancy which is necessary to give it command of its own fortunes."

Except in moments of frenzy, almost all Americans agreed. Even at the height of their enthusiasm for France, in the mid-1790s, almost no Republicans wanted to fight by its side. In the aftermath of the XYZ affair, few Federalists were eager for war with France, although a larger number considered one inevitable. The leitmotiv of Republican diplomacy after the party came to power in 1801 was the search for an alternative to war with Britain. In 1812, Republican senators and congressmen took the nation into such a war only because they could see no acceptable alternative.

Seeking to lessen the chances of involvement, at the very outset of the European war the American government laid down a line of policy far in advance of its day. A proclamation of neutrality issued by President Washington in April 1793 called upon all citizens "with sincerity and good faith [to] adopt and pursue a conduct friendly and impartial toward the belligerent powers." Framing the proclamation produced argument between Jefferson and Hamilton, still cabinet colleagues but moving toward the leadership of rival parties. Hamilton wanted to suspend or even nullify the political alliance of 1778, nominally on the ground that the French government that had concluded it no longer existed; Jefferson preferred — and the president agreed to follow his advice — to evade the issue, at least until France sought the help (it never did) the Americans were pledged to provide. And each privately hoped that neutrality would be so managed that the European power he favored could take most advantage of it. But both agreed that the government should not show partiality and that citizens must avoid actions which would draw the nation toward war.

Such a stance would seem today to be the basic minimum of neutrality. However, in 1793 authorities on international law minimized a neutral's obligations almost to insignificance. In their view, for example, France's American policy from 1775 to 1778 — the dispatch of supplies paid for by the government, tolerance of American commerce-raiding from French ports, and so forth — did not make France unneutral because its armed forces were not engaged. A major power might be able to get away with such behavior, as France did until 1778; the young republic did not dare take the risk, knowing that even technically legal behavior could produce dangerous resentment. Washington's cabinet therefore unanimously agreed to a line of policy which one authority on international law describes as "an epoch in the development of the usages of neutrality."[5]

Madison complained that the president was usurping power not intended to be granted to him by the Philadelphia convention: The Constitution did not give the president authority to proclaim neutrality any more than it gave him the power to declare war. This point also troubled Jefferson. In deference to his sensibilities, the word "neutrality" was not used in the proclamation. Francophiles objected to the suggestion that Americans ought to be impartial, confirming Jefferson's prediction that "A fair neutrality will prove a disagreeable pill to our friends, tho' necessary to keep us out of the calamities of war." Enthusiasts certainly refused to admit that the proclamation barred them from such activities as throwing stones through windows of the British legation. On the whole, however,

5 William E. Hall, *International Law*, 8th ed. (Oxford, 1924), 707.

even among Republicans, Washington's proclamation came to command broad support.

An envoy from France, Edmond Genet, tested the policy almost as soon as it was announced. Genet reached Philadelphia in the summer of 1793, after a four-week overland trip from his landing point, Charleston, during which, in a series of public meetings, celebrations and banquets, he sought to mobilize support for aid to France. "My zeal," he wrote at the time, "never will be satisfied until I shall have drawn [the American people] into the war on our side. The whole new world must be free and the Americans must support us in this sublime design." At the capital, Genet was received in friendly fashion by Jefferson, although the secretary of state cautioned him to show restraint lest he hurt the Republican cause.

"Caution" was not a word known to Genet. Even before he reached Philadelphia, he set out to organize filibustering expeditions by Americans against Spanish territory. He issued commissions to American privateers to sail against enemy commerce; these ships made eighty captures. In the most flagrant case, after allowing Jefferson to understand that he would not do so, he directed a captured British vessel, the *Little Sarah,* renamed the *Petite Démocrate* and armed for commerce raiding, to put to sea. This episode stirred Jefferson to warn Madison that Genet "will sink the Republican interest if they do not abandon him." Above all, the Frenchman, who had a "habit of substituting the rhetoric of public demonstrations for the reality of diplomacy,"[6] repeatedly called on the people not to tolerate the policy of neutrality, and rioters in the streets supported his appeal. Looking back years later, John Adams maintained that only an epidemic of yellow fever, which drained civic vigor, "saved the United States from a fatal revolution of government."

Believing that the administration could not stand against him, Genet demanded a special session of Congress to decide between his wishes and those of the administration. This was too much. The president exploded: "Is the Minister of the French Republic to set the Acts of this Government at defiance, *with impunity*? and then

6 Harry Ammon, *The Genet Mission* (New York, 1973), 58.

threaten the Executive with an appeal to the People? What must the World think of such conduct, and of the Government of the United States submitting to it?" Early in August, Washington and his cabinet, including Jefferson, agreed to demand Genet's recall.[7] Although successors to Genet tried, with no more success than he, to shake Federalist administrations from their chosen path, his failure had been the critical one.

For various reasons, among them doubt about the president's powers and therefore the legitimacy of the detailed directives issued to implement what was largely only a general statement of policy, the Washington administration decided to supplement the Neutrality Proclamation with legislation. The Neutrality Act of 1794 prohibited enlistment in foreign armies, outlawed military schemes like those planned by Genet, and prohibited the arming or strengthening of belligerent warships in American waters. Although Americans were specifically authorized to trade in contraband goods, they were placed on notice that their government would not support them if a belligerent seized these goods on the high seas.

Within a few years the prudence of this form of neutrality seemed clear even to those who initially questioned it. In 1800 the act, originally temporary, was made permanent. In 1817, over objections by friends of the colonial rebellions in Latin America, the prohibitions were extended to wars of revolution. In 1818 a final piece of legislation codified the system.

At times, sympathies or cupidity have led to violations of the code. Latin America's friends violated it. Filibusterers operating in Central America in midcentury, supporters of Fenianism in Canada in the 1830s, backers of Cuban independence movements in the latter third of the nineteenth century – all of them, and others, disobeyed the law. Except in detail, however, the code of neutrality was not changed, and the position laid down in 1793 and 1794 remained in place until World War I and beyond.

In time, other countries endorsed the idea that neutrality meant

---

7 In fact, Genet did not return to France, where he faced arrest and perhaps execution by the new Jacobin government. He retired to New York, married well, and lived out his life as a country gentleman. He became a citizen in 1804.

something more than abstention from hostilities, that it ought, in form at least, to be impartial. In 1823 the British foreign secretary, George Canning, told Parliament, "If I wished for a guide in the system of Neutrality, I should take that laid down by America in the days of the presidency of Washington and the secretaryship of Jefferson." Once again, by serving its own interests the United States had served the interests of others as well.

The almost universal backing for neutrality was early evidence that rival American politicians were not as uncompromisingly committed to the cause of England or France as their opponents charged. Still, they quarreled bitterly for years because they found it difficult to understand and impossible to respect one another, because they were constantly aware of the domestic implications of the success or defeat of the European contenders and because the republic was still young and unsure of itself. Moreover, even though they shared a desire to stay out of the European war and endorsed a new kind of neutrality, within that frame there was still sufficient room for disagreement. Federalist policy was more unfriendly to France than Great Britain, and the reverse was true, though less consistently, of the Republicans. Their quarrels deeply affected American efforts to confirm and to extend the nation's territory, to develop commerce, and especially to hold an even keel during the European storms.

The Profits of Neutrality

During these violent years, the belligerents often treated the Americans brutally. As a result, the United States became involved in an undeclared war with France, a contest that inspired Joseph Hopkinson to write "Hail Columbia," the first national anthem, and a better-known war with England, which evoked Francis Scott Key's tribute to American valor. But the Americans also learned, as a leading diplomatic historian long ago pointed out, that "Europe's distress" could be "America's advantage."[8] They exploited the European wars to reap immense economic benefits. They liquidated

8 This is the theme of Samuel Flagg Bemis, *Pinckney's Treaty* (Baltimore, 1926), which carries the subtitle, *A Study of America's Advantage from Europe's Distress.*

challenges to the boundaries nominally won in 1782 and gained
territory beyond even Franklin's dreams. Both the trials and the
successes were essential to the completion of independence.

Although, as Turgot had predicted, Anglo-American trade increased after independence, commerce with the rest of the world,
including Britain's remaining colonies, languished in the 1780s.
Neither Britain nor France nor Spain shared the American belief in
"the civilizing influence of commercial expansion,"[9] and all continued along traditional mercantilist lines. Then Louis XVI took his
ride in a tumbrel. The new rulers of France, partly as a matter of
doctrine, partly from wartime necessity, opened its colonies and
eased controls on transatlantic trade. Exports to France leapt from $1
million in 1791 to $13 million in 1807. The British, forced to
divert ships to wartime tasks, began in 1795 to encourage annual
proclamations by colonial governors in the West Indies that suspended the legal prohibition on foreign ships, opening what Madison had called a "most natural and valuable" commerce.

More generally, the war increased European demand. Exports of
American goods rose from $19 million in 1791 to $49 million in
1807, bringing prosperity especially to agricultural areas. Reexports
grew even more spectacularly as foreign ships were diverted or, in
the French case, driven from the ocean. The Americans, who
brought goods home before sending them to their ultimate destina-
tions, took over trade between Europe and other parts of the world,
notably the Caribbean. Reexports multiplied thirtyfold in the decade and a half before 1807, reaching a value of $60 million, a level
not again equaled until 1916. Until 1805 the British tolerated this
trade, agreeing to consider the two legs of the journey as separate
voyages rather than one; had they not done so, they would have
believed themselves justified in seizing neutral ships engaged in
carriage from one enemy port to another. By the so-called Rule of
the War of 1756, laid down during an earlier war with France,
Britain had proclaimed that neutral ships could not engage in trade
that had been closed to them in peacetime, as had most commerce

9 Drew R. McCoy, *The Elusive Republic* (Chapel Hill, 1980), 89.

between European metropols and their colonies, without subjecting themselves to seizure.

Wartime neutrality being so profitable, Americans even half regretted a Franco-British armistice in 1801: A Yankee clergyman noted that his parishioners "All rejoiced at the sound of peace and all recollected the great commercial advantages to our Country in the late war. Passion and Judgment struggled without victory." When war resumed, so did profits — for farmers, plantation owners, merchants, and the nation as a whole. One of the most successful war profiteers, William Gray of Massachusetts, built a fleet of thirty-six ships and had an estimated worth of $3 million in 1809. The nation enjoyed unprecedented prosperity.

American trade declined after 1807, thanks to Jefferson's Embargo Act and, later, the war with England. But a strong base had been laid. After the wars ended, American exports resumed their growth, and the merchant marine again played a major role in international commerce. The United States had established itself as a growing factor in the world economy. Like territorial empire, this was very largely a consequence of Europe's wars.

Federalists had no doubt about the value of commercial expansion; Republicans devoted to the idea of an agrarian society welcomed territorial expansion but sometimes had misgivings about foreign commerce. Thus Jefferson, who often resorted to simplicisms belying his intelligence, wrote in 1785 that he wished the nation would "practice neither commerce nor navigation, but . . . stand with respect to Europe precisely on the footing of China. We should thus avoid wars, and all our citizens would be husbandmen. But," he admitted, "this is theory only, and a theory which the servants of America are not at liberty to follow. Our people have a decided taste for navigation and commerce." In short, theory had to give way to avarice.

Particularly troublesome to Republicans was the reexport trade, which, far more than the trade in national goods, led to quarrels with belligerents. Because it benefited only merchants and shipowners, mere "speculators," in Jefferson's view, it also "compromised important republican assumptions about life and labor in what

Jefferson once called 'this agricultural country.'"[10] Consequently, some Republicans wanted to give it up. John Randolph of Roanoke, more Republican than Pope Thomas, described it as "this mushroom, this fungus of war." But the profits were too great to abandon, and the Republican presidents declined to eschew the *champignons* so as to concentrate on native fare.

Avarice, of course, helps explain the "decided taste" Jefferson observed. But so does the belief, expressed by Jefferson at other times, that the precious but precarious republican system – indeed, freedom and independence – could survive only if citizens were prosperous, though not to the extent of "luxury," which was generally deplored. To secure prosperity, Americans looked to a steady increase in exports, particularly, in the case of Republicans, agricultural ones. How nicely united were self-interest and virtuous republicanism.

To protect wartime trade, under almost constant attack from Europeans, both Federalist and Republican administrations fought constant battle. They demanded the broadest possible freedom for neutral commerce. They did so, of course, primarily to defend the nation's interest, but in the spirit of the "Model Treaty," they also saw themselves furthering a melioration of warfare. Their successors would continue to follow the same line on into the twentieth century.

Issues were complex, rights and wrongs unclear. Everyone agreed that neutrals had a right to trade with belligerents, provided that they did not carry goods that had military use, called contraband, or run blockades. But what constituted contraband? How were legitimate blockades to be defined? Did a neutral flag protect cargo owned by a belligerent? – that is, did "free ships make free goods"? If, as authorities agreed, one belligerent's illegal behavior justified its opponent in responding with action that would otherwise violate international law, how far did this right of retaliation extend? Although on a few issues the Americans were cautious, usually they "harnessed doctrines of international law on behalf of national avarice."[11] This led to quarrels, interruptions of the war-engendered

10 Burton Spivak, *Jefferson's English Crisis* (Charlottesville, Va., 1979), ix.
11 Ibid., 12.

prosperity, even to military conflicts during both the Federalist and Republican regimes.

During the Civil War, seeking to suffocate the South, Lincoln's administration radically changed parts of the traditional position. Still, more than any other major power, with the possible exception of tsarist Russia, America has identified itself with broad rights for neutral commerce in time of war. During the Spanish-American War, no complete blockade of Cuba, the Philippines, or Spain was ever proclaimed. While neutral in World War I, America vainly urged Germany and the Allies to accept its definitions as their own, and after entering the war it rather self-righteously declined to employ the most stringent restrictions the Allies had imposed on neutral commerce.

Jay's Treaty

In the United States, from the Genet explosion until Napoleon's final defeat in 1815, differences over foreign policy dominated – nearly monopolized – the political battlefield. Federalists and Republicans had widely different views about the nature of the Republic, but after the Hamiltonian program was in place Federalists took almost no initiatives in domestic policy. When Republicans gained control, they repealed only a few Federalist laws and embarked upon few legislative initiatives. There was too much to do in the diplomatic sphere.

While Genet was appealing to Americans to repudiate their own government, the British embarked on policies that ensured that, once that flamboyant diplomat left the scene, American anger would turn in their direction. Partly because they failed to anticipate the Neutrality Proclamation, expecting instead that the United States would support France, they struck hard at neutral commerce. They ordered foodstuffs bound for France, or countries it dominated, brought into British ports for purchase at regulated prices and, a few months later, subjected to capture all neutral trade with French colonies; both policies defied prevailing views of international law. By the beginning of 1794, several hundred American ships had been seized.

At the same time, the long-festering issue of the border posts and British intrigue with the Indians became more serious. Speaking to a group of Indian leaders, Lord Dorchester, governor-general of Canada, encouraged continued resistance to the advance of American frontiersmen and suggested that, before long, Britain and the Indians would be allies in a war with the United States: "From the manner in which the People of the States push on, . . . on this side, and from what I learn of their conduct towards the Sea, I shall not be surprised if we are at war with them in the course of the present year; and if so, a Line must be drawn by the Warriors." Much to Dorchester's irritation, the text of the speech soon leaked, producing a predictable uproar in the United States. At about the same time, Dorchester ordered a military post established on the Maumee River, close to present-day Toledo, far deeper in American territory than any of the other frontier forts, although news of this development did not reach Philadelphia until a mission to England had been set in train. [12]

Republicans, led by Madison, had been pressing for commercial retaliation against Great Britain since Congress convened in December 1793, and news of the British captures and Dorchester's speech caused nonaligned members of Congress – there were still many – to swing toward the Republican side. Federalists believed a commercial war would be much more harmful to the United States than to Britain, and they feared that it might escalate into a military one. They also thought that the Republicans wanted to align the country with France. "It is all French that is spoken in support of the measure," a Federalist leader grumbled. "I like the Yankee dialect better." For a time it looked as if he and his party would be overborne. In March, Congress passed a thirty-day embargo on trade with Britain and its colonies. Agitation for still further restrictions continued.

12 In the summer of 1794, after a battle with the Indians at Fallen Timbers, General Anthony Wayne advanced on the fort and demanded that the British evacuate it, bringing close a confrontation that might have touched off war in the Northwest and destroyed the negotiations then going forward. However, neither Wayne nor the British commander wanted battle. After a few days the Americans withdrew.

In the middle of April, President Washington nominated John Jay, then chief justice, as special envoy to Great Britain. Federalist leaders who suggested this move to the president had little hope that it would lead to a great diplomatic success. Their principal purpose was political, to derail or at least delay further commercial warfare with Britain. Understanding this, Republicans sought to kill Jay's nomination in the Senate, but they lost, 18–8.

Jay's instructions reflected the Federalist outlook, although they were nominally the work of Jefferson's successor and friend, Edmund Randolph. [13] They omitted any mention of impressment, which only later became an important issue between the two countries, but included a long list of other American desiderata, ranging from evacuation of the posts to compensation for captured ships to terms of a commercial treaty. However, with only two exceptions these were, the instructions stated, "recommendations only, which in your discretion you may modify." They were, in fact, "one of the most open-ended sets of instructions ever written for an American diplomat." [14]

The only two requirements – no direct violation of the treaty with France, no commercial treaty unless American shipping was granted access to the British West Indies – were politically imperative, since open abandonment of the alliance and of West Indian trade, the center of contemporary debate over commerce, would have ruined the administration. For the rest, the Federalists were prepared to seek but not demand. No doubt their fundamental sympathies for Britain and dislike of France affected their stance, although at this time they, like the Republicans, were outraged by English misbehavior. However, the predominant reason was their conviction that the United States lacked the power to force concessions that went to the heart of the imperial system of commerce and war. Their principal, connected purposes were to ease the pressure at home and to avoid being brought into the European conflict. To them, this seemed prudent; to their opponents, it seemed craven.

13 That Washington selected Randolph, rather than a follower of Hamilton, to replace Jefferson when the latter resigned in December 1793 is a further sign of the slow development of partisan division.

14 Frank T. Reuter, *Trials and Triumphs* (Fort Worth, Tex., 1983), 186.

The position of the British government was not dissimilar. Members of William Pitt's ministry, and especially his cousin and foreign secretary, Lord Grenville, although by no means prepared to concede everything the Americans wished, did not want to add another enemy when the European war was going badly. As one government supporter phrased it, after the negotiations with America were under way, "A war with her would be the summit and completion of ruin. England would thereby be more than ever endangered, and the country would be undone both in point of commerce, and perhaps even of internal tranquility." To prevent such an outcome, Pitt and Grenville rejected the importunities of self-interested groups and extremists, much as the Federalist administration rejected those of the Republicans.

By the time Jay reached England in June, Pitt and his colleagues had already begun to move toward accommodation. With Grenville the key player, they had decided that the posts would have to be evacuated. Orders were sent to Lord Dorchester and other officials in Canada to soften their behavior, and similar cautions went to George Hammond, the minister at Philadelphia, who had alienated even the staunchest Federalists by his obstreperousness. A new Order in Council made it easier for American owners to appeal confiscated ships in British courts, and from the outset Grenville accepted that reparations for many seizures would have to be paid. During the negotiations, Grenville went farther: Overriding the objections of West Indian interests and the British East India Company, he offered to open trade with British Caribbean and Asian colonies, and, again defying interested opposition, he agreed to submit the claims of pre-Revolutionary creditors to the hazards of arbitration rather than demand a fixed sum as compensation.

Given the position of the two sides, it is no surprise that a settlement was reached. Nor is it surprising that many issues were simply placed on the shelf, Jay and Grenville concluding that they were too divisive to be pressed. The treaty signed in November 1794 committed England to evacuate the western posts, opened trade with India and (on conditions) the British West Indies, and arranged for arbitration of three matters – the disputed eastern boundary of Maine, the claims of Americans to compensation for ships seized in the West Indies, and the sums owed to British merchants who had given credit to Americans before the Revolution.[15] These terms, the two principal negotiators believed, would make it possible to reverse the trend toward confrontation.

In the end, their calculations proved correct, but it was a "near run thing." Republicans would have objected to almost any settlement with England, but even the administration's friends found Jay's Treaty difficult to swallow. After "much trouble, and many fruitless discussions," Jay had agreed to omit any definition of neutral rights. He raised the issue of impressment, about which his instructions were silent, but only feebly pressed the matter. Moreover, he agreed to a provision which, for the life of the treaty, prohibited discrimination by one nation against the ships and goods of the other, a stipulation that disarmed Republicans of their favorite weapon against Great Britain.

Many years ago the great historian Henry Adams commented, "That Mr. Jay's treaty was a bad one few persons even then ventured to dispute; no one would venture on its merits to defend it now. There has been no moment since 1810 when the United States would have hesitated to prefer war rather than peace on such terms."[16] Except perhaps for the right to trade with British India, Jay did fail to win anything more than what Americans were obviously entitled to, liberation of territory recognized as theirs in 1782 and compensation for seizures even Britain admitted had been illegal. He pried open the British West Indies only at the price of agreeing to prohibit certain American exports, a price even the Federalists soon decided was exorbitant. He accomplished nothing regarding impressment and neutral rights, although in fairness it should be added that he did not accept British pretensions in these areas.

Still, the treaty did remove two major obstacles to smoother relations, trouble on the frontier and over ship seizures, and by doing so reversed the path toward war. The treaty's shortcomings, a

---

15 The first two arbitrations, though marred by contentious dispute between the representatives of the two countries, ultimately were successful, but the third failed, and in 1802 the United States agreed to pay a lump sum to quiet the claims.

16 Henry Adams, *The Life of Albert Gallatin* (Philadelphia, 1879), 158.

historian has written, were "the price paid by the Federalists for a peace which they believed indispensable to the perpetuation of American nationality."[17] Moreover, the successful conclusion of a treaty encouraged the Pitt ministry to alter a wide range of policies. British officials in Canada ceased to intrigue with Indian tribes in the West. London allowed governors of Caribbean colonies to open their ports to American ships, treated American neutral commerce with relative leniency, and forced the Admiralty to return many American seamen who had been impressed by overzealous naval officers.

Beyond this, there was a further American gain, at Spain's expense, which owed a good deal to Jay's Treaty. Following the Revolution, Madrid had seen no reason why it should underwrite Shelburne's territorial generosity. From bases in Florida and Louisiana, Spain laid claim to territory as far northward as the Ohio River, as far eastward as the Appalachian Mountains. Fearing the advance of the frontier, in 1784 it closed the Mississippi River, the chief vent for exports from Kentucky and Tennessee, and encouraged separatism among settlers there. Spain also sought to keep the Southwestern Indians hostile to the United States.

In 1795, Spain found itself in a delicate position, in the midst of a maneuver from the British to the French side. Facing war with England, fearing that Jay's Treaty might presage even closer Anglo-American ties, Spain felt that it could not run the risk that Britain and America would cooperate against it. That Spanish fears were overdrawn is of no moment. They permitted an American envoy, Thomas Pinckney, to gain in October 1795 what had long been withheld, clear title to territory extending west to the Mississippi and south to 31 degrees, the northern border of today's Florida. Spain also agreed that Westerners might export goods over the southern stretches of that river, where it ran through Spanish territory. Thus Pinckney's Treaty "placed the gateway to the riches of the entire Mississippi Valley in the grasp of the United States."[18]

17 Samuel Flagg Bemis, *Jay's Treaty*, 2d ed. (New Haven, 1962), 373. Even so, Bemis excoriated Jay for his supineness.
18 Reuter, *Trials and Triumphs*, 217.

The delayed benefits of Jay's Treaty could not, of course, easily be foreseen in 1794. News of the treaty produced an enormous uproar in the United States. Jay was many times hung in effigy. The Senate approved the treaty by precisely the required two-thirds margin, after Federalist leaders deleted the unpopular West Indian article. The House of Representatives, which had to approve the funds, a mere $90,000, to finance the arbitration machinery, twice came within a vote or two of destroying the treaty, and a Pennsylvania Republican who cast a key vote was, for his betrayal, stabbed in the streets of Philadelphia by his brother-in-law. As time passed and the benefits of the treaty became more clear, and in particular after British troops withdrew from the posts in 1796, the agreement became less unpopular. The Federalists, however, never entirely escaped from the accusation that, motivated solely by a desire to aid Great Britain, they had betrayed the nation, that they had, in Jefferson's phrase, "had their heads shorn by the harlot England."

The French Challenge

The most substantial charge against Jay's Treaty is that in seeking to avoid trouble with one side the United States blundered into it with the other. The treaty hit France like a bolt from the blue, especially since James Monroe, a violent gallophile sent to Paris as a sort of balance to Jay's appointment to London, fed illusions by insisting that his government would not, and in the face of public opinion could not, compromise with England. When France learned that a treaty had been made and, even more astonishing, ratified, it reacted angrily, denouncing the Washington administration as disloyal to republicanism. It struck at American commerce so extensively that French seizures soon outnumbered those earlier made by Britain. The embroglio thus begun is often charged against Jay's Treaty.

This is a half-truth. Most Frenchmen agreed that their country, especially now that it was a republic, had a right to expect support from the United States, at the very least a system of benevolent neutrality akin to Vergennes's policy from 1775 to 1778. Domestic turmoil produced a succession of governments in France during the 1790s, and their tactics toward the United States were various, but not one would have been satisfied by anything less than a permanent American breach with England. Nor could authorities at Paris believe that a regime that defied ties of gratitude and doctrine represented the American people. Finally, in effect ignoring the difficulty of projecting power three thousand miles across the Atlantic, they all believed that, like Holland and various Italian principalities, the Americans would give way when faced with French power. Monroe's biographer, Harry Ammon, has written that the policy of the Directory, the plural executive that came to power late in 1795, was "based on nothing more substantial than irritation, ignorance and an inability to assess the importance of American trade."[19] Very much the same thing could be said of the Directory's predecessors, but it was left to the Directory to convert irritation into something just short of war.

Like most Americans, the Directory expected Washington to run for a third term. Because of Jay's capitulation, Monroe assured them, Washington could be beaten. The French determined to bring this about. Having suspended the treaty of 1778 so as to clear decks for action, the Directory suspended diplomatic relations as well. In August 1796 it ordered Pierre Adet, the minister at Philadelphia, to announce that the forthcoming election presented a choice between friendship and a quarrel, probably a war. Washington, wrote the foreign minister, "must go."

Especially when engaged in ideological crusades, strong states often interfere in the affairs of weaker ones. There are, however, few parallels to France's action in 1796, an open demand, across a wide ocean, unbacked by an invasion threat, that a people follow foreign wishes. The Directory's arrogance roused nationalistic sentiment that virtually doomed its policy from the start, as Republicans saw the moment they read Adet's manifesto.

In September 1796, just before that appeal appeared in American newspapers, President Washington in effect anticipated and took advantage of it by issuing his own Farewell Address. Although couched in broad, even philosophical terms, and though Washington still professed to dislike parties, the address clearly aimed to influence the impending presidential election. In the best-remembered

19 Harry Ammon, *James Monroe* (New York, 1971), 146.

passage the president declared, "It is our true policy to steer clear of permanent alliances." This obviously implied that the alliance of 1778, to which Republicans wished to cling, was out of date. "Nothing," the president stated, "is more essential than that permanent, inveterate antipathies against particular nations and passionate attachments for others should be excluded. . . . Against the insidious wiles of foreign influence . . . the jealousy of a free people ought to be constantly awake." In the context, this was clearly an appeal to the electorate to defy France by rejecting the Republicans.

John Adams, the Federalist candidate to succeed Washington, won the presidency by the narrow margin of three electoral votes. He bitterly resented the close shave — even Jefferson, his defeated rival, admitted that in terms of seniority Adams deserved the post — and he never thanked the Directory for its unintentional assistance. French leaders should have learned, but many did not, that adolescent nationalism is a most dangerous kind to challenge. Early in 1797, just as Adams was inaugurated, they stepped up attacks upon American commerce. The Americans, Paris believed, could be driven to concessions that would reverse the trend in policy begun by Jay's Treaty.

Despite, or perhaps because of, the dangerous tension between the two countries, President Adams's first step was to seek a solution through diplomacy. He considered sending Madison, Republican leader in the House of Representatives, as part of a three-man mission to France, thereby producing near apoplexy among high Federalists, but Madison declined. The choice then fell on a Virginia Federalist, the future Chief Justice John Marshall; Adams's friend Elbridge Gerry, a widely distrusted political maverick; and the elder brother of the successful negotiator with Spain, Charles Cotesworth Pinckney, whom Paris had previously refused to receive as Monroe's successor. Adams directed them to refuse even to discuss repudiation of the treaty with England and to seek compensation for the more than three hundred ships taken by France in the preceding twelve months. "From the French point of view," a sympathetic historian has commented, "the Americans sought much and offered little."[20]

20 Alexander DeConde, *The Quasi-War* (New York, 1966), 45.

What they did offer was not insubstantial: They gave France an opportunity to reconsider, to accept that America's views of neutrality differed from those of Vergennes.

Such possibilities did not appeal to the Directors. In the abstract they, and especially their subordinate, Foreign Minister Talleyrand, wanted peace with the United States. But it must be peace on their terms. They agreed not to settle spoliation claims and to let the jimcrack republicans know that attacks on commerce would continue as long as Jay's Treaty remained in effect. (Talleyrand was less firm on this point, but he did not fight hard for a change.) Furthermore, they passed word to the envoys that, like little states within gunshot of France, the United States was expected to pay for the privilege of negotiating its humiliation. "You must pay money, a great deal of money," an agent informed the Americans. "Millions for defense, but not one cent for tribute," Pinckney is supposed to have replied, but in fact each of the Americans was ready to consider bribery provided that France suspended ship seizures while negotiating. This suggested a reciprocity the Directory would not consider. Marshall and Pinckney broke off their mission in April 1798. Gerry stayed on until July, carrying on discussions with Talleyrand, which the latter never intended to come to any conclusion. "Our present position, half friendly, half hostile, is profitable to us," the foreign minister believed.

Adams withheld from Congress early reports of discussions with the bribe seekers, but in March he did warn the legislators that negotiations were going badly. Foolish Republicans believed that the president was concealing good news, and in April they joined with Federalists quite differently motivated to pass a resolution calling upon Adams to transmit all reports from Paris. After deleting the French agents' names – Messieurs Hottinguer, Bellamy, and Hauteval became "X," "Y" and "Z" – the president dutifully complied, exposing the attempted extortion. Congress voted to make the dispatches public.

A political explosion followed. John Adams, genuinely popular for the first time in his career, developed a mania for the theater, which allowed him to inhale applause from the rest of the audience. After one performance, the British minister's wife wrote, "nothing could equal the noise and uproar, the President's March [Hopkinson's "Hail Columbia"] was play'd, and called for over and over again, it was sung to, and danced to, some poor fellow in the Gallery calling for sa ira ["Ça Ira," the French anthem], was threatened to be thrown over" into the higher-priced seats below. In the fall elections to Congress, Federalists recaptured control of the House of Representatives, almost solely on this issue.

The Quasi War and the Peace of Mortefontaine

The XYZ affair touched off over two years of undeclared and limited war. Congress authorized the capture of French armed ships, although not unarmed merchantmen, and suspended trade with France and its colonies. It also declared the treaties of 1778 void on the ground that France had been unfaithful to them. Heavy French attacks on commerce preceded these acts of retaliation and continued until 1800. In all, about 830 ships fell victim to French warships and privateers, particularly in the Caribbean, although seizures abated somewhat after the British and American navies arranged convoys for the ships of both nations. (The two countries also developed common policies toward the rebellious French colony of Santo Domingo.) For their part, the Americans captured eight armed French ships. Probably most Americans, whether or not they wanted a full-scale war, expected one.

Although Adams twice drafted a war message, he made only modest efforts – a small naval building program, the organization but not the recruiting of a ground force – to arm the country. In the absence of executive pressures, Federalist caucuses in July and again in December 1798 voted against war. By large margins, the House of Representatives twice rejected proposals, not supported by the administration, to seize all French ships, not merely armed ones. Had this action been taken, it almost certainly would have produced a French declaration of war. Like Adams, virtually the entire country, even most Federalists, favored only what Alexander Hamilton approvingly called "a mitigated hostility." When, toward the end of 1798 Hamilton shifted to a more warlike position, Adams commented, "This man is stark mad, or I am." As soon as possible he turned, albeit warily, in the direction of peace.

Largely because thunder across the Atlantic made Paris pay serious attention for the first time, France changed direction almost immediately after publication of the XYZ dispatches. The first approaches were indirect and equivocal. Most of the cabinet, protégés of Hamilton inherited by Adams from the Washington administration, wanted to reject them. The president spurned their advice, and early in 1799 a three-man mission to France was appointed, although its actual departure was made conditional on assurances from Paris that the envoys would be fairly received. Delay followed. Adams went on vacation in Massachusetts, and Secretary of State Timothy Pickering rejected as inadequate the promises forwarded by Talleyrand. At last, in October, the president returned to the capital, then temporarily in Trenton because yellow fever had driven government offices from Philadelphia, overruled his subordinates, and directed the mission to depart. Negotiations actually began only in April 1800.

One envoy was Chief Justice Oliver Ellsworth, for, as Jay's appointment had shown, the nation saw no reason for judges to limit their activities to the courtroom. The others were William R. Davie, a North Carolina politician, and William Vans Murray, a diplomat serving in Europe through whom Adams had first been approached. They were directed to secure compensation for ships taken by France and to end the treaties of 1778, particularly the guarantee concerning the French West Indies. Talleyrand pointed out the illogic in seeking to cancel the 1778 agreements at the same time that one sought damages for seizures largely on the basis that they had been made in violation of those agreements. In sum, he told the Americans they must choose between indemnities and cancellation; they could not have both.

Because they would not choose, the Convention of Mortefontaine, named after the chateau west of Paris at which it was signed in October 1800, did little more than "smother the danger of full-scale war"[21] by arranging an end to hostilities and the resumption of commerce. But the agreement confirmed what had been apparent for some time, that France had given up the arrogant effort to

21 Ibid., 253.

control American policy, more specifically to drive America into confrontation with Britain.

Subsequently, after tangled negotiations, France agreed in 1801 to cancel the 1778 treaties provided that American shipowners' claims against it be paid by the United States government. Because these proved to total $20 million, such was the cost of escaping the alliance that had won American independence. A cynic might observe that there was never a chance that any American government would really fight to save the French West Indies. In any event $20 million, more than was later paid for Louisiana, made the issue moot.

From Adams's point of view, the calendar had been unkind. When he ordered the mission to Paris, he well knew that Federalist ultras would be horrified. Their opposition became virulent, and in May 1800 he demanded the resignation of two of them who were in his cabinet, including Pickering. When the secretary of state protested that he could not afford to give up his $3,500 salary, Adams had to dismiss him. It was the president's misfortune that, having lost the support of many Federalist leaders by agreeing to negotiate, he failed to gain other votes because negotiations took too long. News of Mortefontaine reached the United States only after electors had been chosen. The president ran well ahead of Federalist candidates for Congress, who lost forty seats in the House of Representatives. Nevertheless, Jefferson defeated him. Since the margin was small – outside of New York, where Hamilton betrayed him, Adams won more electors than in 1796 – it is at least possible that an earlier settlement would have returned him to office.

The Federalist Record

The years from 1789 to 1801 are commonly called the Federalist era. In foreign affairs, at least, this is something of a misnomer: Not until about 1794 can Washington's foreign policies be given a partisan label. His first cabinet included both Hamilton and Jefferson. Soon in disagreement over Hamilton's financial program, their antipathy to one another almost immediately spilled over into foreign affairs, but the president did not, as he almost always did on domestic ones, routinely follow Hamilton's advice.

For example, in the first years of the republic Jefferson sought, with Washington's approval, to win commercial concessions from Britain by threatening American economic retaliation. Hamilton, disagreeing with this policy, undermined it by betraying information to a British agent, George Beckwith; by assuring Beckwith that commercial retaliation was not in the cards; and, finally, by distorting messages passing between Beckwith and Jefferson through him.[22]

On the most important issue of the early years, however, Jefferson and Hamilton agreed: They endorsed and helped to create the new, peculiarly American form of neutrality announced in 1793. Although in this instance the two secretaries differed sharply over tactics, at the policy level there was as yet no "Federalist" foreign policy, only a national one.

After Jefferson resigned at the end of 1793, Federalist influence predominated. Edmund Randolph, Jefferson's successor and a man of similar views, was frequently overruled in the cabinet, where Washington threshed out policy questions, but the president also rejected counsel given to him by the most extreme Federalists. Randolph was driven from office by a shabby Anglo-Federalist intrigue in the summer of 1795. French dispatches, intercepted by the British and turned over to a Federalist member of the cabinet, were translated, or mistranslated, in such a fashion that, when presented to the president, they convinced Washington that Randolph was in French pay. The president demanded Randolph's resignation. More important, he ordered formal ratification of Jay's Treaty, a step he had delayed because of renewed trouble with Britain over neutral commerce.

The search for a successor to Randolph was difficult. After at least five men refused appointment, Hamilton wrote to Washington, "a first rate character is not attainable. A second-rate must be taken with good dispositions and barely decent qualifications." This person turned out to be Timothy Pickering, a hard-bitten Yankee and a

22 Later, at the time of the Jay mission, Hamilton was similarly indiscreet, or disloyal. He told the British minister, George Hammond, that the United States would not act in concert with other neutrals protesting British actions, thus removing at least a hypothetical weapon of threat from the American arsenal.

follower of Hamilton. Pickering served Washington loyally, but during Adams's administration he and other Hamiltonian holdovers in the cabinet were frequently at odds with their chief, who was much less eager than they to inflame the quarrel with France. Adams had good reason to fire Pickering in 1800. Indeed, he might have done so earlier.

The Federalist years, then, were not marked by unanimity of views within the administration. Discord was common. But both presidents kept control in their own hands, rejecting extremist advice and thereby creating a record that deserves higher marks than Republicans would have admitted or than some historians have given it.

During these years, years when the new republic was a very feeble thing, major steps were taken toward the confirmation of independence. The United States solidified its control of the West as a result of British withdrawal from military posts south of the Great Lakes and of Pinckney's Treaty, by which Spain abandoned claims in the South. These years also saw liquidation of the alliance with France, perhaps an act of ingratitude toward the nation whose contributions had been essential during the Revolution but one that was more than justified in terms of national interest.

Most important of all, the Federalist presidents kept the United States out of war at a dangerous time. War came close, both with Britain and with France. In both instances, a softening of policy in the European capitals was an essential ingredient in the maintenance of peace, but Washington and Adams also deserve substantial credit. If effect, they clung to the determination, proclaimed in 1793 and clearly of great importance to the very future of the nation, to stand apart from Europe's wars. With justifiable pride, Adams wrote, years later, "I desire no other inscription on my gravestone than: 'here lies John Adams, who took upon himself the responsibility of the peace with France in the year 1800.'"

Of course, the Neutrality Proclamation itself represented a withdrawal from the connection with France, and Federalist policy had what today might be called a pro-British "tilt." But neither Washington nor Adams was moved primarily by sentiment, although both men deplored the excesses of the French Revolution. Adams, in particular, hated the British, and this reinforced his determination, during the undeclared war with France, to avoid British embrace while at the same time cooperating for limited ends. Basically, both presidents simply – and correctly – calculated that the United States could not afford to go to war, especially with Great Britain. For them, this did not mean that the United States should absorb whatever insults Britain chose to offer. Adams consequently lost the support of Hamilton's followers, while at the same time both he and his predecessor alienated the Jeffersonians. Moderation sometimes alienates a majority composed of quite opposing elements, as Adams learned in 1800. He and Washington, however, had served the nation well.

5. Jefferson and Madison: The Diplomacy of Fear and Hope

The canvass of 1800 broke Federalist power, ushering in a quarter century of Republican rule. In March 1801 Thomas Jefferson became president. In 1809 he handed the presidency to his closest collaborator, and Madison, in turn, passed the office to James Monroe in 1817. During all but the first few years of the "Virginia dynasty," contrary to Jefferson's hopes when he was inaugurated, problems of foreign policy predominated. Jefferson expanded the national domain by acquiring the Louisiana country, a magnificent gain. Otherwise he and Madison were failures. Their inept diplomacy produced national disgrace and then a war with England, which, but for good fortune, might well have destroyed the union. Both deservedly left the White House with tarnished reputations. Their continuing fame rests upon earlier accomplishments.

Jefferson, Madison, and the World

The central failure of the two men was an inability to understand the psychology of wartime. Frustrated by America's treatment at the hands of the European belligerents, angered by their failure to react rationally, as he saw it, to his complaints and his menaces, Jefferson railed against their stupidity and even their mental instability. "I consider Europe a great madhouse," he wrote in 1808. Madison was little different. His biographer has written, as if to condone that leader's failures, "President Madison to be successful in his diplomatic strategy needed to deal with men whose understanding matched his own."[1] This is precisely the point: Neither man recognized that "understanding" is often among the first casualties of war; their obtuseness is a heavy charge against them.

1 Irving Brant, *James Madison, the President* (Indianapolis, 1956), 483.

111

As president, Jefferson strangely combined idealism, even uto-
pianism, with cynical craft. Both publicly and privately, he reiterated the Republican creed – limited government, strict construction
of the Constitution, the danger of aristocracy, the rights of man.
Although he sometimes worried that the people of America were in
danger of being corrupted by the pursuit of money, he saw America
as almost the sole repository of virtue in the world.

Yet Jefferson seldom allowed Republican principles to interfere
with pursuit of the national interest as he saw it. He carried through
the Louisiana Purchase even though he believed it unconstitutional.
To enforce the Embargo Act, a prohibition on exports, he carried the
powers of government to heights not even dreamed of by Federalist
predecessors. In principle an isolationist, he twice considered an
alliance with England. Although he decried the rise of trade, except
the export of agricultural goods, he threw the weight of the government behind shipowners and merchants, even those who were trading solely in foreign produce.

Jefferson sought to democratize the presidency. He received a
British minister in carpet slippers and a dressing gown. At his table,
he instituted the system of "pell mell," which meant that when a
meal was announced the guests scurried to take seats wherever they
chose. He reversed the policy of Washington and Adams, declining
to appear in person before Congress. However, despite the opposition of Republican factionalists as well as the declining Federalist
party, Jefferson effectively controlled Congress or, perhaps more accurately, a working Republican majority; unlike Washington and
Adams, who believed themselves to be above party, he saw himself
as a party leader. He preferred private influence – and his was very
effective – to open leadership. Lamentably, during his last months in
office, when leadership was woefully needed, he gave none, and the
legislature wallowed in uncertainty.

Like Jefferson, Madison knew what he thought the nation ought
to do, and in dealing with foreign nations he could be firm and even
rash. But his most loyal supporters did not claim that the president
was a natural leader. During the session of 1811–12, his refusal to
give the nation a lead irritated congressmen who shared his view
that war with Britain was becoming inevitable. Where Jefferson

frequently spurred Congress forward, Madison often remained apparently inert. Never has there been another president who so combined intelligence, personal convictions, and public ineffectiveness.

Neither Jefferson nor Madison was a doctrinaire pacifist, though both strove to keep America at peace. Jefferson professed to believe that war was a mere matter of arithmetic: "When peace becomes more losing than war, we may prefer the latter on principles of pecuniary calculation." In fact, like Madison and the country at large, he reacted to issues of prestige and honor as well as economic factors. After enduring seven years of insult the Republican leaders – Jefferson in retirement at Monticello, Madison in the White House – reluctantly concluded that war could no longer be avoided.

When he became president in 1801, Jefferson certainly foresaw none of this. A European armistice in November of that year adjourned problems of neutral rights, and at first the major concern of the new administration was Tripolitanian attacks upon American commerce. Using military force, but also paying a ransom of $60,000 for American sailors held prisoner, Jefferson was able to end the problem, at least temporarily, in 1805.[2] Before that, however, he had attained a greater triumph, the acquisition of Louisiana.

The Louisiana Purchase

Even before Jefferson became president, many Americans, and perceptive Spaniards as well, recognized that Louisiana, gained from France by Spain at the end of the American Revolution, was singularly vulnerable. In this vast triangle stretching from New Orleans to Canada, Spanish settlers were few, the loyalty of inherited Frenchmen suspect, and Indians troublesome. Madrid could not afford to garrison the territory, and in 1796 only one regiment, a mere fourteen hundred men, stood guard. The real issue was not whether

---

2 This was but one episode in a nearly continuous problem. The Confederation government bought a Moroccan pledge not to attack American shipping in 1787, and Washington and Adams paid tribute to Algiers, Tripoli, and Tunis. After the War of 1812, in 1816, a naval squadron forced Algiers, Tunis, and Tripoli to end, this time permanently, the piratical attacks on American commerce.

Spain would lose Louisiana, but when. It was Jefferson's good fortune that the time came in 1803.

In 1800, recognizing its vulnerability, Spain secretly agreed to return Louisiana to France in exchange for an Italian principality. Rumors of this agreement, wrongly believed also to include transfer of the Floridas, soon spread. Britain's foreign secretary hinted to the American minister that his country might have to undertake a preventive occupation. To this, Rufus King, a Federalist appointee continued in office by Jefferson, responded, "taking for my text the observation of Montesquieu, 'That it is happy for trading powers that God has permitted the Turks and Spaniards to be in the world since of all nations they are the most proper to possess a great empire with insignificance.'" However, he went on, "we should be unwilling to see [the Floridas and Louisiana] transferred except to ourselves." Here was foreshadowed the no-transfer principle, an implicit part of the Monroe Doctrine. The United States claimed an option on the hemisphere, exercisable when and where it wished. Expansion by others was impermissible.

As King's reference to Montesquieu suggested, however, at the moment the Americans were most concerned about commerce. By Pinckney's Treaty the Americans had gained the right not only to use the Mississippi River but also to land goods at New Orleans and to reembark them on ocean-going vessels without paying duties. When they heard of the planned retrocession to France, the Jefferson administration's primary concern was for these privileges.

Near the end of 1802, word reached Washington that the right of deposit at New Orleans had been suspended. Americans mistakenly saw this as a Spanish effort, perhaps ordered by Bonaparte, to clear the decks before the territory became French. (In fact, the Spanish government acted on its own, moved both by American smuggling through New Orleans and by a desire to embroil France with the Americans.) Westerners howled that the free flow of commerce was essential, and they threatened to use force even without administration approval. The president responded with an obvious but effective device, sending a special envoy to France, primarily to allow time for a cooling of "the fever into which the Western mind is thrown by the affair at N. Orleans stimulated by the mercantile, and generally the federalist interest." This emissary, James Monroe, left for Paris in March 1803. To pay his expenses, Monroe had to borrow from his overseer and sell silverware to Secretary Madison.

In return, so to speak, the secretary bestowed two sets of instructions upon him. These reveal Madison and his superior at one and the same time men of limited vision and desperate boldness. Like many Americans, especially other Republicans, Jefferson and Madison believed the future of American society depended upon expansion, but neither even dreamed of acquiring the whole Louisiana territory at this time; that expansion could await the peopling of territory already possessed. Thus the first set of instructions directed Monroe and Robert Livingston, the resident minister at Paris, to try to buy only New Orleans and as much as possible of the Floridas, "France reserving to herself all the Territory on the west side of the Mississippi." The instructions even told Monroe and Livingston that in a pinch they could settle for restoration of the old setup arranged by Pinckney. All Jefferson and Madison really wanted to do was to keep the Mississippi outlet open and perhaps add others through West Florida. Their purposes were limited and commercial.

To accomplish them, however, they were prepared to fight, even to ally with Britain in war against France. Since early 1802, as part of a campaign to induce Bonaparte to abandon his ambitions, Jefferson had warned that French occupation of New Orleans would throw America into England's arms. "From that moment," he wrote in a famous letter intended for French eyes, "we must marry ouselves to the British fleet and nation." The president did not want an alliance, and he hoped that Bonaparte would give way, particularly since the European truce seemed likely to break down. However, in April he and the cabinet agreed that, if France seemed determined on war or "had formed projects which will constrain the United States to resort to hostilities," Monroe and Livingston should open negotiations for an alliance with England, offering even to agree not to make a separate peace with France. If France seemed determined to close the Mississippi, Madison's instructions stated, "your discussions . . . may be held on the ground that war is inevitable."

The planned approach to Britain was foolishly gratuitous, since that country's own interest would make it put a stop to French ambitions. In fact, Britain was planning an expedition against New Orleans, which was to be turned over to the United States without any quid pro quo. Nevertheless, Jefferson's scheme showed that even Republicans were ready to work with Britain and, more important, that while isolationism might be cherished as an ideal it was not yet dogma. "The advantages to be derived from the cooperation of Great Britain," Secretary Madison wrote, ". . . are too obvious and too important to be renounced." So much for isolation when danger threatened or booty offered!

Events outpaced Jefferson and, while passing, bestowed un-earned, even unsought laurels upon him. Bonaparte abandoned his dreams for an American empire in the first months of 1803. The First Consul, as he then denominated himself, had always linked Santo Domingo and Louisiana, the one, via sugar, providing the wealth, the other the granary for the empire he planned. The Santo Domingans, led by men Bonaparte called "gilded Africans," had long been in revolt against French rule. His troops were nowhere near victory, and a reinforcing expedition lay icebound in Dutch ports.[3] Regarding Louisiana, the Americans' violent reaction to sus-pension of the right of deposit and Jefferson's none too subtle hints of an approach to England showed him how difficult an arrangement with Washington would be.

Lowering over all was the European situation. The cease-fire in 1801 had allowed the First Consul to turn his gaze across the Atlan-tic. Had this truce evolved into real peace, Bonaparte might have continued to challenge those he considered inferiors – blacks and Americans. Unfortunately for him but largely the fruit of his urge to dominate Europe, the armistice broke down. In a well-staged scene witnessed by Livingston and other diplomats in March 1803, the First Consul cast down the gauntlet to the British ambassador. Everyone knew that war would soon follow.

This decided matters. In April, Bonaparte ordered a settlement

3 When he came into office in 1801, Jefferson inclined to support the French effort in Santo Domingo; he feared that, if blacks succeeded there, the virus of revolution would reach the United States. Madison took a different, wiser view: Solidification of French power in the hemisphere might be dangerous to the United States.

with the Americans: "I renounce Louisiana. It is not only New Orleans that I will cede, it is the whole colony without any reservation." Livingston, who had no authority to buy, nevertheless did his best to settle before Monroe reached Paris to share the credit. The British ambassador reported, "America is the first to reap the fruit of our discussion with the Government, in consequence of which Mr. Munroe finds the difference which occasioned his mission nearly adjusted." Early in May 1803, Livingston and Monroe agreed to pay approximately $15 million in cash and claims for Louisiana. The acquisition more than doubled the size of the United States and, more than any other event in the Republican era, placed the nation on the road to world power.

Jefferson wrestled with his conscience, a bout he easily won, before deciding to accept the glorious gift. Nothing in the Constitution, he believed, gave the federal government the power "of holding foreign territory, and still less of incorporating it into the Union." It followed that the purchase was "an act beyond the Constitution." Did not Republican principles of strict construction require him to seek an amendment? Urged on by Madison, he decided not, taking consolation in the assumption that "the good sense of our country will correct the evil of construction when it shall produce ill effects." "I infer that the less we say about constitutional principles . . . the better," he wrote his principal lieutenant, "and that what is necessary for surmounting them must be done *sub silentio.*" So much for Republican principles!

Without considering an amendment, and over the opposition of Federalists who expected the new territories to become Republican fiefs, Congress approved the agreement. On December 20, 1803, four weeks after Spanish authorities handed over control to the French, the American flag rose over New Orleans.

Spain understandably accused the Americans of "trafficking in stolen property."[4] The First Consul had not fulfilled his part of the trade by which he gained Louisiana, and he had violated an oath not to sell it to a third party. This scarcely troubled the Americans.

Nor did it prevent them from seeking more. Louisiana's boundary

4 Alexander DeConde, *This Affair of Louisiana* (New York, 1976), 199.

with West Florida was disputed, a matter of little consequence while Spain held both but an opportunity for argument once the United States took possession of Louisiana. Jefferson and Madison tried to force Spain to accept their own expansive definition of the boundary, even to use the quarrel to gain all of Florida. They attempted bribery, procuring a secret appropriation for the purpose. They employed threats. They again considered an English alliance. They encouraged a separatist revolt in a tiny area of West Florida and then annexed it. They occupied more during the War of 1812. They also encouraged but then abandoned a strange project, half revolt and half invasion, in East Florida. But Jefferson's "Florida obsession"[5] was not slaked until 1819, when Monroe's administration purchased the territory.

The Wars Against American Commerce

The war whose resumption won Louisiana confronted Jefferson and Madison with challenges even greater than those faced by Washington and Adams. In an age of power, they appealed to abstract rights and employed — more precisely, misemployed — only weapons of economic warfare. Neither the appeals nor the weapons produced results, and in the end, material losses and spiritual humiliation combined to bring war with England in 1812.

From 1805 onward, Britain imposed controls on American commerce far more draconian than those employed during the earlier phase of the war. It first struck at the reexport trade; in May, in the case of the *Essex,* a British judge, Sir William Grant, held that this vessel, seized while carrying wine from Barcelona to Havana, was engaged in trade between Spain and its colony even though the ship had called at an American port en route. Since trade between Spain and its colonies had not been open to American ships before the war, Grant held, it fell within the prohibitions of the Rule of the War of 1756. The *Essex* principle, applied without warning, led to the capture of scores of ships engaged in trade that the British had previously tolerated, and the result was an uproar in the United States.

5 Noble E. Cunningham, Jr., *In Pursuit of Reason* (Baton Rouge, 1987), 316.

Worse was yet to come. In 1806 Foreign Secretary Charles James Fox declared the entire northern coast of Europe from Brest to the Elbe under blockade. Such a blockade obviously could not be enforced in the manner required by contemporary international law, by squadrons stationed in the near vicinity of the ports declared closed, and the Americans protested vigorously. The next year, in the Orders in Council of November 1807, the centerpiece among British edicts, a new ministry prohibited all trade with France and its satellites (the West Indies were exempted until 1809) save that which passed through British ports, paying duties to the crown. This taxation, naval historian Alfred T. Mahan correctly argued, was "literally, and in no metaphorical sense, the reimposition of colonial regulation."[6] The November Orders were somewhat opaque, but Prime Minister Spencer Perceval quite accurately summarized their meaning: "If you [France] will not have *our* trade, as far as we can help it you shall have *none*. And as to so much of any trade as you can carry on yourselves, or others carry on with you through us, if you admit it you shall pay [us] for it." To enforce the various edicts, the Royal Navy seized ships all over the ocean, as many as two out of every nine leaving American ports in some years.

Napoleon followed a parallel course, although his weakness at sea meant that his pronunciamentos were most often executed against ships so unwary as to enter French ports or those of the large portions of Europe he dominated. By the Berlin and Milan Decrees of 1806 and 1807 — the cities where he issued them suggest the extent of Napoleon's empire — he excluded British ships and goods from the ports he controlled and ordered confiscation of neutral ships that submitted to British regulations or allowed themselves to be searched by the Royal Navy. Although both the British and the French often relaxed enforcement of their decrees, in theory they had combined to outlaw all American trade with their two empires. Small wonder that John Quincy Adams once complained that the rival systems "strike at the root of our independence."

These systems bear only a surface resemblance to those used later,

6 Alfred T. Mahan, *Sea Power in Its Relation to the War of 1812*, 2 vols. (Boston, 1905), 1:178.

notably during World War I. Neither contestant sought literally to deprive the enemy of the means of resistance or even consistently tried to starve him into submission. Most American exports, even reexports, were materials only indirectly useful to the war effort, notably cotton and sugar. There is no parallel to the twentieth century, when goods from America, the world's most productive agricultural and industrial nation, were truly vital factors. In the Napoleonic era the contestants were far more interested in the flow of profits than the flow of goods. Operating on mercantilist principles, each sought to drain the enemy of specie, to bankrupt him.

Thus the emperor did his best to exclude British goods from the Continent but often, when prices were high, encouraged sales to England – food, for example, when there were shortages in Britain. The British, for their part, sought to expand exports to Europe; they even sold supplies – nonlethal ones, to be sure – for the use of Napoleon's armies in Spain. Both struck at neutral trade because it threatened to substitute for theirs or provided cover for that of their enemy. In *War in Disguise; or, The Frauds of the Neutral Flags,* a pamphlet published in 1805 that signaled the beginning of the British system, James Stephen, an admiralty lawyer and judge, anathematized neutral commerce as "channels of a revenue, which sustains the ambitions of France, and prolongs the miseries of Europe." French views mirrored this image.

Despite hundreds of seizures by both sides, trade flourished, except when the Americans suffocated their own commerce. Winds often blew blockading ships from their stations. Merchants and captains became adept at forgery and fraud. There were always neutrals or recalcitrant satellites of Napoleon who opened Continental ports to Americans. Moreover, for reasons of economic policy, primarily to force goods on the enemy, both powers undermined their regulations by issuing, for a price, tens of thousands of licenses suspending them for individual shipments or cargoes. (This made Napoleon's Continental System, the younger Adams complained, "little more than extortion wearing the mask of prohibition.") This cynical selfishness compounded American anger, but the waivers also eased the economic pressure. In sum, American commerce could prosper despite losses to the belligerents, although their systems prevented commerce from becoming even larger. But both challenged American national dignity, even independence, by claiming that they alone had a right to decide what trade the United States might enjoy.

Impressment

British outnumbered French seizures only by a ratio of about three to two, but England alone practiced impressment. Although no one knows the exact total (the British admitted to more than three thousand, but the Americans charged more than six thousand), during the war thousands of Americans were forced to serve under the White Ensign. British boarding officers mustered crews under the Stars and Stripes and then removed for forced service, often for years, perhaps until death, those seamen they considered, or professed to consider, British. At no time, except briefly in 1806, did London consider major changes in what Adams called their "authorized system of kidnapping upon the ocean," and any move in that direction would very likely have destroyed whatever ministry undertook it.

One can understand the pressures upon Britain. About ten thousand new men had to be found for the Royal Navy every year. Impressment, a traditional reliance, seemed to be the solution. Britain never claimed a right to impress Americans, although boarding officers made frequent mistakes, which the Admiralty might set right only after years. The United States, for its part, never denied the Royal Navy's right to impress British sailors on American ships in British ports. Nor did London claim a right to take Englishmen from American warships; the attack on the U.S.S. *Chesapeake* in June 1807 enforced a demand contrary to standing orders. But it would not allow thousands of British sailors – perhaps half the able-bodied seamen in the American marine, Secretary of the Treasury Gallatin estimated – to escape their obligations to the crown by fleeing to foreign ships. The newfangled American doctrine of naturalization, and especially the speed with which citizenship could be obtained, made matters more difficult. Like most nations, Britain denied that a man shed responsibilities to his native land by migrating to another; thus many seamen were claimed as citizens by both countries.

While steadfastly denying the principle of impressment on the high seas, Federalist administrations concentrated on efforts to gain the release of individual Americans wrongly impressed by British standards. Not so Jefferson and Madison. In 1807, having made an agreement to end impressment on the high seas a sine qua non of any settlement, they rejected a wide-ranging treaty negotiated by William Pinkney and James Monroe largely because it ignored the subject. Later in that year, after the attack on the *Chesapeake,* the Republican leaders refused to accept retribution the British were prepared to offer; no settlement, they decided, could be reached unless the British agreed to give up impressment altogether. Small wonder that even a friendly biographer comments, "one is impelled to ask if Jefferson was sufficiently aware that diplomacy, like domestic politics, is the art of the possible."[7]

After 1808 Jefferson and Madison virtually ignored the impressment issue. As late as November 1811, when Madison devoted his annual message, designed to lead the nation in the direction of war, to a catalog of British misdeeds, the kidnapping of seamen passed unnoticed. *Niles' Register,* a newspaper eager for war, complained that the practice had gone on so long that "the acuteness of feeling so natural on account of it, has become blunted. . . . How base and degrading!" And, it expostulated, "How inconsistent with our pretensions of sovereignty and independence!"

The First Failure: The Monroe-Pinkney Treaty

Early in 1806, with Jefferson's encouragement, Congress took up the possibility of economic warfare against Great Britain. A small Republican faction was unwilling to fight for that "fungus of war," the reexport trade. Federalists opposed trade restrictions for whatever purpose, particularly if directed against England. Among the main body of Republicans, some favored a total prohibition on imports from England, while others, probably reflecting Jefferson's

7 Dumas Malone, *Jefferson the President, Second Term* (Boston, 1974), 403.

views, although he kept his own counsel, argued for much more limited action. In April, after three months of wrangling, Congress passed and Jefferson signed the Non-Importation Act.

Randolph, leader of the Republican dissidents, not inaccurately described the law as "A milk-and-water bill, a dose of chicken-broth to be taken nine months hence." The act banned importation of listed British goods, notably excluding those most important both to British exporters and American buyers, and suspended the implementation of the ban until November.[8] It was, in sum, a threat, and a very mild one at that. Still, Republicans hoped that it would cause Britain to mend its ways before November and thereby relieve the United States of even the mild discomfort the bans might cause.

To negotiate such a settlement, Jefferson and Madison selected James Monroe, now minister at London, and William Pinkney, a former Federalist sent to join him. Madison's instructions, prepared in May, verged on the ridiculous, raising a whole laundry list of requests, many clearly unacceptable to the British. One, a favorite idea of Jefferson's, was a suggestion that Britain recognize the Gulf Stream as the limit of American waters and withdraw the Royal Navy behind it. Only two subjects, however, were made sine qua nons of a settlement. The first was some liberalization of treatment of the reexport trade. The second was an end to impressment on the high seas. "So indispensable is some adequate provision for the case," Madison wrote, "that the President makes it a necessary preliminary to any stipulation requiring a repeal of the act shutting the market of the U. States against certain British manufactures." However justifiable the demand, the possibility that Britain would grant it was extremely slim. Two years later, when the instructions became public, Jefferson's enemies charged that they showed that he intended the negotiations to fail. In fact, they demonstrated the Republican leaders' misunderstanding of realities and their excessive faith in the "dose of chicken-broth."

Because the current British ministry was more liberal than any other during the long contest with France, Monroe and Pinkney

8 Further suspensions followed, and the Non-Importation Act did not go into effect until November 1807. It remained in force only briefly.

were able to settle a number of matters. They gained renewal of the
commercial articles of Jay's Treaty, which had greatly benefited
American shipping. They even had success on the reexport trade.
The British agreed to tolerate "broken voyages," provided only that
a small import duty be collected as goods passed through American
ports. Although Lord Holland and Lord Auckland, who negotiated
with the Americans, were prepared to give up impressment on the
high seas, even the Ministry of All the Talents, as it was called,
balked at this. The English negotiators then pleaded with Monroe
and Pinkney to drop the subject. To their surprise the Americans
agreed. As a sort of lagniappe, they were given an official communication, accurately described by Holland and Auckland as "indefinite
but conciliatory," promising "the observance of the greatest caution
in the impressing of British seamen." On the last day of 1806, the
plenipotentiaries signed a treaty on which they had been working
since August.

Jefferson had already decided, when his agents gave advanced
word of their intention to pass over the impressment issue, not to
send the treaty to the Senate. Examination of the finished product
merely strengthened his determination. The treaty included a stipulation binding the United States not to employ commercial warfare,
the favorite weapon of Jeffersonian diplomacy, for a period of ten
years. Moreover, news of Napoleon's Berlin Decree led the British to
hand Pinkney and Monroe an official warning that His Majesty's
Government might retaliate in ways harmful to American commerce
if the Jefferson administration failed to resist that decree effectively.
Consequently, the president told a Senate delegation which called
upon him on the last day of the congressional session, in April 1807,
that he would not seek their advice, preferring to reject the treaty on
his own responsibility. "Our best course," he wrote in a note to
Madison, "is, to let the negotiation take a friendly nap."

Jefferson's decision highlighted the gulf between Federalist and
Republican diplomacy. Like Jay, Monroe and Pinkney failed to at-
tain many important objectives. But the treaty did secure important
commercial advantages, and, more important, Monroe and Pinkney,
like Jay before them, expected the treaty to open the door to further
accommodation. But Jefferson unhesitatingly rejected their handi-
work, whereas the Federalists had grudgingly but decisively ac-

cepted Jay's Treaty. By so doing, the Virginian "missed an opportunity to reforge the Anglo-American accord of the 1790s and to substitute peace and prosperity for commercial restrictions and [ultimately] war."[9] No doubt, in insisting on the fullness of American rights, Jefferson and Madison spoke for the nation's aspirations, but they devised no effective strategy to redeem them. Certainly a "friendly nap" could neither long endure nor prove truly restful.

The *Chesapeake* Affair

The British naval commander on the American station, Sir George Berkeley, soon ensured that sleep would be disturbed. He knew the U.S. Navy frequently enlisted British seamen, including deserters from the Royal Navy; one frigate, the *Chesapeake,* described by a British historian as "a kind of fly-paper for picking up deserters and other wandering British seamen,"[10] had about a hundred Englishmen in its crew. Berkeley ordered that the *Chesapeake* be stopped, by force if necessary, and searched for deserters. Consequently, in June 1807, just as the frigate passed out of American waters off Norfolk, it was brought to by H.M.S. *Leopard.* When its commander refused to muster his crew for examination, the *Leopard* fired three broadsides into the American ship. After *Leopard*'s unprepared opponent hauled down its flag, a boarding party came on board and removed four seamen, one of whom was soon hanged at Halifax for desertion.

The *Chesapeake* affair touched off an explosion of protest in the United States, even in Federalist areas. Years later Jefferson wrote, "The affair of the Chesapeake put war in my hand. I had only to open it and let havoc loose." While sharing the national sense of outrage, however, Jefferson initially hoped to use it not to carry the nation to war but instead to drive the British into concessions out of fear of war. His actions just after the attack aimed to postpone rather than speed a crisis; orders closing American ports to the Royal Navy and cutting off supplies of food and water were about the least he could

9 Donald R. Hickey, *The War of 1812* (Urbana, Ill., 1989), 16.
10 Anthony Steel, "More Light on the *Chesapeake*," *Mariner's Mirror* 39 (1953): 265.

do. It would be time enough to decide on war, he thought, after Monroe had explored the chances of success in negotiations.

By the time news of the affray reached London, the tough ministry headed by Spencer Perceval had taken office. Nevertheless, even before Monroe presented a protest, the foreign secretary, George Canning, told him that the attack had been unauthorized and that his majesty's government, as always in the past, did not claim the right to impress seamen from naval vessels of another country.[11] The men, Canning said, would be released and an indemnity paid. To Monroe, this seemed reasonable, and the affair might have been settled on this basis.

Jefferson and Madison set their sights much higher: They tried to use the danger of war not only to settle the *Chesapeake* affair but also to secure the total cessation of impressment. The secretary of state told Monroe, "As a security for the future, the entire abolition of impressment from vessels under the flag of the United States . . . is . . . made an indispensable part of the satisfaction" required for the attack. Entirely predictably, Canning refused even to discuss such a demand. By asking too much, Jefferson and Madison gained nothing.

Later in the year, Canning sent a special envoy, George H. Rose, to Washington to discuss the affair. Jefferson and Madison now reversed themselves, telling that emissary that they would not insist upon a total end to impressment. However, as Canning had directed, Rose demanded concessions that the president was not expected to make; the entire exercise aimed at delay, not settlement. In the face of Jefferson's refusal, Rose broke off negotiations and returned home in February 1808. The three surviving seamen remained in British hands; one died in service and two were belatedly released as the result of an agreement reached in 1811. The entire affair had been a characteristically inept piece of Jeffersonian diplomacy.

The Embargo

By November, when Congress met, Jefferson knew of Monroe's failure with Canning, and he had received widespread and accurate

---

11 Admiral Berkeley was ostentatiously relieved of his command, but he soon received a more prestigious and lucrative one off the coast of Portugal.

rumors that the Perceval ministry was about to issue new Orders in Council. The president decided that the time for battle had come. But the war he could have had in July was beyond his reach in the fall. As Secretary of the Treasury Gallatin warned while intervening to tone down the opening message to Congress, the public temper had cooled.

After a month's delay, and only four days after a Republican senator assured a friend, "(*in confidence*), the man in the Stone House is of opinion that the die is cast," the president asked Congress not for a declaration of war but for an embargo prohibiting the export of American goods and the departure, except in coastwise trade, of American ships. The proposed legislation was nominally non-discriminatory, and to some degree it was a response to French insults – Napoleon had just begun to enforce the Berlin Decree promulgated a year earlier – but because Britain traded with the United States far more extensively than France did, the anti-British impact of the proposal was obvious.

The Embargo Act was rushed through the Senate in one day, the House of Representatives in three. There was only the barest pretense of rational discussion, and indeed in his message Jefferson had not deigned to give any detailed justification for his proposal. Had Gallatin not pressed him, he would not even have specifically endorsed an embargo, although the administration had already prepared the bill that was subsequently introduced. In this fashion a Republican administration, philosophically opposed to the extension of federal power, carried that power far beyond any Hamiltonian conceptions.

Jefferson's motives, in addition to the political necessity of doing something – anything – after the failures of preceding months, were several. In December 1807 and indeed for the entire life of the Embargo he stressed one in particular: "The great objects of the embargo are keeping our ships and seamen out of harm's way." But when the policy began there was also, as Jefferson and Republican congressmen often said, a less irenic purpose. The Embargo was felt to be and was intended by its authors to be seen by the Europeans as a war warning, a gathering in of resources in anticipation of battle. The threat failed. In ensuing months neither London nor Paris offered concessions, but neither the president nor Congress, however much they sometimes talked of it, was ready to go to war.

When the Embargo Act was passed, relatively little was said about its coercive power. The *National Intelligencer,* mouthpiece of the administration, put this theme in a secondary position: "It is singularly fortunate that an embargo, whilst it guards our essential resources, will have the collateral effect of making it the interests of all nations to change the system which has driven our commerce from the ocean." As the other two justifications faded, and without any declaration of changing purpose on the part of the administration or Congress, the "collateral" justification became the principal one. Over time, Jefferson thought, the loss of American supplies would force the belligerents to modify their policies.[12]

Precautionary and minatory embargoes seldom lasted long, and when the Embargo Act was passed, nobody expected it to be maintained for well over a year. Jefferson repeatedly said that it was only a temporary measure. But a coercive embargo depended upon perseverance, and this in turn required broad political support and a willingness to observe the law. Both soon showed themselves lacking.

The Embargo encouraged a political revival of the worst forms of Federalism, verging on sedition and even treason, and in the congressional elections of 1808 the party doubled its seats in the House of Representatives. At the same time, the Embargo stimulated lawbreaking so extensive as to undermine the Republican regime, perhaps the Constitution itself. Not only shipowners and merchants, but citizens of all occupations, were unwilling to make the economic sacrifices the policy required.

Prodded by Jefferson, who had lost his fear of executive power once he possessed it, Congress responded with acts of increasing ferocity that authorized the president to strike hard against evasion. By a law of January 1809, the most draconian, he was authorized to use the militia for police duty, to order the seizure of goods being

12 A supplementary act, passed in March 1808, among other things, banned exports by land as well as sea. Because it was aimed primarily at trade with Canada, the supplementary act revealed the increasing importance of the coercive motive. This law also tilted the balance even more heavily in an anti-British direction.

carried toward land borders and to sequester ships he suspected might be intending to leave port. No president until Lincoln, during the Civil War, ever possessed equal power over American citizens.

Still the violations and evasions continued, and Jefferson personally approved a prosecution for treason, dismissed in court, of one violator. "I had rather encounter war itself," complained Secretary of the Treasury Gallatin, who disliked the policy but had the duty of executing it, "than to display our impotence to enforce the laws." Jefferson himself came to wonder, as time passed, whether the civic virtue essential to republican government had been destroyed.

Europe failed to react as Americans hoped. Napoleon actually welcomed a policy that withheld supplies from his enemies, but at the same time — this well shows his contempt for the Americans — he used it to justify capture of their merchantmen. His Bayonne Decree of April 1808 essentially maintained that, because the Embargo confined the American marine to port, all vessels flying the Stars and Stripes must actually be disguised enemy ships. Although the British government cynically altered its regulations to encourage American shipowners to violate the law, London never considered serious modifications of the Orders in Council because of lost supplies and positively welcomed the disappearance, violators aside, of competitors of its merchant marine.

An American law of April 1808 authorized the president to suspend the Embargo if conditions so warranted. William Pinkney, who had succeeded Monroe as minister to England, promptly approached Canning. Their talks got nowhere, and in September Canning ended them with a contemptuous, arrogant *non possumus*; in Britain's view, the foreign secretary wrote, "the Embargo is only to be considered as an innocent municipal Regulation, which affects none but the United States themselves. . . . [T]here appears to be not only no Reciprocity but no assignable Relation, between the Repeal . . . of a Measure of voluntary Self-restriction, and the Surrender by His Majesty of his Right of Retaliation against his Enemies."

In April 1809, the British minister in Washington, David Montagu Erskine, reached an agreement with the new Madison administration by terms of which Britain would cease to enforce the Orders in Council against American ships in return for removal of the ban on trade with England and its continuation vis-à-vis France. Madison thought he had won a great victory, but Canning rejected Erskine's unauthorized actions without the slightest hesitation.

Throughout, Jefferson and Madison failed to understand that, from the British point of view, logical or not, the loss of American supplies, though a nuisance, was not vital. The home islands could get along without American goods, and even the British West Indies, though they had suffered during a ninety-day embargo preceding Jay's Treaty, now managed to survive. Britain would have been far more frightened by the loss of American markets, but the Embargo did not prohibit imports (i.e., English exports) in foreign ships. Although imports from Britain declined sharply in 1808, primarily because they had to be paid for in specie rather than by an exchange of goods, they remained well above pre-1807 levels. The balance of trade, the statistic Britain's leaders considered vital, ran heavily in its favor. "The Americans very good naturedly allow us openly to supply their wants," an Englishman commented, "but they will not supply ours in return, except by smuggling."[13] At no time was the Embargo close to success as an instrument of coercion.

The Defeat of Economic Warfare

By the time Congress met at the end of 1808, it was clear that "coercive embargo was flawed by a massive contradiction between the time required to put it to a fair test and the time the American people could be expected to endure it."[14] All parts of the country were suffering from economic distress. In some areas, notably New England, political discontent had reached dangerous levels. Accepting the necessity of repeal, Republicans could not agree on what

13 Even this was not quite true, for Congress allowed the president to permit the departure of ships to carry and goods to be exchanged for imports ordered before the Embargo Act; Jefferson grumbled, but he exercised this authority so liberally that more than six hundred cargoes left legally for Europe.

14 Burton Spivak, *Jefferson's English Crisis* (Charlottesville, Va., 1979), 117.

should follow. Neither the lame-duck president nor the president-elect gave them guidance.

After enormous confusion, just as Jefferson's term came to an end in March 1809, Congress passed the Non-Intercourse Act, a mere sham of a law. Theoretically this act closed both the export and import trade with the belligerents while opening commerce with the rest of the world. In fact, the law merely produced a massive pattern of evasion, for no one could have any idea where a ship would go after leaving an American port. In the first few months of the Non-Intercourse Act, seventy-nine ships sailed from New York in nominal search of a market in the Azores, and many of them, and others that sailed on similarly dubious errands, did not return to the United States while the law remained in effect. Most of their cargoes were sold in European markets. The Non-Intercourse Act lessened but did not eliminate economic distress in the United States, and it did cut into imports from Britain. No more than the Embargo, however, did it force Canning and his colleagues to change course.

By May 1810, the Republicans found even the Non-Intercourse Act too burdensome to continue. The instrument of their retreat was something called Macon's Bill number 2, although Nathaniel Macon, a veteran Republican legislator, only reluctantly introduced it into the House of Representatives as committee chairman. This law removed all restrictions on commerce but pledged the United States to close trade with one belligerent if the other ceased to violate American rights. Ironically this, the weakest effort of all, gained an image – false, to be sure – of success.

At first both Britain and France scoffed at Macon's Bill. Then Napoleon saw a chance to use it to bring about war between the United States and Britain. In August 1810 he had his foreign minister, the duke of Cadore, inform the American minister at Paris, John Armstrong, that French decrees would cease to be applied against American commerce after November 1, provided that the British also suspended their decrees or that the Americans "cause[d] their rights to be respected by the English."

Macon's Bill provided for no such conditional repeal; it authorized the president to act only after a belligerent had demonstrably ended his invasion of American rights. Nevertheless, on November 2, when of course he could have no idea of the situation in Europe one day earlier, President Madison proclaimed that French seizures had ceased; in ninety days, unless London relented, trade with Britain would cease. The president knew his authority to act was questionable, and he rightly suspected that Napoleon, who in fact continued his seizures under what he called "municipal regulations," only sought to embroil America in a war with Britain over continuation of the Orders in Council. However, as he wrote to his predecessor, he "hoped from the step the advantage at least of having but one contest on our hands at a time." The "contest" might well become war, but Madison was not yet resigned to that outcome.

Madison's boldness failed to gain rewards either from France or Britain. Napoleon continued to seize American ships, particularly those which had touched at British ports, and he permitted only a trickle of American goods to reach Europe.[15] Nevertheless, in February 1811 British ships and goods were forbidden to enter American ports. Because of doubts that Macon's Bill had actually been complied with, this was legitimized by legislation. Downing Street, not surprisingly, maintained that the United States had been unfair, that French repeal was fraudulent, and that neither international law nor equity required suspension of the Orders in Council.

The argument dragged on until June 1812, when, just as the United States declared war, Great Britain repealed its decrees. For many reasons, and despite the fact that trade with America had been reopened by Macon's Bill, depression hit England in 1810. The renewed closure of trade with America in 1811 added only mildly to British problems, but opponents of the government argued, in a series of heavy attacks in both houses of Parliament during the winter of 1812, that only a renewed American market could restore prosperity. Sometimes they warned that ministerial policy was driving America to a war that, far more than restrictions imposed by

15 In the fall of 1811, Madison sent Joel Barlow, an intellectual polymath much admired by Jefferson, to Paris to try to clear things up. French officials tergiversated with Barlow for months. In the fall of 1812 Barlow set off eastward to meet Napoleon, who was with his armies deep inside Russia. The meeting never took place, and Barlow died in Poland, where he is buried, in December 1812.

Washington, would destroy trade. Ultimately the government gave way. Its retreat by no means confirms the assumptions upon which Jefferson and Madison had grounded their policy of coercion. A whole series of unfavorable economic developments, not merely the loss of American trade, had been responsible.

The Republican campaign had been an entire failure, an exposition of faulty judgment, lack of nerve, and misunderstanding of what the nation would bear. Because the Embargo had failed, it cannot be surprising that its lesser brethren also failed. Furthermore, since every piece of legislation was accompanied by assertions that war was the next logical step, the campaign created a sort of momentum of its own, one quite different from its originators' intentions. America was driven in retreat from the Embargo and from the Non-Intercourse Act. The aftermath of the Cadore letter made Madison, and the nation, look like fools. In the end, this spirit of humiliation helped to produce war just when revocation of the Orders in Council would have provided a reason for further temporizing.

The "War Hawk" Congress

In negotiations with Augustus John Foster, a new British minister who arrived in Washington in May 1811, Madison and Secretary of State Monroe desperately sought a settlement. According to Foster, Monroe even suggested that an ostensible rather than a real repeal of the Orders in Council would satisfy the United States: "He assured me that if Great Britain would issue such a conditional and ambiguous promise of revocation of Her Orders as France did of the decrees last August, that . . . will be considered enough to authorize the cessation of the operation of the Non-Importation act against her Commerce." Foster was not tempted, and indeed his instructions forbade compromise.

By July, Madison had had enough. Although he did not break off talks with Foster, and until the American declaration of war nearly a year later his secretary of state sought to wheedle concessions from the young minister, he did decide to ready the United States for war or, just possibly, to increase the pressure on Britain by appearing to do so. He ordered the new Twelfth Congress to convene in November, a month before the usual time; the clear, intended implication of this action was that a crisis had been reached, although the inconstant record of the years since 1807 meant that Foster, Americans who wanted war, and those who feared one were doubtful that a conflict would indeed come.

Since states then chose for themselves the date of congressional elections, the Twelfth Congress had been selected over a period of many months in 1810 and 1811. These elections, legend has it, totally transformed the character of Congress, especially the House of Representatives. There, "War Hawks" – new, young, and vigorous Republicans eager for war, men elected because the country repudiated the cowardly, hesitating incumbents – took charge, dragooning elderly survivors into line behind a war movement.

Most of this picture is false. In the young Republic, a 50 percent turnover in congressional membership was common, particularly because members did not see legislative service as a lifetime career, and the proportion of new members in this Congress was about the same as in all the early ones. In a pattern common in the South, John C. Calhoun, a leading "War Hawk," succeeded his uncle, who retired, in what was virtually a family fief. Almost no seats changed hands as the result of foreign policy issues. Henry Clay, soon to be chosen speaker of the House and to use that position to push the legislature forward, was elected unopposed to fill a vacancy created by retirement. Probably no more than a handful of those who convened at Washington really wanted to go to war, although many, like the president, were ready to do so if Britain remained stubborn. Calhoun was twenty-nine, Clay thirty-four, but many of the bellicose members were elderly, and when the House of Representatives finally voted for war the age of supporters and of opponents was almost the same.

In the Congress that met in November 1811, the Federalists were a small minority, although not as weak as they had been before the Embargo. There was also a small antiwar Republican clique led by Randolph. Far larger was a group scorned by its opponents as "scarecrow men." These legislators hoped to frighten Britain into surrender by giving the appearance of preparing for war; some were ready, reluctantly, to go to war if the bluff failed, but others, at least when

Congress met, had not made that decision. The so-called War Hawks, perhaps one-third of the House, also hoped that England would surrender but were from the beginning prepared to go to war. Although they did not want it, they believed that to continue a diet of humiliation would threaten the Republican party and perhaps republican institutions. War, for them, was an undesired imperative – provided that diplomacy failed to produce a quick success. These men were better organized, more consistent than the "scarecrow men," and they had strong leaders in Clay, Calhoun, and a few others. These advantages gained them success in the long run, but the battle was fiercely contested.

The Coming of the War of 1812

Like all presidential communications from Jefferson's time to Wilson's, Madison's opening message was read to Congress by a clerk. The message excoriated British policy and urged preparations for defense, but it did not recommend war then or at any time in the future. Many newspapers considered it little different from a string of presidential messages running back to 1805. From November to June the president lay low. Despite assurances to the contrary from Monroe, the main channel between the administration and Congress, many members believed that the president was essentially one of the "scarecrow men." In fact, although of course Madison would have preferred peace in the unlikely event the British gave way, it now seems clear that from the first he expected war to come in the spring.

The winter session was noisy but only marginally productive. Even though the Federalist band supported preparedness measures, hoping to embarrass their opponents when after a great deal of talk they struck their tents, almost no effective measures were passed. A paper army was created; officers were commissioned but only a few enlisted men recruited. A "War Hawk" proposal to expand the navy fell victim to Republican prejudices against that service. Tax bills were mangled. In March, with great reluctance, Congress passed an embargo intended to gather in shipping before hostilities began, but only after the Senate, with the avowed purpose of giving time for one more approach to London, insisted that it last ninety days.[16] Shortly thereafter, both houses voted to recess, again to allow time for news from Europe, but they differed over the length of the recess. When a "War Hawk," Jonathan Roberts, proposed that members give up pay and travel money during the recess, saving $40,000 for military expenditures, the whole adjournment scheme collapsed.

Understandably, many Americans failed to see that war impended. Equally important, although there were brief flurries of concern, few Englishmen felt any real danger. Foster, who entertained Americans of all political hues, seriously overdrawing his expense account, usually accepted what Federalists told him: The Republicans would back off when the moment of crisis came. In April, he even asked for a six-month leave of absence, since business, he said, was at a stand. His masters saw no reason to challenge Foster's views. As one American diplomat in London wrote, "the general opinion [is] that we do not mean to go to war, notwithstanding all our preparation"; another agreed: "I cannot perceive the slightest indication of an apprehension of a rupture." Thus, although the Orders in Council came under heavy attack on economic grounds, the "scarecrow" hope to frighten Britain into their revocation by raising the specter of war failed. Yet war actually was imminent.

On June 1, Madison asked Congress to hold "early deliberations" on the question of war. He did not formally recommend a declaration; this, he said, was "a solemn question which the Constitution wisely confides to the legislative department." But he did present a catalog of insults aiming to show "on the side of Great Britain a state of war against the United States, and on the side of the United States a state of peace toward Great Britain." Madison mentioned impressment, Indian warfare in the West presumably stimulated by the British, violations of American territorial waters by the Royal Navy, and especially the Orders in Council,

a sweeping system of blockades which has been molded and managed as might best suit [the British ministry's] political views, its commercial jealousies, or the avidity of British cruisers. . . . Such is the spectacle of

16 A large proportion of the merchant marine – 140 ships from New York alone – managed to escape from port before the embargo went into effect.

injuries and indignities which have been heaped on our country, and such the crisis which its unexampled forbearance and conciliatory efforts have not been able to avert.

After seventeen days, the longest such debate in American history, Congress voted for war. The sessions were fierce and raucous, we know, although since the Republican majority dared not expose its arguments to public view they were held behind closed doors. (Federalist congressmen, however, soon published their speeches.) By an essentially party-line vote of 79–49, the House backed a declaration of war. In the Senate, Federalists and schismatics came nearer to success. They almost carried a proposal to fight both England and France, a quixoticism understandable only because it was combined with a scheme to delay action until negotiations were tried one last time. They once carried, then lost, a proposal to fight only a limited war on the ocean. In the end, however, the war resolution passed 19–13.

On June 18, 1812, Madison signed the war bill. Placing a small cockade in his hat, he visited government offices to enspirit the employees, then left only a few days later for his usual summer vacation. Monroe officially informed Foster of the decision; the two men spoke remarkably amicably, and the secretary offered tea to his guest. In this fashion, with a tiny navy, an unrecruited army, no financial plan, the United States set off to war. At almost exactly the same time, Napoleon commenced the invasion of Russia that was to be his downfall, and many years later Madison confessed that, had he foreseen the French defeat, he would not have supported war in 1812.

Causes of the War of 1812

The leadership of Westerners like Clay, accusations against them by the hardly reliable Randolph, the stolid rather than fiery role of other Republicans, President Madison's shunning of an open role — these and other factors give an apparent sectional cast to the decision for war. Westerners were motivated, historians have claimed, by a desire to conquer Canada, either simply to add fresh land or, more plausibly since there was as yet no land shortage in the West, because frontiersmen blamed their troubles with the Indians on Canada-based intrigues.[17]

In fact, insofar as calculations regarding Canada entered into discussion in 1812, they had national rather than sectional relevance. All ten congressmen from the West, it is true, voted for war, but this tiny faction could scarcely have dominated the situation; moreover, in the Senate, three of the six Westerners, fearing that war would mean even stronger Indian attacks, voted against war. When Republicans from all sections pondered an attack on Canada, they sometimes saw it as a means to strengthen national, not merely Western, security by eliminating a threatening British presence; in other words, "what seemed like territorial expansionism actually arose from a defensive mentality, not from ambitions for conquest and annexation."[18] However, even such ideas were less important than the simple fact that an attack on Canada was literally the only way in which the United States could mount an offensive. Canada, in Monroe's words, was not "an object of the war but . . . a means to bring it to a satisfactory conclusion." As a war-minded legislator more floridly put it, the object was to "retaliate on Great Britain the injuries which she has inflicted upon our maritime rights, by an invasion of the provinces, . . . the only quarter in which she is vulnerable."

Legislators' votes were determined primarily by party affiliation. Some who voted no were such confirmed schismatics that they scarcely deserved the Republican label. Only a tiny handful of party regulars deserted. The war bill rolled up its most impressive majorities among those from the South and West simply because these were the most Republican sections. Loyal Republicans everywhere rallied to war, and in the House Pennsylvania provided more votes than any other state. The war was a party war.

17 The most influential statement of the Canada thesis, Julius W. Pratt's *Expansionists of 1812* (New York, 1925), also argued that there was a pact of mutual support between frontiersmen, who desired Canada, and Southerners, who wanted to absorb Florida, but most scholars who stress expansionism have concentrated on the West.

18 Reginald C. Stuart, *United States Expansionism and British North America* (Chapel Hill, 1988), 76.

Since at least 1807, the Republicans had presented a disgraceful picture, threatening and then retreating in the face of European challenges. Since November 1811 they had been announcing that their patience, and the nation's, was exhausted. "After the pledges we have made, and the stand we have taken," Clay asked his colleagues, "are we now to cover ourselves with shame and indelible disgrace by retreating from the measures and ground we have taken?" Even "scarecrow men" felt the lash of this question. To retreat again might well have cost the forthcoming election, perhaps permanently crippling the party.

The Republicans' motives were not simply partisan: They considered their party the custodian of republican principles, their Federalist enemies opponents of those principles. One more defeat might fatally wound the cause of republican government, at home and in the eyes of the world. "If we have no respect for ourselves," commented a young diplomat, "others will have none for us. We shall never write ourselves into the character and reputation our temporizing and cringing policy has lost us."

At the heart of the matter, it seems, lay the Orders in Council and the challenges they posed. Although impressment was one of the oldest issues between America and Britain, Madison did not mention the subject in the message with which he welcomed Congress, and it was only infrequently raised in Congress until the spring, when all grievances were piled together to complete the case for war. Another alleged British challenge, support for Indian attacks on frontier settlements, was also at most a minor theme during the winter, not least because what Americans charged could not be proved and was in fact not true: The British had no desire to provoke the United States by setting fire to the West. The predominant theme of congressional debates, overwhelmingly so, was the Orders in Council. Years later, Madison said that they were the only issue sturdy enough to bear a declaration of war.

The Orders were, of course, a direct blow to American interests, although, since shipowners and merchants had learned to adjust to and evade them, not quite so savage a one as "War Hawks" and others proclaimed. Moreover, they could be, and were, blamed for economic difficulties actually produced by domestic forces. Still, although commerce never regained 1807 heights, both exports and imports were well above peacetime levels, and seizures under the Orders were not especially numerous in 1811 and 1812. Moreover, on the whole America had prospered during the European war – at least when America itself did not close down trade – and, in any event, war against the world's greatest naval power was unlikely to benefit commerce. In sum, the economic impact of the Orders in Council, though serious and rightly resented, was neither catastrophic nor a sensible reason for war.

What was catastrophic, in the view of most Republicans and many citizens, was the challenge to the honor of the nation, to the effectiveness of republican polity. In the words of a congressional manifesto, the Orders were not only "sapping the foundation of our prosperity"; they also "went to the subversion of our independence." Boycotts, bargaining, and complaint all had failed to secure repeal of the Orders. Britain continued to treat the United States as an inconsequential power, not far removed from a colonial condition. It appeared to seek, as one "War Hawk" earlier phrased it, "a monopoly of our commerce, and the destruction of our freedom and independence." Thus there developed "the theme of British diabolism, . . . the key in June 1812 in justifying a final call to arms."[19]

Perhaps the Republicans were right; perhaps neither the party nor the American form of government could have survived further humiliation. If so, the fault lies with them for encouraging and tolerating insult. They might argue that they had tried to find an alternative to war, but the option they selected, commercial warfare, was badly conceived, accomplishing none of its ends and contributing to the sense of frustration and dishonor. Fully as much as authorities in London, they made the War of 1812 a second war for independence.

"Mr. Madison's War"

The war went badly. Republican factionalism and the opposition of Federalist governors plagued the administration. Madison proved,

19 Ronald L. Hatzenbuehler and Robert L. Ivie, *Congress Declares War* (Kent, Ohio, 1983), 126.

in Clay's words, "unfit for the storms of war"; he never managed to control or rally the war effort. The Americans failed to conquer Canada, an easy task as long as the British armies were facing Napoleon; because there were only five thousand Redcoats in Canada in 1812, its conquest should have been little more than the "mere matter of marching" Jefferson expected it to be. General William Hull, who was supposed to attack eastward from Detroit in 1812, surrendered to a greatly inferior force. After General William Henry Harrison succeeded in a similar effort in 1813, clearing much of Upper Canada (today's Ontario), the volunteers who made up almost all of his forces returned to their homes, and the territory was abandoned. Efforts to strike north from New York, clearly the wisest strategy, were botched and ineffectual. The most important victory of the war years was gained at the expense not of the British but of the Creek tribes; Andrew Jackson's campaign against them in 1814 destroyed their military power in the area near the Gulf Coast.

On the ocean, the U.S. Navy won several single-ship duels with slightly overmatched vessels, forcing the Admiralty to issue secret orders against this type of combat, and privateers reaped a rewarding harvest of British merchantmen. When the British got down to business, however, their blockade stifled the American navy and merchant marine. In 1814 a tiny amphibious force sacked the nation's capital, one squadron courteously firing a 21-gun salute as it sailed past Washington's tomb at Mount Vernon. A London paper commented, "were it not that the course of punishment they are undergoing, is necessary to the ends of moral and political justice, . . . we should feel ashamed of victory over such ignoble foes." On the other hand, a mismanaged counterstroke from Canada failed at Lake Champlain in 1814, and unfortunately for America's moral improvement, an 8,000-man force that landed near New Orleans was defeated by Jackson in January 1815, just before news arrived that a treaty had been signed.

The Treaty of Ghent

Efforts to stop the war began even before the first shots were fired. However, it was not until August 1814, at Ghent in the Netherlands, that representatives of the two powers met to negotiate peace. America's position appeared desperate. The Treasury was empty. Sedition was rife, and no one knew whether more important areas would follow Nantucket Island, which had declared its neutrality. Napoleon's fall ("To us alone this brings misfortune," wrote Jefferson) freed British troops for American duty and stimulated demands for revenge on those who had stabbed England in the back in an hour of peril.

Yet the situation was less bleak than it appeared. Britons were not prepared to pay a large price, in terms of money and endurance, to obtain the victory they wanted, and the government was very conscious of the difficulties. The cabinet of the earl of Liverpool, who succeeded Perceval after the latter's assassination by a madman in 1812, wanted to lower taxes. Ministers sought relief from what one of them called the "millstone of an American war" so that they might concentrate on the restoration of pre-Napoleonic Europe being negotiated at the Congress of Vienna.

Moreover, as negotiations proceeded London became less and less confident that the United States would collapse internally. This was especially so after ministers learned that President Madison had made public early accounts from Ghent that showed how much England had asked. Although extremists continued to plan for a convention at Hartford in December to consider antiwar, anti-Republican measures, Madison's tactics rallied many Federalists behind his administration. For example, the *United States Gazette,* a Philadelphia journal whose Federalist credentials dated back to the 1790s, declared that "No alternative is left us but to resist with energy or submit in disgrace." The Liverpool ministry spoke harshly, as Britons demanded. It was willing to delay a few months, to speculate on success in the summer campaigns of 1814. But its underlying wish was to end the war before another campaigning season began.

The long negotiations perfectly reflected the setting: First the Americans withdrew, and then, after their military dreams evaporated, the English followed suit. The five American envoys, a strong group including Albert Gallatin, Henry Clay, and John Quincy Adams, essentially fought a skillful defensive battle. Their personalities clashed — perhaps more accurately, Adams's personality clashed with the others.[20] They differed over tactics, and their disagreements at this level became the stuff of legend. Still, even Adams, whose penchant for quarrels was inveterate, admitted that "upon almost all the important questions we have been unanimous." Until nearly the end of the negotiations, none expected success; their principal purpose was to place Britain in the wrong when their mission ended.

Although their instructions, rather weakly, directed them to seek the cession of Canada, the American diplomats never presented this demand. They even denied, when the British raised the point so as to reject it, that the conquest of Canada had ever been contemplated. They did not raise issues of maritime rights, issues of little practical importance now that the European war had ended but extremely important symbolically and perhaps for the future. They never mentioned impressment. Old instructions from Secretary Monroe had said, speaking of impressment, "If the encroachment of Great Britain is not provided against, the United States have appealed to arms in vain," but all the American commissioners were prepared to ignore the question. They were spared the necessity to violate their orders by the arrival of new ones just as negotiations began. These, written by Monroe immediately after learning of Napoleon's defeat, permitted them to settle for silence. By resisting as long as impressment was actually practiced, the secretary argued, America had sufficiently proved its determination.

British surrenders took more time. At the outset London made it a sine qua non that its Indian allies be parties to the peace and have their boundaries recognized. It might be best, the instructions added, to create an independent Indian state between Canada and the United States. British commissioners at Ghent elevated the buffer state proposal into a sine qua non, even led their superiors to believe the Americans might accept it. When London came to realize that the Americans would break off negotiations rather than

20 "They sit after dinner," he complained in his diary, "and drink bad wine and smoke cigars, which neither suits my habits nor my health, and absorbs time which I cannot spare."

agree, the ministry backed off. It passed word to Gallatin and his colleagues that the buffer state idea was only a proposal for discussion — which of course meant that it was no longer discussed.

The momentum of surrender, plus the fact that many tribes had already agreed to abandon the British, soon led the ministry to give up its original sine qua non. No tribes were parties to the treaty, and the United States merely promised to restore lands they had held in 1811. So much for British obligations to the "sable heroes" who had been their allies! Two years later, when renewed American advances made the Indians ask for help, a British official wrote, "If . . . the American Government admitted the Indians . . . to return to their former Situation for a week or a month they complied with the Treaty literally." The arrangement, like Jackson's victory at Horseshoe Bend, meant that American settlement could press westward.

When negotiations began, Britain dreamed of conquest. By the time the Indian question was disposed of, the invaders of New York, so confidently expected to slice the union in two, had turned back following a small but sanguinary naval battle on Lake Champlain in September. The British commissioners were directed to demand only minor bits of territory. Even these demands, though humiliating to the Americans, were difficult to justify in terms of the military situation.

At this time, fearing that Bonapartist terrorists would attack their ambassador in Paris, the duke of Wellington, the ministry decided to call him home. To mask the reason for his flight, the duke was offered command in America. If he accepted, Liverpool explained, he would "go out with full powers to make peace, or to continue the war, if peace should be impracticable, with renewed vigour." Wellington replied that he had little hope for military success. He scoffed at the reasoning that led the ministry to believe Britain could extort territorial concessions. "I shall do you little good in America; and I shall go there only [to] sign a peace which might as well be signed now," he wrote. This response provided a screen behind which, without any signs of distress, his superiors withdrew their demand for territory.

At the end of November the Americans learned of this retreat. The British continued to ask confirmation of their prewar right to use the Mississippi River as an outlet from Canada, and the prospect of Englishmen traveling among Indian tribes of fragile loyalty chilled the Americans, particularly Clay. However, this demand was largely a ploy to make it logically difficult for the Americans to insist upon reaffirmation of another prewar privilege, Yankee fishing on the coasts of British North America. Yet this is what the Americans, dragooned by Adams, tried to do. Except for him, their hearts were never really in it, and one of his colleagues accused Adams of a willingness to "barter the patriotic blood of the West for blubber, and exchange trans-Alleghany scalps for codfish." In the end, both sides agreed to pass over the two questions in silence.

After twenty weeks of negotiation, a peace treaty was signed on Christmas eve, 1814. It essentially ignored all major issues or simply restored the prewar status quo. Few would have guessed that it marked the end of the last Anglo-American war. John Quincy Adams, reflecting the views of his colleagues at Ghent, described it as "an unlimited armistice [rather] than a peace, . . . hardly less difficult to preserve than to obtain."

The British ministry welcomed a peace that allowed it to concentrate on European and domestic problems. Some supporters even argued that the war had been a victory since the Americans had won neither objective – Canada and an end to impressment – for which presumably they had gone to war. On the first curtain at the Covent Garden theater, an allegorical figure of America was painted in to join other defeated powers crouching at Britannia's feet.

News of the treaty reached Washington in February 1815, shortly after reports of Jackson's victory and of the milk-and-water outcome of the Hartford Convention. It was quickly ratified. The fortunate conjunction of events drowned out critics who maintained that the war had not attained a single object of national importance. The quasi-official *National Intelligencer* argued, like ministerial supporters in Britain, that silence on the major issues was really a victory: The United States had defied British demands and continued the war until insult ceased because of the European peace. "Peace has come in a most welcome time to delight and astonish us," one Republican wrote; "We have stood the contest, single-handed, against the conqueror of Europe; and we are at peace, with all our blushing victories thick crowding on us." Seldom has a nation so successfully practiced self-induced amnesia! Within only a few years another Republican journal, *Niles' Register,* even had the effrontery to argue that "we did virtually dictate the treaty of Ghent."

In a more modest sense, the American people did have a right to celebrate. They had escaped disaster by being militarily just efficient enough to show Liverpool and his cabinet that half measures would not succeed. As a result, they emerged from the morass into which Thomas Jefferson had plunged them, and the very miseries of the prewar years made the wartime record look better than it deserved. Thus the War of 1812 revived the nationalism born in the era of the American Revolution and destroyed a sense of tentativeness about the Constitution that the nation could ill afford. "In 1815," Henry Adams later wrote, "for the first time the Americans ceased to doubt the path they were to follow."[21]

21 Henry Adams, *A History of the United States,* vol. 9 (New York, 1891), 220.

6. *To the Monroe Doctrine*

Like most American wars, the War of 1812 was not followed by a period of repose, but rather by one of nationalism, here marked by efforts to foster American trade, expand territorially, and develop influence in parts of the hemisphere previously of little concern. These endeavors culminated in the Monroe Doctrine of 1823. In his annual message of that year, President James Monroe asserted principles that, though not shouted to the world, had often influenced and even guided his predecessors. By giving public expression to these themes, he proclaimed a policy of diplomatic independence stronger than any his predecessors had dared.

At the very beginning of the period, in 1815, there occurred an incident that, though substantively trivial, expressed the new spirit. Monroe, still secretary of state, directed negotiators of a commercial convention with England to insist upon the principle of the *alternat*. By this principle, when major states made treaties, the name of each alternately took precedence in the text and, on the signature page of the copy it was to keep, each delegation signed on the preferred left-hand side. Although partially followed in Pinckney's Treaty with Spain and completely in the Louisiana agreements, most American treaties, including those ending the Revolution and the War of 1812, did not follow the *alternat* – Europeans took precedence. Monroe considered this demeaning, as did John Quincy Adams, one of the negotiators at London. Adams's colleagues, Henry Clay and Albert Gallatin, were prepared to ignore their instructions and Adams's opinion, but he brought them around by a threat to withhold his signature from the convention. Two years later, when he had become secretary of state, Adams inserted a requirement of the *alternat* in standing instructions for American negotiators. That he and Monroe had insisted upon this recognition of America's entry into the company of respectable powers was fitting, since they were

147

the primary architects of the nationalistic policies of the next decade.

James Monroe and John Quincy Adams

Monroe was, and was recognized to be, a fitting symbol of the new
nationalism. The last president active in the Revolution (he was
wounded at the Battle of Trenton in 1776), he reminded Americans
of that great experience. In earlier years a violent, scheming Republican partisan, he had mellowed in middle age and now presented a
reassuring presence. As a consequence of his balance and energy he
was the only member of Madison's administration to emerge with an
enhanced reputation from the War of 1812. Because the Federalists'
seditious behavior during that conflict had ensured their political
death, Monroe, the Republican candidate, easily won the presidency
in 1816.

No president since Washington had risked a trip beyond his own
section of the country. Monroe dared to do so. He processioned
through the North in 1817, to Maine and as far west as Detroit,
receiving enthusiastic welcomes everywhere, even in Boston. Not
only John Adams but also Timothy Pickering, a quintessential Federalist relic, attended a public dinner in the president's honor. In
1820, running for reelection, Monroe gained all but one electoral
vote, and the senior Adams was an elector on his ticket in Massachusetts. Although the fabled "Era of Good Feelings" lasted at most
a very short time, the squabbles of the period sprang almost exclusively from sectional and personal rivalries. Monroe was above them,
the personification of national unity.

But Monroe was more than a mere symbol. Although a toplofty
Harvard historian once dismissed him as "one of those men of persistent mediocrity from whom useful and attractive Presidents have
been made,"[1] this is far from fair. Monroe did not have a creative
mind. "He was," George Dangerfield writes, "the third of the Virginia Dynasty, in the order of intelligence no less than in that of

1 Edward Channing, *A History of the United States,* vol. 4 (New York, 1927), 314.

succession."[2] By 1817, however, he was a man of good judgment, and, perhaps because he had reached the pinnacle of politics, he was relaxed and self-confident. Although, unlike his two predecessors, he very rarely negotiated directly with foreign emissaries, he kept full control of policy. He discussed all important matters with his cabinet, made the final decisions himself, and then permitted the secretary of state to manage negotiations. Even John Quincy Adams had little critical to say about Monroe in an almost universally acerbic diary.

Adams took over the Department of State from the secretary ad interim, Richard Rush, in September 1817. His eight years of diplomatic service abroad – at St. Petersburg, Ghent, and London – had, despite pleasant conversations with that autocrat par excellence, Alexander I, merely strengthened his devoted, even extravagant, nationalism. Adams believed that the Washington government must, for material as well as moral reasons, fight an aggressive war for American commerce. More than almost anyone else, thinking to the future but also attempting to establish America's moral virtue, he sought in a series of futile negotiations to induce Britain to agree to American views on neutral rights, including impressment. He believed, further, that the nation should expand territorially until it possessed all of North America; it was, as he saw it, "a physical, moral, and political absurdity that [European colonies, British and Spanish] should exist permanently contiguous to a great, powerful, enterprising, and rapidly-growing nation."

Adams believed, finally, that outside of North America the United States should serve as a "beacon of liberty," an example for all but not an active combatant in the struggle for freedom. In a Fourth of July oration at the Capitol in 1821, Adams rang the changes on the iniquities of colonialism and on European, especially British, politics as well. He also warned America against adventurism:

Wherever the standard of freedom and independence has been or shall be unfurled, there will her heart, her benediction, and her prayers be. But she goes not abroad in search of monsters to destroy. She is the well-wisher to

2 George Dangerfield, *The Awakening of American Nationalism* (New York, 1965), 20.

the freedom and independence of all. She is the champion and vindicator only of her own.

If America sought dominion, he said, "She might become the dictatress of the world. She would no longer be the ruler of her own spirit."

Postwar Nationalism: Bank, Navy, Commerce

Even before Monroe became president in 1817, the war-engendered nationalism began to be evidenced. In the message presenting the Treaty of Ghent to Congress, James Madison asked the legislature to consider a whole string of measures to strengthen the nation, several involving the repudiation of traditional party views. Most dramatically, he asked for, and in 1816 procured, the chartering of a new national bank, although he had been a leading opponent of such an institution when Hamilton proposed it and had allowed the first Bank of the United States to die when its charter ran out in 1811. Only such an institution, Republicans now believed, could mobilize national resources in time of need.

Madison also asked for appropriations for land and naval defense well above prewar levels. Although the navy, in particular, had been no favorite of early Republicans, Madison was able to push through a program that, though never fully implemented, nevertheless provided the nation with more and larger ships, including a 74-gun monster, than Federalists had ever proposed. A bigger navy, Americans believed, would reflect the nation's importance. It would also provide protection for American commerce, most immediately against the depredation of "Barbary pirates." Finally, a naval force in being would provide a core of strength should another British war occur, as many anticipated. As Clay told Congress in 1816, "That man must be blind to the indications of the future, who cannot see that we are destined to have war after war with Great Britain, until, if one of the two nations not be crushed, all grounds of collision shall have ceased between us." Even Rufus King, an elderly Federalist who had worked for Anglo-American understanding as minister in London from 1796 to 1803, agreed in forecasting "repeated struggles upon the Ocean before the undisputed Trident reposes in our Possession."

In his message of 1815, President Madison also reversed Republican principles by calling for a protective tariff. The tariff of 1789, although it fostered American shipping, had contained virtually nothing to protect producers against import competition; Hamilton had dared not seek more. The tariff of 1816, although by later standards quite moderate, levied protective rates on a range of goods, particularly textiles generally imported from Britain. Although the immediate problem was the alleged "dumping" of underpriced British goods on the American market, the longer-range purpose was to encourage national self-sufficiency. War had made manufactures patriotic; even Jefferson now favored them. Most interesting in the debates of 1816 was the nationalistic oratory of Southerners led by Calhoun, in the past and definitely in the future to be bitter opponents of protectionism.

Nationalism also showed its force in a campaign to open the British West Indies to American ships. At the end of the Napoleonic wars, Britain once again closed colonial ports to foreign shipping. During the negotiations at London in 1815, Adams, Clay, and Gallatin were unable to arrange for repeal or relaxation of the prohibition. As a consequence, beginning in 1817 Congress passed a series of laws designed to coerce Britain; the last, in 1820, virtually wiped out trade with its American colonies. The program elicited grumbling in port cities, which lost business, and raised the possibility that Britain would retaliate with legislation harmful to exporters, say, of southern cotton. Shipowners alone stood to benefit if the campaign succeeded, but even they had little to gain from access to what was no longer a very important trade. Yet the Americans persevered until settlement finally was reached in 1830, opening the islands but leaving the British free to give tariff preferences to goods carried by their ships. This long struggle, "a dispute in which principles were more significant than the practical interests involved,"[3] showed perhaps even better than the tariff the strength of American nationalism.

3 Harry Ammon, *James Monroe* (New York, 1971), 519.

Florida

The sole territorial gain of the Monroe administration, no match for the Louisiana Purchase in grandness, was accomplished by an even more open demonstration of American determination and menace. And the treaty by which Spain ceded Florida — in contemporary usage, "the Floridas," East and West — also drew a boundary between the United States and Spain's Mexican colony all the way to the Pacific Ocean, a major step on the road to continental empire.

Jefferson and Madison had nibbled away at the Floridas, and many Americans expected to acquire the entire peninsula someday. There was however no real sense of urgency before the War of 1812. The major fear was that a nation more powerful than Spain might acquire East Florida, thus presenting an effective challenge to American expansionism. Concerns about France evaporated after the Louisiana Purchase. Later, President Madison became alarmed by false reports that Britain had its eyes on Florida. At his request, in January 1811 Congress passed a secret resolution declaring that "the United States . . . cannot, without serious inquietude, see any part of the said territory pass into the hands of any foreign power"; the administration was authorized to use force, if necessary, to prevent it.

In a sense, this resolution was a forerunner of the Monroe Doctrine, especially the portion of it that denied Europeans the right to establish colonies in the hemisphere. The Monroe Doctrine, however, proclaimed universal rules, whereas the resolution of 1811 dealt only with a single, specific area. Still, the two sprang from a similar spirit, and in time the No-Transfer principle was generalized. In 1870 Secretary of State Hamilton Fish explicitly united it with the Monroe Doctrine.

Nothing came of European threats to East Florida, and after the War of 1812 the Monroe administration decided to try for the territory itself. Exhausted by the Napoleonic Wars and involved in conflict with its Latin American colonies, Spain was ready to leave. In return, Spain wanted a favorable boundary for Mexico, not yet in revolt; its idea of a proper one was the Mississippi River, a fatuous idea the implementation of which would have negated the Louisiana Purchase. Not surprisingly, for a long time negotiations got nowhere. Of Luis de Onís, the Spanish negotiator, Secretary of State Adams complained, "his morality appears to be that of the Jesuits as exposed by Pascal."

In the spring of 1818 Onís went for a vacation in Pennsylvania, doubtless as exhausted as Adams by their colloquies. The holiday did not last long, thanks to General Andrew Jackson. In December 1817 the administration had directed Jackson to crush Seminole Indians who were terrorizing border areas even if he had to enter Florida to do so. Just before his appointment, Jackson had urged Monroe to seize the opportunity to conquer Florida: "This can be done without implicating the government. Let it be signified to me through any channel . . . that the possession of the Floridas would be desirable to the United States, and in sixty days it will be accomplished." The Tennessean later claimed to have received the approval he sought. The administration, with somewhat more plausibility, denied his story, but Washington certainly did not respond to his letter with a warning against impetuosity. Monroe and Secretary of War Calhoun should not have been surprised by what followed: The feisty general entered Spanish territory with three thousand men, and after dispersing the Indians he went on to seize St. Marks and Pensacola. He also executed, in April 1818, two Englishmen who fell into his hands, Robert Ambrister, a soldier of fortune, and Alexander Arbuthnot, a trader with the Indians.[4]

Hastening back to Washington, Onís awoke Secretary Adams in the middle of the night to demand an interview. The next day, he insisted upon return of the posts and "a satisfaction proportioned to the enormity of the offenses, together with lawful punishment of the general." Most of Monroe's cabinet was prepared to meet these demands – Calhoun was particularly angry with his subordinate – but Adams vigorously argued that Spain's inability to keep order in Florida justified Jackson's action. Eager to keep pressure on Madrid, the president accepted this argument.

Monroe had Adams pass word to Onís that the next Congress would probably vote to take Florida and insist on a western bound-

4 Jackson later regretted that he had not, in addition, hanged the Spanish governor.

ary at the Rio Grande. A bit later the secretary, refusing to allow news of his mother's death to delay him in his task, drew up a lengthy pronunciamento for delivery by the American minister to Spain.[5] This paper, soon released to the public, was strident, self-righteous, and defiant. To start with, Adams informed Madrid that "The President will neither inflict punishment, nor pass censure upon General Jackson, for that conduct, the motives for which were founded in the purest patriotism." His chief purpose, however, was to warn Madrid that Spain must control the Indians or "cede to the United States a province, of which she retains nothing but the nominal possession, but which is, in fact, a derelict, open to the occupancy of every enemy, civilized or savage, of the United States, and serving no other earthly purpose than as a post of annoyance to them." This menace may have been unnecessary, since Jackson's invasion had already shocked Madrid into giving Onís orders to make a settlement. In any event, real negotiations began in January 1819.

Both bargainers, taking for granted the cession of Florida, sought to best the other in drawing a boundary between the United States and Mexico. Thus, as George Dangerfield puts it, "like two wrestlers in some half-lit ring, . . . they . . . struggled to and fro across Melish's map," the standard but inaccurate authority.[6] Adams was characteristically difficult — to the end he insisted that the Mexican shore of rivers, not their center, be the boundary — but agreement was reached in February. The United States gained the Floridas, in return not for money but for the assumption of $5 million in claims against Spain by its citizens, and a transcontinental boundary that began at the Sabine River, now the eastern border of Texas, and proceeded irregularly to the Pacific Ocean at 42 degrees, the present southern boundary of Oregon.

John Quincy Adams, who could not know that Onís had authority to concede even more, considered this his greatest achievement as secretary of state. Drawing a boundary to the Pacific, he wrote in his diary, "forms a great epocha in our history." Indeed, the very concept

5 In printed form, it occupied twenty-nine pages.
6 George Dangerfield, *The Era of Good Feelings* (New York, 1952), 151.

of a transcontinental republic was new and ambitious, and his decision to break loose from Monroe's original idea of a north–south boundary comparatively near the Mississippi was extremely important. The secretary did surrender what is now Texas, although, if pressed harder, Onís might have given it up. Adams was later criticized for this, rather unfairly, since Monroe and the cabinet had made that decision against his advice. In 1819, however, even Jackson, never generous toward Spaniards, thought a good bargain had been made. The Senate unanimously approved the treaty two days after Adams and Onís signed it.

That did not quite end the matter. Spain delayed ratification, seeking as a price American promises not to aid – certainly not to recognize – the rebellious colonies in Latin America. The United States challenged enormous new land grants to grandees, which Spain insisted it recognize. At one time, it seemed likely that the Americans would take the territory by force. In the end, Spain gave way, and the treaty was signed again – on Washington's birthday, 1821, chosen by Adams as symbolic – and reapproved by the Senate.

Revolutions in Latin America

"The all-absorbing problem in foreign affairs during Monroe's Presidency," his biographer observes, "was that created by Spain's crumbling American empire. Nearly all his major decisions either centered on this issue or had to be closely correlated with the questions it raised."[7] One aspect of the "problem," really an opportunity, of course was Florida; another was the series of revolutions in Latin America. These uprisings, which began during the Napoleonic Wars, naturally aroused enthusiasm in the United States; they were seen, in Jefferson's words, as "another example of man rising in his might and bursting the chains of his oppressor." When, freed by Napoleon's downfall, Spain mounted a counterrevolutionary campaign, one that at times seemed close to success, many in the United States were alarmed. Restoration of colonialism in Latin America, coming as it did on the heels of the destruction of democracy in

7 Ammon, *Monroe,* 409–10.

France, would be a severe blow to Americans' vision of the world, to the crusade they themselves had begun in 1775.

Sympathetic to anticolonialism though they were, almost no Americans proposed that the nation should extend military support to the Latin Americans. (A few volunteers or adventurers did join rebel armies, and a number of seamen, sensing the opportunity for profit, did serve under flags of the rebel regimes.) Isolationism was already too far ingrained to permit of intervention; the United States preferred to be "the beacon on the hill," providing a guide for those struggling in the world below.

Moreover, few Americans believed that the southern rebels were capable, at least not yet, of truly following the beacon. In the American view, "The somnolent populations of that region, debilitated by their heritage [under Spain] and enervated by a tropical climate, neglected their rich natural resources, while the Catholic faith lulled them into intellectual passivity." Miscegenation had made things worse. "All [Latin] American countries fell under censure for lax racial standards and indifference to the social consequences of polluting the blood of whites."[8] They were, in a word, inferior, and their future was unpromising. Consequently, many if not most American commentators combined "sympathy for the Latin-Americans' cause with . . . skepticism about their ability to make good use of their independence, if they won it."[9]

Such views spread across the political spectrum. John Randolph, the always acid old-style Republican, predicted in 1816 that Latin America was headed for "a detestable despotism. You cannot," he said, "make liberty out of Spanish matter – you might as well try to build a seventy-four out of pine saplings." The *North American Review,* the most self-consciously intellectual magazine of its day, warned the next year that success in an anticolonial revolt was "no proof that the people are capable of a better." Latin Americans, the *Review* continued, are "destitute of that moral structure of character, which is the basis and indispensible requisite of a stable, free poli-

8 Michael H. Hunt, *Ideology and U.S. Foreign Policy* (New Haven, 1987), 59.
9 Arthur Preston Whitaker, *The United States and the Independence of Latin America* (Baltimore, 1941), 187.

cy." John Quincy Adams used similar reasoning to support his argument for delay in recognizing the new states, at least until the Florida matter was settled. "So far as they are contending for their independence, I wish well to their cause," he told Henry Clay, the foremost advocate of prompt recognition, in 1821; "but I have not yet seen and do not now see any prospect that they will establish free or liberal institutions of government." Even Clay agreed with the basic premise; while he hoped that, in time, the nation's southern neighbors would progress, for the moment he considered those lands "place[s] of despotism and slaves, of the Inquisition and superstition."[10]

Still, Americans hoped the armies of Spain would be defeated, for good practical reasons as well as because of their dislike of colonialism. Trade with Latin America rose sharply after the War of 1812, although in fact most of it flowed to Cuba, still firmly under Spanish control. Especially in New Orleans and Baltimore, the ports most deeply involved, there were hopes of further increases if Spain did not manage to restore its monopolistic system. Optimists dreamed of an "American system," a grouping of states that would take their lead from Washington, certainly cooperate to thrust off European influence, even if the subordinate members were not certified republicans by American standards. This kind of reasoning disgusted Adams: "As to an American system, we have it; we constitute the whole of it; there is no community of interests or principles between North and South America." But from the beginning he and Monroe were ready to recognize Latin American states when the time was ripe.

On several occasions, the first in 1810, Washington sent special missions to investigate conditions in Latin America and to urge the rebels to establish republican governments. "Agents for seamen and commerce" and, occasionally, consuls were appointed to serve in ports held by the rebels. A neutrality proclamation issued in September 1815, slanted in the insurgents' favor, recognized their rights of belligerency. On the whole, however, the United States remained cautious, for fear of provoking Spain while the Florida

10 So Clay described Mexico in 1821.

issue remained unsettled. Outrages committed by privateersmen, many of them Americans sailing in ships that had been armed in American ports, angered the United States, and one of their bases, Amelia Island, near the border between Florida and the United States, was broken up by force in 1817.

Although Monroe's cabinet discussed full-scale recognition of one or several of the rebel governments as early as 1817, and although there was much pressure to do so, in Congress and out, the president held back. As he wrote to his old colleague, Albert Gallatin, in 1820, "With respect to the Colonies, the object has been to throw into their scale, in a moral sense, the weight of the United States, without so deep a compromitment as to make us a party to the contest. . . . I am satisfied that had we ever joined them in the war, we should have done them more harm than good, as we might have drawn all Europe on them, not to speak of the injury we should have done to ourselves." This cautious approach, so characteristic of Monroe by this stage in his life, was heartily endorsed by his secretary of state.

Finally, with Florida in American hands, with the tide of battle in the southern continent running decisively against Spain, Monroe and Adams decided that the time had come to recognize the most solidly established Latin American regimes. Their purposes were several: to establish American influence and undercut that of Europe, to assist commerce, and though hopes were not high, to encourage the growth of republicanism. In March 1822, Monroe asked Congress for funds, funds that were enthusiastically granted, to support diplomatic posts in five of the new states – Argentina, Chile, Gran Colombia, Mexico, and Peru – and in January 1823 he nominated ministers to those countries. Among the nominees was Andrew Jackson, named to go to Mexico; but the general, apparently a better judge of his own character than Monroe and Adams, declined the diplomatic appointment. Even before those who were confirmed took up their posts, the administration officially received Manuel Torres as chargé d'affaires from Gran Colombia in June 1822. Shortly thereafter it extended recognition to Mexico.[11]

11 Mexico, where earlier risings had been suppressed, revolted successfully in
   1821. That it was a monarchy – indeed, styled itself an empire – did not deter

Although the revolutionary regimes in Latin America had recognized one another, no other nation had as yet done so. American recognition, delayed though it had been, was not without elements of risk. Despite defeats, Spain refused to abandon its imperial hopes. Fears grew that the Continental European powers, joined together as the Holy Alliance, would give Spain military assistance. What, then, would the United States do? Dared it either accept or challenge an imperialist, monarchist "rollback" in the hemisphere? The question became pressing, or at least appeared so, in 1823, and the administration's answer was presented in Monroe's annual message to Congress on December 2.

The Monroe Doctrine: Noncolonization

In that message, however, Monroe did not, when he presented his thoughts on international relations, confine himself to problems in Latin America. The Monroe Doctrine, as only many years later it came to be called, staked out positions in two other areas as well; taken together, these asseverations marked out a pattern of policy reflecting contemporary nationalism and, though implementation was sometimes delayed, marking a course for the future. Taken together, too, they amounted to a declaration of diplomatic independence.

One of the questions at issue in 1823 concerned territory on the Pacific Coast. The Spanish treaty of 1819 had fixed the southern limit of American claims in the Far West, but to the north the United States faced British and Russian competition. The Americans had a small post at Astoria, near the mouth of the Columbia River, which had been established in 1811, but otherwise their presence was limited to ships that cruised the shores, fishing and trading with Indians. British activities, overland from Canada, and Russian ones, southward from Alaska, were far more developed. In 1821, largely because it was irritated by the activities of American

Monroe and Adams. Within less than a year, the royal system was overthrown. In 1824, the United States recognized the empire of Brazil. In time, official recognition was extended to all of the American states, although not to black Haiti until 1862.

mariners, Russia, which claimed the Pacific Coast as far south as 51 degrees, ordered American and other foreign vessels to stay away from those shores. America's resistance to this challenge in an area three thousand miles from the nation's heart, well north of today's border with Canada, shows how greatly the nation's ambitions had expanded.

As early as 1819, at a cabinet meeting, Secretary of State John Quincy Adams declared that the world must be "familiarized with the idea of considering our proper dominion to be the continent of North America." In 1821, as part of a continuing and often acerbic dialogue on territory beyond the Rocky Mountains, he told the English minister, Stratford Canning, "that we certainly did suppose that the British government had come to the conclusion that there would be neither policy or profit in cavilling with us about territory on the North American continent." And in July 1823, contesting the Russian decree, he told the tsar's envoy, Baron Tuyll, that "we should contest the right of Russia to any [new] territorial establishment on this continent." A few months later, Monroe decided, at Adams's suggestion, to echo these sentiments in his message to Congress. The message asserted to the world that "the American continents, by the free and independent condition which they have assumed and maintained, are henceforth no longer subjects for any new European colonial establishments."

Thus was framed and announced one component of the Monroe Doctrine, the noncolonization principle. It was striking in its audacity, logically because it rested on an argument the United States itself refused to admit – that "free and independent" governments, worthy of respect, existed among Indian tribes – and politically because it challenged nations far more powerful than America. And it was cynically selfish, for it denied the right of expansion to European powers only; as a British paper later commented, "The plain *Yankee* of the matter, is that the United States wish to monopolize to themselves the privilege of colonising . . . every . . . part of the American Continent."

Arrogant though this might be, the declaration did not carry antiimperialism or national selfishness to unreasonable lengths. By using the word "henceforth," Monroe made clear that for the moment the United States did not intend to challenge existing European colonies. There was, indeed, less talk of acquiring Canada than in, say, 1776 or 1812. But even in areas not currently colonized, in any meaningful sense, Monroe and Adams had to compromise. They had already agreed, in 1818, to extend the Canadian-American border along the forty-ninth parallel as far as the Rocky Mountains, and, in negotiations carried on after the Monroe Doctrine and completed in 1824, the United States recognized Russian claims on the Pacific Coast as far south as 54 degrees, 40 minutes. Nevertheless, the self-confident nationalism of the declaration of 1823 was striking.

The Great Flirtation

In 1822 and 1823, reports circulated that conservative European monarchies, led by Russia and France, which had already intervened in Spain to restore the powers of its reactionary king, Ferdinand VII, intended to come to the aid of Spain in Latin America. The fears kindled by these reports are now known to have been unfounded, for the Europeans never came close to carrying out intervention, certainly not by strong military action. [12] In their reports from Europe, some American diplomats guessed as much, but others disagreed, and the newspapers were filled with rumors. Honest fears were felt by all American leaders with the exception of John Quincy Adams, and the British, who had already made clear their opposition to the activities of the Holy Alliance, seemed to share them.

In March 1823, George Canning, who had succeeded Lord Castlereagh as foreign secretary after the latter's suicide, made public instructions recently sent to the British ambassador at Paris. In

---

12 A few European statesmen, notably the French foreign minister, toyed with what is called "the Bourbon monarchy scheme." A small naval and military force, according to this scheme, would proceed from country to country in Latin America, by menace and negotiation creating kingdoms ruled by members of the Bourbon family, though not by Ferdinand and his court. No less an authority than the duke of Wellington thought this might fairly easily be done. Although certainly a less unrealistic scheme than a massive invasion of the continent, even this one had only limited support in European chanceries.

his letter to Sir Charles Stuart, Canning wrote that, although the question of formal British recognition remained to be decided, "events appear to have substantially decided [Latin American] separation from the Mother Country." Because he was far in advance of colleagues in the Liverpool ministry, Canning had to move cautiously; the Stuart letter neither warned Spain to end its efforts to put down the rebellions nor threatened to prevent European assistance to it. Still, the letter enlisted Canning on the side of the rebels, a development warmly received in the United States. "The course which you have taken in the great politics of Europe," the British representative in Washington reported, "has had the effect of making the English almost popular in the United States." "Even Adams," he added with some astonishment in a private letter, "has caught something of the soft infection."

In August, encouraged by such reports, Canning approached Richard Rush, the American minister at London. He proposed that they issue a joint declaration, essentially an internationalization and extension of the Stuart letter. "For ourselves we have no disguise," Canning suggested they agree to state. "We conceive the recovery of the Colonies by Spain to be hopeless. . . . We aim not at the possession of any portion of them for ourselves, [but] we could not see any portion of them transfered to any other Power, with indifference." Rush refused to take upon himself responsibility for accepting Canning's proposal, although he would have done so had the foreign secretary been willing to give formal recognition to one or more of the Latin American states. He did, however, forward the offer to Washington, and he and Canning exchanged views on the matter for some weeks thereafter. There had begun what Canning himself called a "great flirtation," the proposal of a union that would give pause to European plotters and at the same time further improve Anglo-American relations.

Rush's reports reached Washington early in October, just before Adams returned from a visit to his father in Massachusetts. The president sought the advice of his mentors, Jefferson and Madison. He did not explicitly commit himself to Canning's text, but he did incline toward the view that "we had better meet the proposition fully, & decisively." He welcomed Canning's invitation to the company of world powers and the opportunity to guarantee Latin American independence. The ex-presidents agreed, although Jefferson correctly pointed out that the self-denying portion of the proposed declaration would prevent the United States from taking over Cuba.

Nonintervention and Isolation

Early in November, Monroe returned to Washington from a Virginia vacation. During the next few weeks he discussed the mix of problems facing the administration with four members of his cabinet, Adams and Secretary of War Calhoun dominating the discussions. Because they had only Rush's dispatches, a handful of reports from other American diplomats in Europe, and some newspaper clippings to inform them, they were in a sense feeling their way in a dimly lit room. Seldom have such important decisions been taken by such a small and incompletely informed group.

When the cabinet sessions began, Monroe apparently inclined to accept Canning's initiative. Adams disagreed. He did not believe the threat real, nor did he believe that, if undertaken, an attack could have much success. If the rebels were so weak as to need help, it was further argument against "embarking our lives and fortunes in a ship which . . . the very rats have abandoned." In any event, to join Britain as a junior partner – and all the world would see it so – was undignified: "It would be more candid, as well as more dignified, to avow our principles explicitly to Russia and France, than to come in as a cock-boat in the wake of a British man-of-war." In response, Calhoun argued strongly that the United States should not throw away an opportunity to save Latin America from a counterrevolutionary attack, and although the president deferred a final decision, he seemed to agree with the secretary of war.

Just at this time, further dispatches arrived from Rush, reporting that Canning had cooled off. Monroe and Adams interpreted this news, correctly, as evidence that Britain believed the danger of intervention had passed. Adams's arguments, the news from Europe, and perhaps, in addition, fear of the political consequences of a connection with England led the president to decide not to accept Canning's proposal.[13] The United States would strike out on its own.

13 When, however, shortly after the president's message, new reports of French

While these discussions were going forward, Adams worked on a response to a recent declaration of Russian policy received from Baron Tuyll, the tsar's envoy in Washington. This circular, described by the secretary of state as "an Io Triumphe over the fallen cause of revolution, with sturdy promises of determination to keep it down," of course posed an ideological challenge; it also might be read as further evidence that intervention impended. Adams did not believe so, but he saw an opportunity to state American opposition to intervention without seeming simply to follow Canning's lead. He therefore prepared, and Monroe approved, an extremely strident note to Tuyll defending republicanism and warning that the United States "could not see with indifference, the forcible interposition of any European Power, other than Spain, . . . to restore the dominion of Spain over her emancipated Colonies in America."[14]

This, Adams thought, was enough – America was on record. But Monroe decided to issue a public warning to Europe. In his annual message, adopting Adams's ideas and using much of his language, the president announced that "we could not view any interposition for the purpose of oppressing [Latin American states], or controlling in any other manner their destiny by any European power in any other light than as the manifestation of an unfriendly disposition towards the United States." Thus was proclaimed the nonintervention principle of the Monroe Doctrine.

When Adams saw a draft of Monroe's proposed message, he was on the whole gratified by what he found, but one passage troubled him. Monroe proposed to condemn the French intervention in Spain that had restored Ferdinand VII to his throne and to praise the Greek struggle for independence from the Ottoman Empire. (The Greek

intentions to send a small army to Latin America were received, at Monroe's direction Adams wrote Rush that the time that would necessarily elapse while the expedition was organized "may yet be employed, if necessary, by Great Britain and the United States, in a further concert of operations, to counteract that design, if it really existed." What Adams, to say nothing of Monroe, really had in mind at this point is unclear. Thus, although the Monroe administration decided to move independently at this time, "America's . . . prospective relationship with Britain . . . remained ill-defined" (Ernest R. May, *The Making of the Monroe Doctrine* [Cambridge, Mass., 1975], 228).

14 This note also included a statement of the no-transfer doctrine, which, although akin to nonintervention, was not included in Monroe's message.

cause was very popular in the United States; Albert Gallatin even proposed that naval vessels be loaned to the Greeks.) Adams objected, arguing both against the risks of involvement in European politics and that the force of the demand that Europe stay out of Latin America would be logically undermined by American intervention in transatlantic affairs. Consequently, after blandly affirming "sentiments the most friendly, in favor of the liberty and happiness of their fellowmen on that side of the Atlantic," the message as delivered continued, "In the wars of the European powers, in matters relating to themselves, we have never taken any part, nor does it comport with our policy, so to do." Thus the message restated the isolationist theme and identified it with the Monroe Doctrine.

The Monroe Doctrine

Monroe's message of December 2, 1823, fifty-one paragraphs long, was for the most part either a dreary summary of events over the preceding year — he was perhaps the worst stylist among our early presidents — or a series of recommendations on domestic policy. But one paragraph announced the noncolonization doctrine, and another section devoted a paragraph each to nonintervention and to isolation.

Both passages angered European statesmen at the time, and for decades European states denied that the Monroe Doctrine had any legitimacy other than as a statement of American ambitions. In the 1850s a British foreign secretary loftily declared that "The Doctrine . . . could be viewed only as the dictum of the distinguished personage who announced it, and not as an international axiom which ought to regulate the conduct of European states."

Monroe's contemporaries in Europe knew that intervention in Latin America was never in sight, and they resented his gratuitous warning against it. This was particularly true of Canning. When Rush refused to respond to his flirtation, he quickly turned in another direction. In November, Paris approved a memorandum of talks between the foreign secretary and the French ambassador in London, the prince de Polignac. In this paper, the ambassador assured Canning that his country had no plans to intervene in Latin America. Ten days later, of course in ignorance of the Polignac memorandum but comforted by Rush's earlier report that the situation was brightening, Monroe sent his message to Congress. Canning resented the fact that Monroe had stolen a march on him, particularly since he feared that it might lessen British influence in Latin America. Consequently, in March 1824 he made the memorandum public, and shortly thereafter he convinced his reluctant colleagues to agree to British recognition of three of the new nations. In subsequent years he worked, successfully, to convince the Latin Americans that it was Britain, not the United States, whose role had been most important in 1823.

European conservatives reacted especially negatively to the American version of an "Io Triumphe," the vainglorious assertion of republicanism. In a famous statement, the Austrian chancellor, Prince Metternich, wrote:

These United States, whom we have seen arise and grow, . . . have suddenly left a sphere too narrow for their ambition and have astonished Europe by a new act of revolt, more unprovoked, fully as audacious, and no less dangerous than the former. They have announced their intention to set . . . altar against altar. . . . In permitting themselves these unprovoked attacks, in fostering revolutions wherever they show themselves, . . . they lend new strength to the apostles of sedition, and reanimate the courage of every conspirator.

The American reaction was rather different. Congress failed to give formal support to the principles espoused by the president. In 1824, when Colombia suggested an alliance based on the nonintervention principle, it was turned down, as was Brazil when it made a similar proposal the next year. In 1826, an administration proposal to send delegates to a congress of American states at Panama provoked violent debate in Congress, culminating in a duel, fortunately bloodless, between John Randolph and Henry Clay. Approval of the mission was so delayed by concern about the dangers of political connections that, though the envoys' appointments ultimately were approved, the only one who actually traveled to Panama arrived after the meeting had ended.[15] But in 1823 the nation responded favora-

15 Racist concerns also played a part. Senator Thomas Hart Benton objected to American participation in a conference including representatives of "five nations who have already put the black man upon an equality with the white, not only

bly to the principles Monroe expressed. "The explicit and manly tone," the British chargé reported, "has evidently found in every bosom a chord which vibrates in strict unison with the sentiments . . . conveyed. They have been echoed from one end of the country to the other."

For a generation, the various parts of the Monroe Doctrine were seldom used as charts for American foreign policy.[16] Until the nationalist and republican European uprisings of 1848, it was not even imaginably necessary to warn the American people, as had been done in the context of the Greek revolution, of the dangers of involvement in transatlantic affairs. (The American reaction in 1848 combined vocal enthusiasm with a total disinclination to do anything.) The noncolonization doctrine played no part in the discussions with Britain over Oregon's future or those with Russia which fixed the southern limit of Russian Alaska at 54 degrees, 40 minutes. Britain's occupation of the Falkland Islands in 1833 and its efforts to expand the Central American colony Belize in the 1830s attracted little attention, and certainly no opposition from Washington.

The nonintervention doctrine was, so to speak, redundant before it was born, at least so far as a major European effort was concerned. Canning had seen to that, although even his actions were probably supererogatory. Not for many years, until a contest with Britain over influence in Central America in the 1850s, and especially in the 1860s, when Napoleon III of France attempted to create a satellite empire in Mexico, did it seem necessary to hark back to the pronunciamento of 1823. European interventions resulting from commercial grievances – for example those by France in Mexico and Argentina in 1838 – were viewed without alarm.

Nor did announcement of the nonintervention doctrine secure for the United States the political and economic advantages for which Monroe and others hoped. Although all the Latin American states

in their constitutions but in real life . . ., who have . . . black generals in their armies and mulatto senators in their congresses!"

16 The first history of American diplomacy, Theodore Lyman's *The Diplomacy of the United States* (Boston, 1828), did not mention Monroe's message, and as late as 1849 William H. Seward, in a biography of John Quincy Adams, still felt it possible to omit the subject.

save Brazil, which established a monarchy maintained until 1889, formed what were nominally republican governments, with rare and short-lived exceptions power was held by military leaders and oligarchs. If the United States had hoped to stake out a republican hemisphere, it had succeeded in name only. Trade, which had flourished during the wars for independence, declined thereafter, fulfilling Adams's earlier warning that "they want none of our production, and we could afford to purchase little of theirs." British manufactures and British credit came to dominate the southern continent until the development, after the Civil War, of American industry. "By the late 1820s," one historian recently observed, "a mutual disillusionment prevailed in many facets of relations between the United States and Latin America. To North Americans, trade, institutions, and British predominance in Latin America were disappointments. For Latin Americans, North American arrogance, high tariffs, and either expansionism or lack of interest had dashed earlier, higher hopes."[17] Not until the end of the nineteenth century, and then in ways often resented by the Latin Americans, would the United States begin to play a major role in the southern countries.

In one sense, the president's message was simply an important signpost on a very long road. Isolation from world politics had long been an American ideal, and both the noncolonization and nonintervention doctrines clearly had roots in earlier years. Monroe, indeed, felt that he was responding to immediate dangers, not inventing grand new principles. For the moment the principles he here restated were expressed defensively – what other powers could not do, what the United States would not do – but in the future they would become weapons of American expansion as well as hemispheric defense. Though hackneyed and negative, however, the principles as stated in 1823 laid out a system of foreign policy remarkably congenial to the national temper. Although implementation was delayed, the Monroe Doctrine "was never . . . to lose its original and valiant quality of committing the United States – prematurely, indeed, in 1823 – to a leadership in world politics."[18]

17 Peggy K. Liss, *Atlantic Empires* (Baltimore, 1983), 221.
18 Dangerfield, *The Era of Good Feelings*, 308.

Monroe's declaration was a fitting climax to a long search reaching back to 1776. The nation had created a viable government. It had consolidated and expanded its territory. It had survived controversies over neutral rights with two great powers. Now, almost for the first time and certainly more clearly than before, it spoke boldly and on its own to major issues. President Monroe's "policy statement [was] a diplomatic declaration of independence." At last the nation had "reached the point seen so distantly in 1776: it had achieved an American identity."[19]

19 Ammon, *Monroe*, 491–2.

7. Manifest Destiny

The idea of territorial expansion was born when America was born. The charters of most British colonies in America granted them dominion as far as the Pacific Ocean. The Articles of Confederation explicitly reserved a place in the new nation for Canada. In 1801, Jefferson looked "forward to distant times, when our rapid multiplication will . . . cover the whole northern if not the southern continent, with people speaking the same language, governed by similar forms, and by similar laws."

When Jefferson wrote, the United States possessed 838,000 square miles, an area already about eight times as large as the kingdom from which it had separated. The purchases of Louisiana and Florida more than doubled the national domain, but the grandest acquisitions, geographically at least, took place between 1845 and 1848. Annexation of Texas, settlement of the Oregon boundary, and the conquests of the Mexican War, all accomplished in the administration of James K. Polk, raised the land area of the United States to three million square miles. Later, in 1867, the Alaska Purchase brought holdings on the North American continent to their present extent of three and a half million square miles. Brazil, Canada, and China are about the same size, but only Russia, twice America's size even after breakup of the Soviet Union, possesses a significantly larger domain.

The Meaning of Continentalism

The processes of American expansion underline the role of power rather than, as many citizens liked to think, that of virtue or moral principle. Only the small Gadsden Purchase from Mexico in 1853 and the acquisition of Alaska were – and even this could be argued – freely negotiated transfers. Bonaparte's decision to sell Louisiana –

170

the sale of stolen goods, in any case – was influenced by American menace. West Florida and Texas were acquired when rebellious American settlers in foreign territory set up their own governments and then sought the sheltering arm of the United States. Threats of force were important in the acquisition of the rest of Florida and confirmation of title to the Oregon country. An invasion of Mexico capped by occupation of the enemy capital brought about the vast expansion into California and the Southwest.

Not only Spaniards, Canadian employees of the Hudson's Bay Company in Oregon, and Mexicans felt the lash or saw the shadow of American power. Fewer than two thousand Spaniards lived in Florida when the Americans took over; only a few dozen Hudson's Bay employees were in that portion of Oregon gained in 1846; eleven thousand Mexicans lived in California at the time of the American invasion. Far more numerous were the Indians, also more feared and hated, more brutally treated and more forcefully pushed aside. For example, about one hundred thousand Indians lived in California in 1846: Only a third remained by 1860.

In the political theory of the United States government, the tribes occupied a strange position. Because they were not considered sovereign, the State Department did not handle relations with them – that was the responsibility of the War Department – but until 1871 they were treated as "nations" that made war and peace and negotiated treaties, primarily land cessions for white benefit. The doctrine of preemption, largely developed by Jefferson, "recognized the legal right of Indian nations to the land they possessed and at the same time the legal right of the . . . intruder to purchase the land, free from the fear that the land might be sold to a rival . . . power."[1] Purchase treaties were often accomplished by an application of force, menace, and trickery. Even so the buyers frequently failed to carry out their part of the bargain.

Webster's Dictionary defines "imperialism" as "the acquirement of new territory or dependencies . . . or . . . the extension of [a nation's rule] over other races of mankind." These need not be the same thing, although both usually have unfortunate consequences for the

1 Wilcomb E. Washburn, *Red Man's Land/White Man's Law* (New York, 1971), 56.

original inhabitants. The majority of imperialisms, including that of the United States in 1898, involved control by an alien minority over populous areas occupied by "other races of mankind." In their "acquirement of new territory" on this continent, the Americans sought to push aside or to eliminate rather than exploit the Indians, and, although Chicanos suffered severe discrimination, they were soon reduced to a small minority by an influx of American settlers and therefore never dominated the labor pool in the new territories opened to exploitation.

Additionally, although a leading critic of the American record sarcastically refers to "the traditional equation between liberty and expansion" in American thought and rhetoric,[2] the linkage was not merely hypocrisy. The Northwest Ordinance of 1787, perhaps the sole important accomplishment of Congress under the Articles of Confederation, established the principle that all territory held by the United States should ultimately gain statehood "on an equal footing with the original States in all respects whatever." Until it embarked upon overseas empire in 1898, the United States did not plan to keep new lands in subjugation – settlement by its own citizens anyway made this impossible – and ultimately all gained statehood.[3] None of this is to condone American behavior, only to distinguish it from imperialism of a different kind.

In America's early years, expansion had a very special meaning for Jefferson and many others. As his letter of 1801 shows – "governed by similar forms, and by similar laws" – he expected the American system to expand but did not expect his successors to be presidents of a continental empire. How could representative government function if legislators had to spend a great deal of their time traveling by carriage or on horseback between their constituencies and the capital? He and like-minded persons anticipated a system of separate republics peopled from the United States, following its example and basking in its sun. In 1825, a leading advocate of expansion, Senator Thomas Hart Benton of Missouri, declared:

2 William Appleman Williams, *The Roots of the Modern American Empire* (New York, 1969), 87.
3 Alaska is an exception, although it too, of course, ultimately became a state.

The Western limit of the republic should be drawn [at the crest of the Rocky Mountains], and the statue of the fabled god, Terminus, should be raised upon its highest peak, never to be thrown down. . . . In planting the seed of the new power on the coast of the Pacific ocean, the new government should separate from the mother Empire as the child separates from the parent at the age of manhood.

Sharing these sentiments, Monroe had proposed to state the principle of separate republics in his annual message of 1824. That his cabinet, especially Adams and Calhoun, opposed this was a sign that the old idea was losing strength.

By the 1840s, it had been defeated. This did not mean that Americans, at least most of them, proposed to extend the area of freedom by indiscriminate conquest. Because everyone expected new regions to become states, at least ideally they ought, if populated at all, both to possess institutions similar to American ones and to seek admission. In the prevailing view, "any hurried admission to the temple of freedom would be unwise; any forced admission would be a contradiction in terms, unthinkable, revolting."[4] Of course Washington often prodded the process along, but the Americans did not seek to create a centralized empire resting on force.

One further factor, racism, also worked, in a perhaps paradoxical way, to limit the extent of territorial ambition. Mexicans were, contemporaries believed, an inferior and motley race in which were mingled Indian, Spanish, and black blood. As such, they should make way for *norteamericanos*. However, to bring within the national boundaries of the United States large numbers of such people – "barbarous and cruel, . . . sordid and treacherous . . . , destitute of noble impulses," in the view of an Ohio congressman – would present two equally unpalatable alternatives: Either they would, like other citizens, join in the political process, thereby debasing it, or the United States would have to convert itself into an empire, ruling colonials, thereby abandoning a fundamental principle.

Unwillingness to confront either of these alternatives made many Americans reluctant to exploit to the full the military victory in the

4 Frederick Merk, *Manifest Destiny and Mission in American History* (New York, 1963), 25.

Mexican War. "More than half the Mexicans are Indians, and the other is composed chiefly of mixed tribes," said John C. Calhoun. "I protest against such a union as that! Ours, sir, is the Government of a white race." In the end, the United States took about half of Mexico's territory, only a very tiny fraction of that country's population. A Democratic newspaper expressed pleasure that the nation had managed to acquire "all the territory of value we can get without taking the people."

In both the Jeffersonian and later forms, expansionism was – like most broad political movements before the Civil War – largely a farmers' crusade, although in the 1840s it also gained support, and even some leadership, from urban segments of the Jacksonian coalition. Sometimes, as in 1803, agriculturists supported drives for territory that secured routes to foreign markets. Usually, however, they wished to gain new territory for themselves and men like them. Neither Texas nor Oregon nor California offered markets, nor did they provide useful ports for the export of farm goods from older areas.

The commercial community, their views often expressed by the Federalist and later the Whig party, tended to oppose territorial expansion. Businessmen did not find Texas at all alluring. Oregon and California – the Pacific Coast – were perhaps another matter; some Whigs were tempted by the charms of Puget Sound, San Francisco Bay, and San Diego. Even before President Jefferson sent Lewis and Clark to find a route to the Pacific Ocean in 1804, Americans had dreamed of a rich traffic with the Far East, a trade that must necessarily be in high-cost goods, since transportation of bulk cargoes like agricultural produce then seemed impossible. For this trade, ports were essential.

When negotiating with the British and the Mexicans, President James K. Polk sought to gather in as many ports as possible. Yet Polk, of course, was a Jacksonian Democrat, as were most fervent expansionists, primarily interested in opening new areas for American settlement. His emphasis on ports may have been at least in part a way of gaining the support of those who sought commercial opportunities. Whatever his purpose, the opportunity to acquire ports on the Pacific Coast helps to explain not only the comparative weakness of Whig opposition to the acquisition of California but also the support some Whigs gave to the cry for Oregon, just as it also explains their unwillingness to continue the fight for territory north of 49 degrees. In any event, as practical politicians, Whig leaders knew that their constituents, including many of their supporters, shared the enthusiasm for expansion expressed in the term "Manifest Destiny."

Manifest Destiny

During the administrations both of John Quincy Adams and Andrew Jackson, there were fruitless, because comparatively half-hearted, efforts to buy Texas from Mexico. There was, as well, some concern over the Oregon country. However, for twenty years after the Transcontinental Treaty, territorial expansion was neither a major political nor emotional issue. Then, between 1845 and 1848, came the greatest surge of territorial expansionism in the nation's history, one that won Texan annexation, the vast conquests of a war with Mexico, and clear title to areas in the Northwest previously challenged by Britain.

Nor did these acquisitions sate the expansionist appetite. Some Americans talked of all of Mexico, of Yucatán and Cuba and Nicaragua, of Hawaii and Okinawa, even – this was the pet project of Matthew Maury, the great oceanographer and proslavery imperialist – of a hemispheric empire reaching as far as Brazil. These projects failed – indeed, usually commanded little support – partly because many would have meant control over "other races of mankind" for which, slavery in the South apart, Americans were not ready. Nevertheless, agitation did continue, in part because many people believed that, as an Indiana congressman put it in 1847, "When we cease to extend, we will cease to be, what we now are, a united and ascendant people."

By the 1840s, even earlier, there had emerged what historians call the "second party system." Democrats, essentially descendants from Jefferson's Republicans, spoke the language of Jacksonianism. They were opposed by Whigs, less clearly the heirs of Federalism. In the political arena, expansionism was overwhelmingly a Democratic crusade; the projects were carried by Democratic votes in Congress. Whigs, professing to believe that expansion was both desirable and bound to come, argued that existing institutions (and territory) should be consolidated before the nation extended its boundaries and – this was a related concern – that expansion at this time would jeopardize the delicate balance of slave and nonslave interests within the union. It was the Whigs' position, their organ, the *North American Review,* declared in 1845, that "for the mere acquisition of territory they will not consent to disturb the harmony and relationship which now exist among the States." "You are rushing headlong and blindfold upon appalling dangers," a Whig congressman warned expansionists in 1847. "You are rekindling the slumbering fires of a volcano."

Many Whigs, particularly legislators who did not hold safe seats, found it necessary to mute these themes, sometimes going along reluctantly, at other times emphasizing that their opposition was to the modes rather than the principles of expansion. They clearly recognized that to oppose expansion was, in the setting of the 1840s, politically dangerous. "We must not place ourselves in an *anti national* attitude," a leading strategist, Thurlow Weed, warned his Whig colleagues in 1845. And national the sentiment for territorial expansion surely was. Even the philosopher Ralph Waldo Emerson believed it "certain that the strong . . . race which have now overrun much of this continent, must also overrun [Texas], & Mexico & Oregon as well." Deploring though he did the methods of many expansionists, he nevertheless admitted, "It will in the course of ages be of small import by what particular occasions & methods it was done."

The 1840s, years of "freedom's ferment,"[5] embraced religious revivalism and mounted crusades against slavery, drink, and other evils. Expansionism was part of this ferment, a crusade to improve foreign lands by bringing them into the American system. In Emerson's words, "in every age of the world, there has been a leading nation, one of a more generous sentiment, whose eminent citizens were willing to stand for the interests of general justice and human-

5 Alice Felt Tyler, *Freedom's Ferment* (Minneapolis, 1944), 548.

ity. . . . Which should be that nation but these States? . . . Who should be the leaders, but the Young Americans?"

If the "beacon of liberty" concept, the predominant theme of an older generation, never disappeared, it certainly stood aside for "manifest destiny." First used by John L. O'Sullivan, a New York Jacksonian who edited the *Democratic Review,* in 1845, that phrase encompasses many subthemes, sometimes contradictory or at least unrelated. Taken together, however, they demonstrated, as O'Sullivan put it, "our manifest destiny to overspread the continent allotted by Providence for the free development of our yearly multiplying millions." No longer should Terminus stand on the Rocky Mountains! America must spread into neighboring lands, not merely influence them. Doing so, she would "distance the United States from European influence, . . . promote greater economic freedom, and . . . preserve democracy."[6]

Doctrines of Manifest Destiny are difficult to treat with respect today, especially when expressed in the self-righteous language of the 1840s. They were nevertheless strongly held; they had to be, in order to overcome tugs of sectional selfishness, which led Northerners to be doubtful about Southern expansion and vice versa. O'Sullivan and other expansionists argued that a mere glance at the map would show that God had laid out the continent with the United States in mind. More moderate and as it turned out more prescient men believed the presence of the Rio Grande showed, at least to the southward, the deity's view of the nation's proper limits. Whatever the boundaries, once talented and virtuous American farmers had possession of the land they would turn it to the most productive possible use, redeeming it from waste and exploitation by Indians, trappers, and peons. They would, in Thomas Hart Benton's words, use it "according to the intentions of the CREATOR."

Above all, by expanding, Americans would, to employ a phrase apparently coined by ex-President Jackson, be "extending the area of freedom," whether by rooting out Catholicism – as Know Nothings wished to do within the republic – or by eliminating tyrannical, corrupt, colonial, or simply monarchical governments. Because new

6 Thomas R. Hietala, *Manifest Design* (Ithaca, 1985), 8.

territories would invite a vast increase in farming, the threat to true freedom posed, in the view of many Jacksonians, by the rise of an industrial, urban order would be abated. Consequently, by the mid-1840s "American leaders were coming to accept a close relationship between liberty and the active promotion of national greatness defined more and more in terms of territorial expansion."[7] Summing up this theme, James K. Polk declared in his inaugural address in 1845 that "foreign powers do not seem to appreciate the true character of our government. To enlarge its limits is to extend the dominions of peace [and freedom] over additional territories and additional millions."

Ideas alone did not create expansionism. Prime land, mineral resources, access to commercial routes — these and other material interests attracted expansionists. Moreover, expansion seemed necessary to assure the nation's future. Even though vast areas of the Louisiana Purchase remained unsettled, the steady pressure of the westward movement seemed to require it, to provide insurance against the future or to bring back into the union those who had emigrated beyond national boundaries to take up virgin land. Population had nearly doubled between 1820 and 1840, and this caused concern; without expansion, men like O'Sullivan asked, how long could the United States continue to serve as a haven for Europe's oppressed? These powerful motives for expansion were almost certainly insufficient in themselves. The doctrines of Manifest Destiny "enabled the nationalist to pursue expansion without a sense of heresy to his original ideal. . . . Moral ideology was the partner of self-interest in the intimate alliance of which expansionism was the offspring."[8]

Texas

First came Texas. Beginning in 1821, just after Mexico broke from Spain, Americans were encouraged to enter its northern province. A law of 1825 offered newcomers as much as forty-four hundred acres

7 Michael H. Hunt, *Ideology and U.S. Foreign Policy* (New Haven, 1987), 30.
8 Albert K. Weinberg, *Manifest Destiny* (1935; repr., Chicago, 1963), 12.

for a mere two hundred dollars in legal fees. By 1830 thirty thousand immigrants, far more than the number of native Mexicans there, had settled in Texas. Fearing to lose control, the Mexican government sharply curbed immigration, whether by settlers or the slaves some of them brought with them. (About one-quarter of the immigrants owned slaves, and many others hoped to.) This and other measures designed to keep the Americans subordinate instead had a different but predictable result: They stimulated revolution.

An abortive revolt took place in 1832, a more serious one in 1835. The Mexican president, Antonio López de Santa Anna, marched north to put it down, telling a British consul before his departure that, if the United States or its citizens helped the rebels, he would "continue the march of his army to Washington and place upon its Capitol the Mexican flag." President Jackson considered the revolt "rash and premature," although of course his basic sympathies were with the Texans, but he did fairly effectively enforce the neutrality laws. In April 1836 a Texan army commanded by a protégé of "Old Hickory," a pallbearer at Rachel Jackson's funeral, Sam Houston, who had mysteriously emigrated to Texas while governor of Tennessee, defeated the Mexicans at San Jacinto. Santa Anna, a prisoner before whom Bowie knives and guns were displayed, agreed to a treaty recognizing Texas's independence, although he and indeed all Mexicans soon repudiated it on the not unreasonable ground that it had been extorted under duress. Still, in a practical sense, Texas had won independence. "The old Latin mistake had been repeated, of admitting Gauls into the empire."9

Texas existed as a ramshackle republic for a decade. It had ten capitals during that time, most of them villages; at one, the British and American ministers shared a room with four other men. Its future appeared uncertain – Mexico would not recognize its independence and often talked of reconquest, and for some years the United States shied away from annexation. What was clear was that Texas was too weak to stand alone for long.

In discussions of Texas's future, Houston, the most important figure, played an enigmatic hand. He continues to baffle historians;

9 Frederick Merk, *Slavery and the Annexation of Texas* (New York, 1972), 180.

the two names, "the Raven" and "Big Drunk," bestowed upon him by the Indians among whom he often resided suggest the difficulties of analysis. A leader of the annexationist forces in the United States, Robert J. Walker, said of Houston in 1844 that, "When *sober,* he was for annexation; but when *drunk* or in liquor, he would express himself strongly against the measure." Still, Houston, who later confessed that he had "coquetted a little with Great Britain," and the lesser men who sometimes occupied the presidency at least professed to consider permanent independence buttressed by a connection with England. London at times encouraged such a course, though always very cautiously and without any real commitment.

The Texans' maneuvers may have been serious, but at least sometimes they were tactics to frighten the United States in the direction of annexation. For example, Anson Jones, the former dentist who was Texas's last president, said at a time when things were not going well in Washington, "I will have to give them another scare. One or two doses of English camomel . . . have to be administered." At all times, the population as a whole clearly desired to return to old loyalties, and it is unlikely that, whatever their wishes, politicians could have prevented annexation if and when the United States was ready for it.

In that country, the question slumbered for some years, primarily because perceptive people saw that to awaken it might plunge the country into a crisis over slavery. Then, in 1843, President John Tyler, a political maverick who had succeeded to office on the death of William Henry Harrison, a Whig, opened negotiations with Texas, primarily to create an issue that might gain him a second term. In April 1844 John C. Calhoun, named secretary of state specifically for the purpose, completed a treaty of annexation.

The two front-runners, the Whig Henry Clay and the Democrat Martin Van Buren, soon announced their opposition – at least until Mexico reconciled itself to Texan independence. Both stressed that, in Clay's words, "annexation and war with Mexico are identical." Both also made it clear that they did not want a sectional issue to tear the nation apart. Calhoun, however, showing "his characteristic attitude of monomaniac intransigence on the subject of slavery,"[10]

10 Ibid., 60.

made sure the sectional issue would be clear. In a letter to the British minister, simultaneously released to the public, Calhoun defended slavery as a positive good and announced that Texas was being annexed to foil abolitionist plotting by England. He was determined to make the North admit its obligation to support the "peculiar institution."

Calhoun badly miscalculated. The rising expansionist spirit might well have carried his treaty through the Senate had he kept silent or even limited himself to denouncing British machinations in Texas. But he asked the Senate and the country to admit what many expansionists were trying to ignore, that annexation meant the incorporation of a territory where slavery already existed and – worse yet – the extension of the slave system into vast areas beyond Texas's traditional boundaries if its claims to the Southwest as far as Arizona and New Mexico were "annexed" as well.[11]

A few months later Senator Thomas Hart Benton, a Missourian whose expansionist pedigree went back at least two decades, said that "he was in favor of annexation, but for none of the . . . *nigger* reasons" given by Calhoun. Returning the compliment, one of Calhoun's followers, Robert Toombs, declared that he did not care "a fig about Oregon," which many expansionists sought. "I don't want a foot of Oregon or any other country [after Texas], specially without niggers." Democrats who shared Benton's views joined with almost all of the Whigs to send Calhoun's treaty down to crushing defeat, 16–35, in June 1844.

Van Buren's opposition to annexation cost him the Democratic

11 To meet these concerns, the indefatigable expansionist, Walker of Mississippi, developed a sophisticated if not sophistical argument. The annexation of Texas, he prophesied, would draw off slaves from the Old South and, so doing, ultimately lead to its extinction by dilution. The unthinkable alternative, he argued, was a struggle culminating in emancipation and racial conflict, even in the North, to which many freedmen would certainly go. Thus both North and South shared an interest in Texas annexation. How many Northern expansionists accepted this reasoning is not clear; one who did was O'Sullivan, and another was Senator Breese of Illinois, who prophesied that "by the noiseless and unceasing operation of such causes as He has set in motion, the whole black race . . . will find a refuge . . . where they may realize such liberty as they may be capable of appreciating."

nomination, at proslavery Southern hands. Out of a pack of contenders there emerged, thanks largely to Senator Walker's energetic
management and ex-President Jackson's endorsement, James K.
Polk, a party wheelhorse from Tennessee. The party platform, also
largely Walker's work, was stridently expansionist. It called for the
"reannexation of Texas," a reference to the alleged surrender of the
territory by John Quincy Adams in 1819, and the "re-occupation of
Oregon," where too Adams had allegedly surrendered American
rights, this time in an 1818 agreement with Great Britain. By
linking the two issues, Walker — and the party — sought to mobilize
the spirit of Manifest Destiny nationwide and to mollify Northerners troubled by the priority given to Texas and the slave interest.

During the campaign, Polk and his spokesmen constantly stressed
the party's devotion to expansion, although appeals for Oregon did
not equal those for Texas. The wobbling of Polk's Whig opponent,
Henry Clay, suggests that Clay's sensitive antennae divined that
opposition to expansion was impolitic. In the end, Polk won by 170
electoral votes to 105, although the popular vote was much closer
and as always the outcome was not decided by a single issue.

Nevertheless, lame-duck President Tyler told Congress that the
people had spoken. He asked the legislators to evade the two-thirds
rule by approving the substance of the rejected treaty in a joint
resolution that, when accepted by Texas, would unite the two countries. Antiannexationists and senators concerned about their pre-
rogatives howled. So, following a course first suggested by Walker,
the joint resolution scheme was coupled with a Benton proposal for
further negotiations with Mexico over Texas. Choice between the
two courses was left to the president. The president-elect, already in
Washington, threw his weight behind the scheme, among other
things using promises of appointment in the new administration
"with faultless virtuosity to exert the last ounce of pressure for
Texas."[12] He also let word circulate that he intended to follow
Benton's plan, thereby securing just enough votes to secure passage
of the two-headed monster in March 1845. Walker, a newspaperman
reported, looked like "the happiest man this side of a Methodist

12 Charles Sellers, *James K. Polk, Continentalist* (Princeton, 1966), 208.

revival." Although no one expected Tyler to act in the few days before he left office, he ignored the Mexican option and sent an offer of annexation to Texas.

Polk did not withdraw this offer. Indeed, to ensure Texas's approval, he promised to support its claim to all the territory south and west to the Rio Grande, a claim that encompassed vast territories as far as Santa Fe, although as a province of Mexico Texas had not extended beyond the Nueces River, more than a hundred miles above the Rio Grande.[13] Polk's endorsement of this claim demonstrated his "anxiety to complete annexation not only at the earliest possible moment, but also as offensively to Mexico as possible."[14]

Just at this time, Britain finally convinced Mexico to recognize Texan independence, provided Texas promised not to join any other power. Some of its leaders were tempted to follow that route. In the summer of 1845, however, a specially elected convention voted almost unanimously to accept the American offer. By the end of the year the deal was complete.

The country, especially the North, rang with denunciations. There was some justice in the charge that the United States was annexing war with Mexico, even though every major power had recognized Texas's independence, which presumably meant that it had a right to determine its own destiny. The real issue, however, lay deeper. As early as 1843 John Quincy Adams, back in Washington as a member of the House of Representatives, had, with twelve colleagues, declared annexation "identical with dissolution" of the union and called upon free states to refuse to submit to it. Few Northerners were abolitionists, most were negrophobes, but many resisted the extension of slavery – more precisely, an extension of the

13 Commodore Robert F. Stockton, ordered to the Texas coast by Polk, sent an agent to President Anson Jones urging him to send troops to the Rio Grande. Many years later, Jones recalled that he replied, "'So, gentlemen, the Commodore, on the part of the United States, wishes me to *manufacture a war* for them'; to which they replied affirmatively." In fact, only a few days later, Jones proclaimed an armistice with Mexico. There is no evidence to prove – or to disprove – that Stockton's suggestion was authorized by Washington, although most authorities believe the naval officer exceeded his instructions.
14 Sellers, *James K. Polk,* 224.

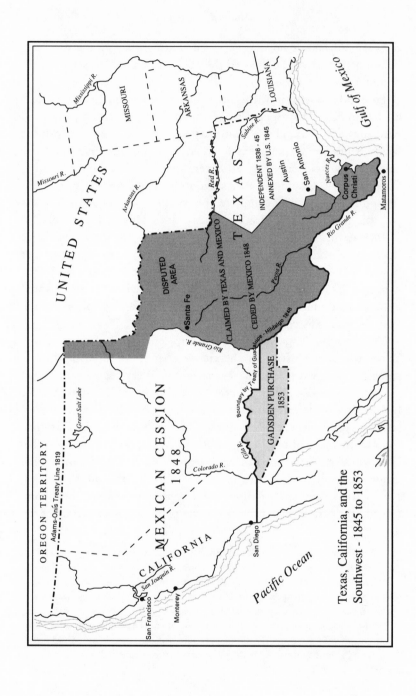

Texas, California, and the
Southwest - 1845 to 1853

area of slavery under the American flag — for reasons which to them seemed morally and politically imperative. Was the United States to become a nation in which the slave power, slave interests, predominated? They succumbed to forces of Southern expansionism and, because other Northerners deserted them, of Manifest Destiny generally. Those Northerners who fought for Texas in what they considered the higher cause of national growth would feel betrayed when, in 1846, Southerners and President Polk did not reciprocate by holding firm in the dispute with Britain over Oregon.

James K. Polk

As president-elect and president, James K. Polk played a critical part in the Texas denouement. As in later negotiations over Oregon and in his management of affairs with Mexico, Polk showed himself a remarkable but not empathetic person. He had served loyally in the ranks of Jacksonianism for years, although, at forty-nine, he was the youngest president so far. Having forced his way to the top, he now expected, as "Young Hickory," to command obedience. Polk trusted and respected no one, allies as well as foes, and his diary is virtually a catalog of denunciations of others. He knew where he wanted to go, and in domestic affairs as well as foreign he accomplished most of his purposes.

Polk had important failings already visible during the Texas affair. Having, though a slave owner himself, no deep feelings about the slavery issue, he did not understand how others could have them. When, during the Mexican War, Congress spent days debating a ban on slavery in territory that might be acquired from Mexico, thus delaying military appropriations, Polk complained that, "instead of coming up to the mark as patriots, they are . . . discussing the abstract question of slavery." His other major failings were "narrow partisanship, lack of candor, and [a] proclivity for secrecy and evasiveness."[15] He thereby won, a contemporary observed, a reputation for "sly cunning which he thought shrewdness, but which was really disingenuousness and duplicity." The Benton men had suffered this

15 John H. Schroeder, *Mr. Polk's War* (Madison, 1973), 4.

during the Texas debate, and the ardent Oregon men would soon have cause to complain of it.

In his first months in office, Polk watched approvingly as annexation went forward and, through Secretary of State James Buchanan, began Oregon negotiations. In December 1845, in his first annual message, he reasserted, with a revealing twist, principles laid down by Monroe in 1823. He revived Monroe only in part to rebuke Britain and France for intrigues in Texas designed to prevent absorption by the United States.[16] In a conversation with Benton he said that above all he meant to reassert "Mr. Monroe's doctrine against permitting foreign colonization," adding that "in doing this I had California and the fine bay of San Francisco . . . in view." His own yen for this Mexican province made him take seriously insubstantial, erroneous indications of British ambitions there.[17]

In this message, Polk reasserted the separateness of European and American politics and declared that "the people of this continent alone have the right to decide their own destiny." If any portion of them, "constituting an independent state," sought to join the union, he asserted, "this will be a question for them and us to determine without any foreign interposition. We can never consent that European powers shall interfere to prevent such a union." He quoted and then, in even stronger language, reaffirmed Monroe's noncolonization principle: "It should be distinctly announced to the world as our settled policy that no future European colony or dominion shall with our consent be planted or established on any part of the North American continent."

Polk's message initiated a period in which "the defensive theme of the Monroe message was extended so as to unite with the theme of

16 In his annual message of 1842, with Texas in mind, President Tyler wrote, after noting that the United States did not interfere in European politics, that "we may be permitted to hope an equal exemption from the interference of European Governments in what relates to the States of the American Continent." This was mild language, indeed, compared to that used earlier by Monroe and soon to be used by Polk.

17 In October 1842, in response to rumors that California had been ceded to the British, Commodore Thomas ap Catesby Jones occupied Monterey for two days, withdrawing in some embarrassment when he learned that the reports were erroneous. He received no real punishment for this unauthorized behavior.

advance."[18] More explicitly than before, European powers were warned not to tamper with areas upon which the United States had its eyes, and Latin Americans understood and resented his meaning. Polk's statement "reinvigorated the message of 1823, . . . inaugurated the fashion of citing it in diplomatic documents, and set it in the way of becoming a generally accepted dogma."[19] At the same time, Polk began the progression by which the United States offered not only to defend the hemisphere but claimed a right to dominate it.

The Onset of "Mr. Polk's War"

When Polk sent his message to Congress, it was already clear that the "theme of advance" was to be played at Mexico's expense. Indeed, the president warned that war might become necessary. Just after Polk's inauguration the Mexican minister demanded his passports, announcing that his country intended to maintain its claim to Texas "by every means in her power." His opposite number soon left Mexico City. The severance of relations was total, the clash direct.

Polk clearly had his eye on California. The province was very weakly held by Mexico; both the Mexican settlers and Americans who had begun to seep into the north were restive, and they frequently defied Mexican authority. Sometimes the president hoped that these conditions would lead Mexico to sell the province, particularly when purchase offers were accompanied by menace. Sometimes he hoped for a Texas-style revolution. Secretary of the Navy Edward Bancroft forwarded to a naval commander in the area, for distribution to citizens who might be interested, a copy of the Texas constitution helpfully translated into Spanish. Secretary of State Buchanan told the American consul at Monterey, Thomas O. Larkin, that "if the people should desire to unite their destiny with ours, they would be received as brethren."[20] A small military expe-

---

18 Frederick Merk, *The Monroe Doctrine and American Expansionism* (New York, 1966), viii.

19 Dexter Perkins, *Hands Off* (Boston, 1948), 87.

20 Buchanan added the phrase, "whenever this can be done without affording Mexico any just cause of complaint" – but no doubt he reserved to himself a right to define "just cause."

dition under Captain John Charles Frémont was sent westward in the summer of 1845, nominally to explore transportation routes; Frémont reached California toward the end of the year.

Finally, it is certainly not beyond the bounds of possibility that Polk sought a war with Mexico, one that could be converted into a war of conquest. This is suggested by his support of Texas's preposterous claim to a boundary at the Rio Grande, far beyond its limits while a Mexican province. Annexation was provocative enough from the Mexican point of view, but Polk's endorsement of the Rio Grande claim virtually obliterated chances of a peaceful settlement. Which of the three possible courses predominated in the president's mind at any point is uncertain. Probably he was willing to use whichever seemed most promising at the time, most likely to bring California under the Stars and Stripes.

Despite an anti-American tumult in Mexico, at the end of 1844 a moderate administration had come to power, displacing Santa Anna. Polk received word that, if he sent an informal representative to Mexico City, a way might be found to settle the two countries' differences. For this task, he selected John Slidell, a tough Louisiana expansionist. The language of Slidell's instructions was utterly contemptuous toward Mexico, and the envoy considered his principal mission to be "to throw all the responsibility and odium of the failure of negotiations on the Mexican Government." Slidell was authorized, if President José J. Herrera's government declined to sell California, to put that issue off to another day; perhaps revolution would solve the problem. He was told to agree to cancel claims against Mexico by American citizens, claims of $2 million plus accumulated interest, if Mexico would agree to extend the boundary along the Rio Grande beyond El Paso. East of that point, however, he was neither to compromise nor offer compensation: Mexico would have to give in, accepting Texan independence and ceding territory beyond the historic boundaries of that province, or face the consequences.

Herrera dared not receive Slidell formally, but his refusal to do so did not save him. At the end of 1845 his government was displaced by a less conciliatory one. Slidell again applied to be received; again he was refused. "Depend upon it," he wrote home, "we can never get along well with them, until we have given them a good drubbing."

The Mexican course appears foolish, and Polk at least could pose as a reasonable man. However, things were not as they seemed. The Herrera government had offered to receive an informal envoy; Polk required Mexico to accept Slidell as a full-fledged minister, thus conceding that the issue over which it had broken relations – annexation – was closed. If the Mexicans refused to receive his envoy, the president appears to have believed, as Slidell did, the onus of a breach, even war, could be placed on them. The offer to settle for the Rio Grande line, demanding though it was, may well have been pure window dressing, designed for later display to the American people. If this is so, the whole affair is highly characteristic Polkian behavior.

The Mexican government could at least temporarily have escaped war by accepting the Rio Grande line, but no regime in Mexico City would have dared to accept this humiliation. Herrera's successor, Mariano Paredes, certainly had no inclination to do so. Mexicans enormously underestimated American military power; most believed they could foil an invasion by the U.S. Army, then only a force of seven thousand men. They also indulged the fatuous hope that one or more European countries would come to their aid or that an Anglo-American war would break out over Oregon.[21]

Following Mexico's refusal to talk with Slidell, Polk stepped up the pressure. He ordered a naval squadron to Vera Cruz and directed General Zachary Taylor, who commanded American troops in Texas, to advance from Corpus Christi, on the Nueces River at the northern edge of the territory under dispute, to the Rio Grande. Although Polk cautioned the general not to commence hostilities, he also told Taylor to consider any Mexican crossing of the Rio Grande an act of war. The army's advance clearly was an act of menace, probably a deliberate act of provocation. American troops reached the mouth of the Rio Grande unmolested, but in April 1846 the Mexican com-

---

21 Most Americans also thought victory would come easily. Polk advised his brother not to return from Italy to enlist since the war would be over before he arrived.

mander across the river demanded that they withdraw. Taylor refused and, when the Mexicans denied him use of the river, blockaded its mouth. On April 25 a Mexican force crossed the river and attacked an American patrol.

On May 9, the day after Slidell returned to the capital, before news arrived from Taylor, Polk decided to ask Congress for a declaration of war. He proposed to ground it on Mexico's refusal to receive Slidell and on its failure to fulfill promises to American claimants. He planned, in reality, a war of aggression.

A few hours after Polk and his cabinet had decided on war, Taylor's report reached Washington. The president and his advisers congratulated one another on their luck: Mexico had provided the United States with a far better justification for war. Although regretting "the necessity which had existed to make it necessary for me to spare the Sabbath in the manner I have," Polk worked away at his message to Congress on Sunday, May 10. He sent it in the next day. The message "epitomized Polk's whole policy toward Mexico since his inauguration, by assuming what was not yet proved, by thrusting forward to throw his adversary off balance, and by maintaining a show of reluctance and sweet reason to placate moderates and pacifists at home. Naturally, Polk did not mention California."

In other words, "for all the uninformed reader might have guessed, the Mexicans could have completely satisfied him at any time by paying several million dollars of claims or by yielding a few square miles of barren borderland."[22] After summarizing American grievances, the message continued: "The cup of forbearance had been exhausted even before the recent information from the frontier," but the president did not reveal that he had planned to ask for war as a result. "Now, after repeated menaces, Mexico has . . . invaded our territory and shed American blood upon American soil. . . . War exists, and, notwithstanding all our efforts to avoid it, exists by the act of Mexico." Such was the result of the president's endorsement of the Rio Grande claim and his orders to General Taylor.

As a matter of practical politics, it would have been – as it always

22 David M. Pletcher, *The Diplomacy of Annexation* (Columbia, Mo., 1973), 386.

has been – nearly impossible for Congress to reject a presidential call for a declaration of war. Nevertheless, to be doubly sure, only in the last stages of debate on a military appropriations bill did the Democratic leadership propose to add a preamble, which declared that "by the act of the Republic of Mexico, a state of war exists." Members of Congress did not easily swallow this, and about a third of the House and twenty senators opposed the amendment. In the end, however, most members felt compelled to accept the bill – it would hardly do to withhold supplies from a military force already in battle. Still, a few did oppose. About forty more abstained, including some strong Texas men like Calhoun, who complained, in a letter to his son, "Never was so momentous a measure adopted, with so much precipitancy; so little thought; or forced through by such objectionable means." Clearly there would be more troubles in the future.

Conquests and Discord

As many legislators had anticipated, the country, except perhaps in New England, was swept by patriotic fervor. Crowds rallied in many cities, and the army could not accept all those who volunteered. In Tennessee, where thirty thousand sought to enlist, only three thousand could be accommodated, because of a quota system developed in Washington. By the end of the year, however, as the realities of the prewar maneuvering and the implications of expansion by conquest became understood, dissent developed throughout the country, most noisily in the North. The Democrats lost their majority in the House of Representatives in the elections of 1846. When Congress reassembled in December, Whigs took up the cudgels against the president. Senator Thomas Corwin of Ohio declared his sympathy for any Mexican who said "we will greet you with bloody hands and welcome you to hospitable graves."

No doubt much opposition was merely partisan, a Whig effort to destroy Polk. A large part was genuine conviction, made deeper by fear that war would lead to a further extension of the slave system. Many Northern Democrats willing to annex Texas, where slavery was a fact, shrank from extending it into areas where it did not exist, in large part because they believed that citizens of their states would be unwilling to take up lives there alongside slave owners and slaves. As early as August 1846 one of these men, David Wilmot, a Democrat from Pennsylvania, who wished to reunify the nation behind expansionism by exorcising the divisive issue that threatened it, moved to prohibit slavery in any territory that might be acquired from Mexico. He, like-minded Democrats, and Whigs carried the "Wilmot Proviso" in the House of Representatives, but a filibuster prevented the Senate from acting before adjournment. The issue, however, did not go away. Indeed, the House twice more passed the proviso, only to have it again blocked by the Senate.

A good deal of the furor could have been avoided if Polk had not refused to clarify his war aims. Shortly after the war began, Buchanan proposed that the president renounce all territorial ambitions — beyond, that is, the extravagant claims for the boundary of Texas. Polk scornfully rejected this proposal, declaring that, "though we had not gone to war for conquest," Mexico must be made to pay for its aggression by the cession of California, at least. Subsequently the president and his cabinet discussed various territorial settlements, but they never settled on one.[23] To the public and to Congress, the president spoke only of "indemnification for the past and security for the future," at most of the necessity to "defray the expenses of the war which [Mexico] by her long continued wrongs and injuries forced us to wage." Very belatedly, in his annual message of December 1847, Polk stated that the United States must insist on the Rio Grande line, California, and New Mexico. Even then he left the door open for more, and he surely was thinking in more expansive terms.

Had Polk announced at the outset that California was the limit of

23 In the summer of 1846 the U.S. Army recruited a regiment for service in California, where the soldiers were to be discharged when their enlistments ended. This indication of the administration's ambitions contributed, at least briefly, to the campaign against the war as a war of conquest, but opposition to the acquisition of California was never as strong as that directed against other acquisitions from Mexico.

In August 1846, after the conquests of New Mexico and California, American commanders issued proclamations annexing those areas, and they also organized new local governments. (In 1847, New Mexicans revolted against the harsh rule and depredations by American soldiers.) The proclamations seem to have been largely ignored or considered purely military measures.

his (not immoderate) ambitions, much of the opposition would have been destroyed. For many, "the dilemma was to strike a happy balance between the desire for Mexico's land and resources and the demand that masses of nonwhite people be excluded from the union."[24] California, like all of Mexico's northern provinces, was thinly populated. Its acquisition, it might be argued, would only slightly accelerate the Texas-like process certain to take place as soon as American settlers predominated. To go beyond that was a different matter: The United States would have to rule in Mexico as an imperial power or admit to the political process millions of people whose inferiority was axiomatic.

Those who worried about this prospect became increasingly alarmed when, late in the war, some politicians talked of taking over Mexico, lock, stock, and barrel. The All-Mexico movement was never strong. That it existed at all, and in particular that its strength was concentrated in the Northeast, which had little material interest in the proposed conquest, showed the strength of Manifest Destiny expansionism. "The 'conquest,'" declared a Boston paper –

The "conquest" which carries peace into a land where the sword has always been the sole arbiter . . . , which institutes the reign of law where license has existed, . . . must necessarily be a great blessing to the conquered. It is a work worthy of . . . a people who are about to regenerate the world by asserting the supremacy of humanity over the accidents of birth and fortune.

What we know about this unknowable man suggests that Polk never succumbed to the All-Mexico virus, although he did dream of greater annexations than those he actually procured. He neither led nor discouraged the movement. His failure to disavow All-Mexico talk or, put the other way around, his failure to emphasize his overriding concern for California deepened the turmoil and suspicion surrounding the war.

Peace with Mexico

Shortly after the war began, American settlers in northern California revolted. Frémont, already on the scene, delayed a bit, so as not to

24 Hietala, *Manifest Design*, 158.

seem responsible, then gave his support and indeed took command. Northern California was quickly cleared, and after his companion, the scout Kit Carson, kept his hand in by scalping three local inhabitants, the young captain and his men marched southward. There they joined a force under General Stephen Kearny, which had come overland by way of Santa Fe, and by early 1847 the whole province was in American hands.

With California conquered, the president sought peace. Much earlier, in the fall of 1846, he had opened an intrigue with Santa Anna, then in exile in Cuba. Approached by an agent for Santa Anna, the president and his cabinet, incredibly, managed to convince themselves that, if properly rewarded, Santa Anna would make peace on their terms. The exile was given money and permitted to pass through the American blockade to his homeland; he soon regained power.

In April 1847, to treat with Santa Anna's government, Polk sent a commissioner, Nicholas P. Trist, to join General Winfield Scott's army, which had just landed at Vera Cruz for a march on Mexico City. The president had thought of sending Secretary of State Buchanan, but this seemed too risky. Trist, formerly Jackson's private secretary and consul to Havana but in 1847 chief clerk of the Department of State, apparently was selected simply because he was expected to be an obedient mouthpiece of imperialism. He was directed, as a minimum, to require, in return for a payment of up to $30 million, American acquisition of California and New Mexico as well as a right of transit across the Isthmus of Tehauntepec.

Trist and Scott twice arranged armistices with Santa Anna, only to have that wily man use them to improve his military position. When the Mexicans did discuss terms, they were unwilling to cede more than the traditional Texas boundary and a small portion of California; in other words, they required the Americans to evacuate a great deal of conquered territory. Angry at Santa Anna's chicanery and apoplectic when Trist forwarded the niggardly Mexican offer, Polk ordered his agent home in November. A few weeks earlier Scott had taken the Mexican capital, yet peace still seemed unattainable.

When Polk's orders reached Trist, Santa Anna had been overthrown. His successor, Manuel de la Peña y Peña, who defied his countrymen's pride in order to forestall national destruction, asked Trist to reopen negotiations. Trist decided to ignore his recall, an act of considerable audacity. Failure to settle with Peña y Peña might well have meant still another return to power by Santa Anna, a prolonged occupation of much of Mexico, perhaps even consummation of the All-Mexico project. None of these appealed to Trist. On February 2, 1848, he signed the Treaty of Guadalupe Hidalgo. Mexico accepted the Rio Grande line and, in addition, ceded California and the Southwest, about a third of its domains. The United States paid Mexico $15 million and assumed responsibility for the claims of its citizens against that government.

Although furious at Trist's "infamous conduct," Polk was in a dilemma. The treaty conformed in all important respects with his original instructions. To press for more would have made the war so obviously a war of conquest that opposition, which had recently won a vote in the House of Representatives declaring that the war had been "unnecessarily and unconstitutionally begun by the President of the United States," was bound to become even worse. Refusal to submit the treaty to the Senate would throw the issue into a presidential campaign, to the advantage of the Whigs. So, although Buchanan and Robert J. Walker, now secretary of the treasury, wanted to bury the treaty, Polk reluctantly decided to send it to the Senate.

After a day's delay occasioned by John Quincy Adams's funeral, the Senate took up the treaty. Some Whig senators wanted to renounce all territory beyond the Rio Grande; some Democrats wanted a larger piece of Mexico and did not, like the president, see the dangers of continuing war to get it.[25] The one thing they did not disagree on was the payment of money to Mexico: To Democrats, it was "an evidence of American liberality," whereas, to Whigs, it was "conscience money for the wrongs done to Mexico by the administration."[26] Fortunately for the treaty, both sets of dissi-

---

25 In the Senate, fifteen Whigs supported an amendment to forswear all conquests, and eleven Democrats voted for an amendment proposed by Jefferson Davis calling for more. Between them, of course, they composed more than one-third of the Senate.

26 Merk, *The Monroe Doctrine and American Expansionism,* 192.

dents feared that an even worse one, from their quite opposite points of view, might follow rejection of Trist's settlement. In March, by a vote of 38–14, over equal numbers of die-hard Whigs and die-hard Democrats, the Senate recommended ratification.

One editor hailed "the sublime spectacle of national magnanimity in not keeping possession of all of Mexico." Calhoun more accurately described the treaty as a "fortunate deliverance." His view was widely shared. On July 4, returning from ceremonies celebrating the beginning of construction of the Washington Monument, Polk received word that Mexico, too, had ratified the Treaty of Guadalupe Hidalgo. The war was formally over.

Thirteen thousand American soldiers had died, about seven-eighths of them from disease. However, Mexico received only $15 million for an immensely valuable territory, and even the costs of the war were not burdensome, although they produced a federal deficit in 1847 larger than in any other year before the Civil War. But the conquests, the means by which they had been acquired, and the use to which they should be put cleaved the nation, setting in train events culminating in the attack on Fort Sumter.

Whether slavery could have established itself in the new territories is highly problematic. The plantation system was ill-adapted to conditions in the Southwest and California, although at the time many Southerners caught up in the spirit of Manifest Destiny never even considered this problem. While a few visionaries thought slaves could be used to mine gold and silver, it is hard to believe that a system of slave labor in the mines could have survived alongside a large nonslave agricultural population. Calhoun and other thoughtful Southerners had virtually no hope or expectation that slavery could be carried beyond Texas. Waddy Thompson, a former minister to Mexico, said that "he would consent to be gibetted, or, if dead, that his bones be dug up and made manure of, if ever a slaveholding State were formed out of any portion" of the new territories. As these men saw it, expansion actually would further the already threatening predominance of the nonslave section of the nation.

Calhoun and those who subscribed to his views of course opposed the "All-Mexico" talk. Acknowledging the strength of Manifest

Destiny, however, as practical politicians they felt compelled to accept the acquisition of California and the Southwest. "For the sake of unity within his home state [and, for that matter, within the South], Calhoun subscribed to an imperialist grab that he knew was fraught with danger for his own section."[27] He, and all Southerners, did however insist that, whatever the prospects for success, the new territories be open to slavery.

What was at issue was not reality but fear and principle. Southerners, whether or not as perceptive as Calhoun, wanted a right to take their system anywhere in the nation; they insisted that it be protected by the federal government; they feared being overwhelmed by the power of nonslave states. Even though they did not insist on abolishing slavery where it existed, Northerners in increasing numbers refused to give national blessing to an extension of the system. The battle was joined over territory acquired as a result of "Mr. Polk's War."

The Tennessean, hard and unimaginative, failed to anticipate this. To Congress in July 1848 he spoke complacently of his accomplishments, declaring that they would be "productive of vast benefits to the United States, to the commercial world, and the general benefit of mankind." And indeed it is probably true, as Samuel Flagg Bemis, a nationalistic historian, observed after cataloging Polk's sins, "Despite all this it would be well-nigh impossible today to find a citizen of the United States who would desire to undo President Polk's diplomacy, President Polk's war, and the treaty of Guadalupe Hidalgo negotiated by President Polk's disobedient chief clerk of the Department of State."[28] Observing his preelection pledge not to seek a second term, Polk left the White House in 1849. He died within three months, long before the full extent of the nation's danger was clear.

27 Ernest McPherson Lander, Jr., *Reluctant Imperialists* (Baton Rouge, 1980), 175.
28 Samuel Flagg Bemis, *A Diplomatic History of the United States,* 5th ed. (New York, 1955), 244. Trist finally received $13,647 in back pay and appointment as postmaster in Alexandria, Virginia, from the Grant administration.

Last Spasms of Expansionism

From this time onward the story of expansionism changes, becoming essentially a study in frustration. To be sure, in his inaugural address in 1853, Franklin Pierce announced that his administration would "not be controlled by timid forebodings of evil from expansion," but its accomplishments fell short of its dreams. To secure a good southern route for a railroad to the Pacific Ocean, this administration arranged, through its agent, James Gadsden, to buy a small slice of Mexican territory. (Santa Anna, in power for the last time, was the seller.) Other projects, directed at Cuba – a target since Jeffersonian days – or Mexico or parts of Central America, all failed, in Pierce's time as in that of his successor, James Buchanan.[29] They aimed at lands heavily populated by peoples the Americans were unwilling to rule as true imperialists or admit into the rites of the republican cathedral. Above all they became tangled up in the slavery issue, drawing support from those who wished to extend the "peculiar institution" into areas where, Cuba aside, it did not exist but thereby inviting the even stronger opposition of those who did not. Few but Southerners supported such projects.

After the Civil War, in 1867, Secretary of State William H. Seward completed the process of continental expansion, the purchase of Alaska from Russia. "It was a question," the Russian negotiator said, "of our selling . . . or our seeing them seize it." The purchase ran into difficulty in Congress, and intensive lobbying and bribery were necessary to get it through. Walker, still serving the expansionist cause, was one of the lobbyists; he received $23,000 for his efforts but lost much of it to pickpockets. If Seward had had his way, further acquisitions would have been made, but his schemes regarding the Virgin Islands and Santo Domingo failed. Manifest Destiny adjourned.

The expansion that carried the United States from the Atlantic Ocean to the Mississippi River, then to the Rocky Mountains, and

---

29 Buchanan's support, in his annual messages of 1858, 1859, and 1860, for the purchase of Cuba was almost pathetic in its impracticality and the lack of enthusiasm it evoked.

finally to the Pacific Ocean was the product of greed, of often unscrupulous leadership, and of the disparity of power between the nation and those who stood in its way. It was also based upon a set of beliefs of which the most notable was a conviction that republicanism was both a superior form of government and an exceedingly demanding one, difficult if not impossible to maintain if the nation included a large alien population. This conviction doomed geographically ambitious dreams of empire beyond North America. Until the end of the nineteenth century, Alaska apart, the expansionism that transformed the nation aimed to extend republicanism, expand the area of American farming, and strengthen the nation generally, not to establish dominion over others or to incorporate different peoples into the Union.

8. Britain, Canada, and the United States

After 1825, the Americans resolutely turned their backs on Europe. The opportunities, and problems, lay in their own hemisphere. In 1835, confessing to an omission from his great work *Democracy in America,* Alexis de Tocqueville explained that "the Union . . . has, properly speaking, no foreign interests to discuss." Half a century later, another foreign analyst, James Bryce, wrote in the *American Commonwealth,* "The one principle to which the American people have learnt to cling in foreign affairs is that the less they have the better."

At first sight, Bryce's comment seems exaggerated. After all, the preceding decades had been studded by disputes with Europe, especially with his own country. Yet in a world-political sense he was right: With extremely rare exceptions, America only tangled with European powers over interests near at hand, over territory and influence in neighboring areas, or − during the Civil War − over issues emerging from that national trial.

The Pursuit of Commerce

The most persistent exception to this generalization lies in the field of foreign trade and commerce. After 1812 the American merchant marine lost the advantage − and it had been an advantage despite the depredations of preceding years − of neutral status while Europe was at war. Nevertheless, after a brief slump the marine grew rapidly, and Americans took pride in the fact. This growth reflected an explosion in international trade, vigorously shared in by the United States itself, rather than the superior competitiveness of American shipowners. They were, for example, slower than their rivals, particularly the British, to adapt to steam; in 1860, only 4 percent of American merchant ships were stream-driven. Although even as late as the beginning of the Civil War American ships carried roughly two-thirds of the cargoes entering and leaving American ports, the proportion had fluctuated downward for years. After 1861 the risks posed by Confederate cruisers and a consequent rise in insurance costs drove many ships to foreign registry. Some of those transferred to the British flag and engaged in blockade-running to the Confederacy. In 1864, for the first time, more foreign than national tonnage entered American ports. The change became permanent. A major characteristic of the nation's youth had passed.

Despite checks in periods of depression and falling prices, and despite, too, the virtual disappearance of the traffic in reexports, which had fueled prosperity before 1812, trade prospered. As early as 1816 the United States sent more of its produce abroad than ever before, and by 1835 it had doubled the prewar high. In 1860 the United States exported domestically produced goods worth $316 million, about half going to Britain and another quarter to the rest of Europe. As it had for years, cotton provided about 60 percent of the total. America imported substantially more. Expansion of the domestic economy was so great that, comparatively speaking, foreign commerce never played as important a role as in the years before 1812. Still, the growth was remarkable, exceeding in percentage terms that of Great Britain. The United States had become, even more than before the War of 1812, an important part of the international economy.

For the most part, individual producers, traders, and shipowners, rather than the government, could claim credit for the commercial expansion. Americans continued to value international trade both for economic and ideological reasons, and some alarmists argued that, if the United States did not act vigorously, Great Britain would create a system of "informal empire," tying the world to London by commercial bonds, including preferential trade agreements. Such warnings rarely stirred the government to energetic action, however, and "America's assault on the British Empire and attempt to establish an informal empire of its own generally failed before the Civil War."[1]

1 Kinley J. Brauer, "The United States and British Imperial Expansion, 1815–1860," *Diplomatic History* 12 (1988): 34.

This is not to say that the government did nothing. With forty or fifty largely antiquated ships, the U.S. Navy bustled around the globe, protecting and encouraging trade, usually simply showing the flag but sometimes employing force. In the single year 1832, for example, naval action took place against Javanese authorities and, in the Falkland Islands, against Argentina. The navy established a Mediterranean squadron in 1815, and by 1835 permanent forces cruised in the Caribbean, off Brazil, on the Pacific Coast, and in the Far East. As always, a major concern of American diplomats was to foster trade. In the forty-five years after the Treaty of Ghent, they concluded commercial agreements at the rate of about one per year. In less formal ways, too, by collecting useful information, sometimes also by exerting their influence with foreign governments, consuls and other diplomats aided American merchants and skippers.

Only rarely, however, did commercial concerns become full-fledged matters of policy. American threats to retaliate forced most countries to abandon discrimination favoring their own ships, at least with the exception of trade between colonies and metropols. Even in the latter field some progress was made, most notably the agreement of 1830 regarding the British West Indies. Although not completely successful in its aspirations, since not all restrictions on American ships were removed, the nation had driven Britain from an age-old devotion to colonial monopoly.

During Andrew Jackson's administration the unwillingness of France to pay damage claims, many of them dating back to the Napoleonic period, led to a war scare. At one point Jackson even asked Congress for the power to seize French ships. In 1836 the French finally paid American businessmen and shipowners about $5 million.[2]

The 1840s and 1850s saw the beginning of sustained, although still minor, interest in the Orient. The first American ship reached Canton in 1784. In subsequent years, although only enjoying a

---

2 By the same settlement, Beaumarchais's heirs, who alleged that the Continental Congress had not paid him for the supplies he furnished on his own account, received $270,000.

minimum of official support, Americans built up a small trade, largely an exchange of Chinese tea for specie and for opium purchased in Turkey. When, early in the 1840s, Britain forced China to relax barriers that had limited trade, the Americans took the cue: By the Treaty of Wanghia (Wangxia) in 1844, a special envoy, Caleb Cushing, gained similar privileges for commerce and the right of extraterritoriality (exemption from trial before Chinese courts) for his countrymen. By an astute mixture of persuasion and menace, Commodore Matthew Perry broke down Japan's isolation in 1853, creating, at least in theory, new opportunities for American trade.

Neither accomplishment produced much immediate advantage. Both missions had been dispatched by commerce-minded Whig administrations. The Democrats, in power during most of the years before the Civil War, did not follow them up or particularly value them. Reflecting their disinterest, Franklin Pierce's annual message of 1853 dismissed news of Perry's success in two sentences. The Chinese and Japanese episodes really are important only in hindsight, because they were the first steps toward deeper involvement in the Orient a half century later. Even so, they were more dramatic than actions elsewhere in the world.

Europe After Vienna

How could America so consistently avoid involvement outside its own bailiwick? Historian C. Vann Woodward has called this the era of "free security,"[3] one in which the Royal Navy's domination of the oceans made it unnecessary for the United States to arm for defense or for support of the Monroe Doctrine. England, in other words, became "the unwitting protector of American isolationism. Given Britain's imperial concerns, defense of the high seas and of the American continent against European interference was always in that nation's interest."[4] It is by no means clear, however, that Continental powers needed the silent discipline of the Royal Navy. As

3 C. Vann Woodward, "The Age of Reinterpretation," *American Historical Review* 66 (1960–1): 3.
4 Lawrence S. Kaplan, *Entangling Alliances with None* (Kent, Ohio, 1987), xvii.

Woodward notes, three thousand miles of ocean made it extraordinarily difficult if not impossible for Continental states to project their power to North America.

Equally fortunate for the United States was the state of European politics. The Vienna settlement of 1815 closed an era of wars so large they spilled beyond Europe. No European war for the rest of the century lasted as long or so deeply troubled international trade as the American Civil War. America could stand aloof. The Crimean War in the 1850s created trouble only when the English minister at Washington sought to raise recruits in the United States. The Franco-Prussian War of 1870 ended so quickly that it had almost no impact, save that Americans found occasion to applaud the collapse of Napoleon III, disliked both for his imperial pretensions and for his pro-Confederate sympathies during the Civil War.

At the same time, however, the diplomatic cauldron steadily simmered, making European diplomats reluctant to invite difficulties with the United States that would embarrass their power nearer to home. During the Civil War, for example, British leaders, concerned about the driving ambition of Napoleon III and by controversy over Poland, were restrained by "the need to keep relations with America quiescent in order to strengthen Britain's diplomatic position in Europe."[5] Until well after Appomattox, the state of Europe permitted Americans to mind their own affairs.

Nor did European ambitions in the Western Hemisphere, save those of Britain, pose a serious threat or even the appearance of one. For some years after 1823 Spain feebly continued to contest Latin American independence, but none of the Continental powers intervened in any serious fashion in the affairs of the Western Hemisphere, at least until, in the 1860s, Napoleon, joined at first by Britain and Spain, moved against Mexico. These two factors – the absence of major wars in Europe and the virtual disappearance of European ambitions in America – allowed the Americans, more than at any other time in their history, to determine the pace and geographic focus of their own foreign policy.

5 Brian Jenkins, *Britain and the War for the Union,* vol. 2 (Montreal, 1980), 398.

The British Setting

The one European power with which the United States often engaged in dispute was Great Britain, that nation which presumably gave the Americans "free security." For this, the neighborhood of Canada was primarily responsible. So, too, were British ambitions in Central America and its role, preeminent among Europeans simply because of its industrial and naval strength, during the Civil War. Very often, Britain was the target of denunciations by Irish-Americans, nationalistic editors, and apostles of world republicanism. Even conservative Americans of British descent, men and women who favorably contrasted the island kingdom with Continental Europe, were often suspicious. Like the rest of the nation, they had "inherited a historic hostility to the British oppression which had provoked so many American symbols of patriotic pride from the Declaration of Independence to the *Star Spangled Banner*."[6] The tinder was there; that the glowing sparks never burst into flame after 1815 was a tribute to Anglo-American statesmanship, particularly that of successive British ministries.

"Britain will never be our Friend, till We are her Master," John Adams predicted in 1816. He was quite wrong. Of course, many Britons detested the United States. They scoffed at its cultural pretensions; America had, the Reverend Sidney Smith wrote in the *Edinburgh Review* in 1820, "done absolutely nothing for the Sciences, for the Arts, for Literature, or even for the statesman-like studies of Politics and Political Economy." (The apoplectic American reaction to such strictures can readily be imagined!) After the panic of 1837, when eight states and the territory of Florida defaulted on millions of dollars of foreign-held bonds, Britishers howled. Smith, still going strong, declared that Americans had "no more right to eat with honest men than a leper has to eat with clean men." If Lincoln succeeded in reuniting the nation, a conservative paper asked in 1861, "who can doubt that Democracy will be more arrogant, more aggressive, more leveling and vulgarizing, if that be possible, than before?"

6 Cushing Strout, *The American Image of the Old World* (New York, 1963), 134.

Fortunately other sentiments – and factors transcending sentiment – made for peace. Those who wished to broaden the franchise in Britain often praised America's accomplishments, although at the same time pointing to the dangers of complete democracy, and they worked hard to develop friendship. During debates over the reform bill of 1867, which doubled the number of voters, supporters frequently cited the North's success as proof of the advantages of a broadly based government. Although Liberals and republicans would become less sympathetic as the United States moved toward the age of McKinley and Rockefeller, in midcentury their role had been important.

Above all, this was, to employ two catchphrases, the age of "Little England" and of the "imperialism of free trade." Peace with the United States was especially precious, since Britain was more dependent on the Americans for supplies than at any other time except during World Wars I and II. Imports from the United States roughly equaled those from Britain's own empire. Foodstuffs were much needed, a major reason for repeal of the Corn Laws, a tax on imports, in 1846. The American South provided about three-quarters of the cotton that fueled the textile industry, chief engine of England's economic expansion. In addition, the United States took more exports than any other nation. Increasing amounts of British capital were invested in America, despite problems caused by the panic of 1837, especially the defaults. By the 1850s Englishmen owned more American government securities than those of all the rest of Europe combined. In 1857, securities of seven American railroads were listed on the London stock exchange, reflecting British investors' involvement, to the extent of £80 million, in the growing railroad system. Anyone "who wishes prosperity to England," the British premier, Lord Liverpool, declared just after the Treaty of Ghent, "must wish prosperity to America."

Although it would be wrong to suggest that they were any more devoted to economic developments than their opponents, and although their backbenchers were rather consistently anti-American, conservative leaders held power on almost every occasion when major accommodations with the United States were reached. Lord Castlereagh, foreign secretary in Lord Liverpool's ministry, directed a major reorientation of British policy after the War of 1812. Lord Aberdeen, foreign secretary in the government of Sir Robert Peel, was more than any other individual in either country responsible for settlements that defused dangerous controversies in the 1840s. Such men were conservative in style as well as philosophy, and, although some of their ministerial colleagues only reluctantly went along, jingoism, almost symbolized in the mid-nineteenth century by Lord Palmerston, a Liberal, was less prevalent than in their opponents' ministries.

All British governments were aware that Canada served, in a very real sense, as a hostage to peace. Successive ministries sought to build a system of land fortifications, especially important after the Great Lakes were demilitarized by agreement in 1817, but the efforts were halfhearted. In 1861 inquiries revealed that two key forts had been converted into prisons, while another was in use as an insane asylum.[7] Although during the Civil War troop strength was built up to 17,600, usually fewer than 5,000 men were in Canada. Britain had "clearly and consciously surrendered the mastery of the North American continent to the United States."[8] During every controversy with Washington, London was restrained by knowledge that the first consequence of war, at least barring the resurrection of Madison as commander in chief, would be the loss of Canada.

Fortunately for Britain – and for Canada – the Americans did not, even in the heyday of Manifest Destiny, entertain thoughts of conquest. They did hope, or at least many did, that Canada would throw off imperial shackles. Some happily speculated that a liberated Canada might seek union with its neighbor. When a revolt, a very ineffectual one, broke out in Canada in 1837, American sympathies were with the rebels, who often operated from bases south of the border and enlisted Yankees in their ranks, but Washington care-

---

7 For their part, the Americans built massive works at the northern end of Lake Champlain; unfortunately, thanks to faulty surveying, "Fort Blunder" stood on what should have been Canadian territory. In 1842 Britain agreed to accept the crooked line as the northern boundary of New York, so the Americans kept their fort.

8 Kenneth Bourne, *Britain and the Balance of Power in North America* (Berkeley and Los Angeles, 1967), 302.

fully avoided any involvement. In the late 1840s, when a small group, largely merchants in Montreal, sought to create an annexationist movement, their efforts foundered in part because they received so little support south of the Great Lakes.

Americans also expected their economy to move toward convergence with the Canadian one, creating a sort of informal, incomplete union in which the United States would be the major partner. A reciprocity treaty concluded in 1854 was the major formal evidence of this expectation. Beyond that, no federal officials and only a few citizens were prepared to go.

The Years of Castlereagh

The new pattern began immediately after the War of 1812, thanks in large part to the efforts of Foreign Secretary Castlereagh. Like his cabinet colleagues, and indeed his country, Castlereagh worried far more about domestic problems and European developments than he did about relations with the United States. Unlike almost all of his predecessors, however, he did give them serious thought in their own right, not merely as offshoots of more important concerns. As a leading diplomatic historian, Sir Charles Webster, observes, Castlereagh was "the first British statesman to recognize that the friendship of the United States was a major asset . . . , and to use . . . with her a language that was neither superior nor intimidating."[9] The foreign secretary believed, as he wrote a minister assigned to duty in Washington, that "there are no two States whose friendly relations are of more practical value to each other, or whose hostility so inevitably and so immediately entails upon both the most serious mischiefs."

The best-known postwar settlement put a stop to naval building on the Great Lakes. Many Britons as well as Canadians argued that, since the United States could more easily throw substantial land forces into battle, England must strive for superiority on the water. Castlereagh rejected this reasoning. In 1817 his representative,

9 C. K. Webster, ed., *Britain and the Independence of Latin America,* vol. 1 (London, 1938), 42.

Charles Bagot, and Richard Rush, temporarily in charge at the State Department, signed an agreement ending the building race that was a legacy of the War of 1812 and limiting naval forces to those necessary to enforce revenue laws.

The Rush-Bagot agreement did not create a defenseless frontier, and in a sense its canonization has been excessive. In addition to continuing to build land defenses, both sides sometimes stretched or even violated the agreement. For example, the Americans launched an oversize ship on Lake Erie in 1843, and the British responded by subsidizing construction of three ships easily converted to military purposes. Moreover, like most arms control agreements, this one reflected rather than caused changes in the international situation. Still, this transaction, coming as it did only two years after the end of a bitter war, demonstrated the good sense of those involved, particularly Castlereagh, and it did change forever the military setting along the frontier.

At least equally important was a less famous agreement reached the next year. In 1818 Albert Gallatin, then minister to France, journeyed to London to join Richard Rush, now stationed there, in wide-ranging discussions. The negotiators – Castlereagh left the business to underlings while he went off to a European conference – failed to settle several issues. But they did agree to extend a commercial convention of 1815, which regulated Anglo-American trade, and settled, albeit temporarily, the fishery question Ghent had failed to resolve. Most important, they drew the boundary between British and American territory along the forty-ninth parallel from the Lake of the Woods to the "Stony Mountains," a distance of eight hundred miles, and left territory beyond the Rockies "free and open . . . to the citizens and subjects of the two powers" for a period of ten years. This provision, extended indefinitely in 1827, left a final settlement of the Oregon question to what Rush rightly called "time . . . , the best negotiator." While he was Monroe's secretary of state, John Quincy Adams had several acidulous exchanges on the subject with the British minister in Washington. On the whole, however, disputes over the faraway country dwindled until the 1840s.

During the American campaign for Florida, Castlereagh again showed his wisdom. When, during Jackson's incursion, the general executed two British subjects, the English press exploded against the Americans. Castlereagh later claimed that "such was the temper of Parliament, and such the feeling of the country, that . . . war might have been produced by holding up a finger." Even if this is an exaggeration, his refusal to make an issue of the executions prevented a nasty confrontation. After the Florida cession had been arranged, he told Rush that while Britain would have preferred to see a weak power there, London recognized that this was impossible, welcomed a peaceful settlement, and hoped the treaty would be ratified. When the Spaniards delayed, Castlereagh warned them that their foolishness might cause the Americans to take Florida by force.

Castlereagh's success in settling or muting controversies was notable, particularly considering the bitter legacies of the War of 1812 and the presence, in the Department of State, of John Quincy Adams. After Castlereagh slit his own throat in 1822, George Canning succeeded to his office. Many Americans expected trouble, remembering that Canning had been a domineering foreign secretary in the cabinet that framed the Orders in Council of 1807. They did not get it, and the "great flirtation," as Canning described his approach to Rush, showed that he too had changed. After the wooing failed, after the Monroe Doctrine's tone and principles alienated Britain, the rapprochement cooled.

In a sense it had been fragile, because both sides – particularly the Americans, who rejected Canning's overture of 1823 partly because they feared he might double-cross them – never lost their suspicion of one another. "The crucial element lacking . . . was mutual trust," but also important was an American belief, largely unjustified at least as far as the London government was concerned, "that Britain refused to recognize the United States as a nation as worthy of respect as a European state."[10] Still, by contrast with the past, the accomplishments had been notable, and their impact remained. In his first annual message to Congress, Jackson expressed the view that, "With Great Britain, . . . we may look forward to years of peaceful, honorable, and elevated competition. Everything in the condition of the two nations is calculated . . . to carry con-

10 Howard Jones, *To the Webster-Ashburton Treaty* (Chapel Hill, 1977), xi–xii, xiii.

victions to the minds of both that it is their policy to preserve the most cordial relations." The astounded editors of the *Times* of London commented that "never since Washington's day, had a message included so much that was valuable and so little that was offensive."

Lord Ashburton and Secretary Webster

That a new crisis arose late in the 1830s was a function not so much of the continuing suspicion as of the new mood of assertiveness that culminated in the war with Mexico. For example, brawling between rival lumberjacks escalated into the "Aroostook War" over the almost unpopulated area of extreme northern Maine, where the boundary with New Brunswick was disputed. (A compromise line suggested by the king of the Netherlands, though acceptable to Jackson, had been rejected by the Senate in 1836.) Fortunately, although Congress appropriated $10 million and authorized the president to enlist fifty thousand volunteers, the quarrel remained a war of imprecations rather than blood, though no one could be sure that would always be the case. Late in 1840, in upper New York, a Canadian, Alexander McLeod, who allegedly had taken part in a raid across the Niagara River against supporters of the rebellion of 1837, was arrested for murder. Lord Palmerston, then foreign secretary, informed the British minister in Washington that "McLeod's execution would produce war."[11]

To lower the international tension, a new British government and the Tyler administration arranged for negotiations in 1842. The Tory ministry named Lord Ashburton, scion of the great banking house of Baring, which had large investments in the United States. Throughout his political career, Ashburton, who had an American wife, worked to improve relations with the United States; he even

11 Secretary of State Daniel Webster attempted to have McLeod released but could not control the New York courts, and Governor William H. Seward refused to intervene, although he very secretly told intimates that he would pardon McLeod if a jury convicted him. Fortunately, McLeod was found innocent in November 1841. His acquittal, observes the chronicler of this episode, "opened the way for Britain and the United States to clear up other disagreements" (Kenneth R. Stevens, *Border Diplomacy* [Tuscaloosa, Ala., 1989], 158).

favored the cession of Canada on the grounds that only thus could repeated clashes be avoided. "What seems most important," he wrote at this time, "is that there should be a settlement of some sort, and I do not attach [much] importance . . . to the precise terms." In Washington, Ashburton negotiated with Daniel Webster, who stayed on as secretary of state solely to seek an accommodation with England when the rest of the cabinet resigned shortly after President William Henry Harrison's death.

Not surprisingly, therefore, the two men reached agreement in August 1842. The McLeod issue had already evaporated with his acquittal, and Ashburton gave a qualified apology for the border crossing in which he had allegedly taken part. The negotiators' greatest difficulty – aside from Washington's summer heat, which nearly prostrated Ashburton – was with agents of Maine and Massachusetts, which had incorporated Maine until 1821 and still had land rights there. In effect, the negotiations became triangular and, consequently, "among the most disorderly on record."[12] In the end the two states were soothed with payments from the federal treasury, a most unusual procedure, and Webster agreed to a boundary in northern Maine that mildly favored Britain. Another disputed section of the boundary, between Lake Superior and the Lake of the Woods, was drawn in such a fashion that the Americans received the Mesabi district, although Ashburton was at most only dimly aware of the tremendous iron deposits there. Ashburton failed to gain one of his objectives, permission for the Royal Navy to search suspected slave ships flying the American flag; instead, a cumbrous, ineffective system of joint squadrons was established. He and Webster also failed to settle, because London's instructions were too demanding, the question of Oregon.

In both countries, opponents of the government attacked the Webster-Ashburton treaty as a surrender. First the American and then the British government produced ancient maps, the latter's being more convincing, purporting to prove that it had not receded from the boundary intended by negotiators of the Treaty of Paris in

12 Wilbur Devereux Jones, *The American Problem in British Diplomacy* (Athens, Ga., 1974), 20.

1782. However, only nine senators voted against ratification. On the whole, the country seems to have accepted the treaty as reasonable. That such a storm could have arisen over insubstantial issues in the first place, however, presaged more trouble in the future.

Oregon

While negotiating the Convention of 1818, which fixed the Canadian-American boundary as far as the Rockies, the American negotiators, Richard Rush and Albert Gallatin, sought unsuccessfully to extend the 49-degree line to the Pacific Ocean, into what was called the Oregon country. Subsequent negotiators had no better luck. The matter did not seem especially pressing until the 1840s: Settlement was almost nonexistent, the country far away, communication difficult. Then overland migration began, and by 1844 there were several thousand Americans in Oregon. Soon, it was believed, railroads would link the Northwest and its seaports with the rest of the country – and make possible political representation in Washington. The failure of Webster and Ashburton to settle, even really to come to grips with, the Oregon question "allow[ed] the solution of the . . . problem to drift away from . . . the momentum of the achievements won in [their] negotiations, and into the era of . . . the politics of expansionism, and the war crisis of the Polk administration."[13]

The United States had a shadowy title as far north as 54 degrees, 40 minutes, fixed in 1824 as the line of division between its claims and those of Russia, the proprietor of Alaska. However, American diplomats had often offered to divide Oregon with Britain at the forty-ninth parallel. Britain's claim extended south only to the Columbia River. The area truly in dispute, containing valuable ports on Puget Sound and the southern tip of Vancouver Island, lay between the Columbia and the forty-ninth parallel. In the end, the Americans won almost all the disputed territory, largely because fur trapping declined there (beaver hats in any case were going out of style) and English leaders concluded that the game was not worth

13 Frederick Merk, *The Oregon Question* (Cambridge, Mass., 1967), 215.

the candle. Before the denouement, however, President Polk played a dubiously honest, dangerous, and diplomatically unnecessary game.

In 1844, because Van Buren opposed Texas annexation, he was deprived of the Democratic nomination. To assuage Van Buren's Northern supporters and to nationalize the demand for expansion, the man who had managed Polk's successful campaign for nomination, Robert J. Walker, pushed through the convention a plank that declared, "our title to the whole Territory of Oregon is clear and unquestionable." In the campaign, particularly in the North, Democratic orators coupled "the reoccupation of Oregon and the reannexation of Texas." The appropriately labeled "Foghorn Bill" Allen, senator from Ohio, declared for "Fifty-four forty or fight!" When Polk won, by a narrow margin in an election contested on many issues, his success was construed as a mandate for expansionism. His election, the *Times* of London expostulated, represented (with the exception of his party's support of a lower tariff) "the triumph of every thing that is worst over every thing that is best in the U. States of America" – Southern and slave interests, debt repudiation, Texas annexation. From the *Times*'s point of view, worse was still to come, over Oregon.

After he became president, Polk followed a tortuous and complex policy regarding Oregon. From the Hermitage, Andrew Jackson urged "Young Hickory" to "dash from your lips the counsel of the timid. . . . *temporizing will not do.*" Polk was of less stern stuff than his mentor, although he followed a policy of public threats and bellicose posturing, which encouraged "innocent demagogues" like "Foghorn Bill" Allen, the expansionist senator from Ohio, to think he was at one with them. "The trouble with Polk's policy of bluff," his biographer observes, "was that it required a lack of candor toward his own countrymen as well as toward Britain. . . . It created serious . . . difficulties from both a moral and a pragmatic standpoint."[14]

The president's extravagant language stimulated Calhoun to direct an incumbent senator to resign so that he himself could return to the Senate, principally for the purpose of organizing a peace

---

14 Charles Sellers, *James K. Polk, Continentalist* (Princeton, 1966), 359.

bloc. With the assistance of others, notably Benton of Missouri, he promptly succeeded. The strength of the opposition was soon understood by the British, whereas if the president had followed a policy of quiet firmness he might well have had the diplomatic advantage of a united country behind him. Moreover, his public bluffing was undermined, as far as Britain was concerned, by repeated private hints of weakness. He was extraordinarily fortunate to escape with victory.

In his inaugural address, despite bombast on the Oregon question that made him seem a "fifty-four forty" man, Polk did not explicitly endorse the platform's demand for the "whole of the Territory of Oregon." Shortly thereafter, in deep secrecy, he asked Calhoun, a Southerner whose interest in Oregon was less than minimal, to go to London with full powers. This request, though refused by Calhoun, shows Polk's true feelings. Then he had Secretary of State James Buchanan present to the British minister, Richard Pakenham, an offer to settle at 49 degrees. Polk claimed that he felt bound by previous administrations – in other words, no president from Jefferson to Van Buren had seriously dreamed of insisting on 54 degrees, 40 minutes – but the proposal greatly weakened his policy of menace. When Minister Pakenham foolishly refused even to forward the offer to London, Polk returned to 54 degrees, 40 minutes and began to rattle the saber – or at least to brandish the scabbard. Buchanan, a man of truly marvelous weakness and inconsistency, was astounded; to Polk's declaration that he would "leave the Oregon question to God and the country," Buchanan replied that God was not much to be relied on north of 49 degrees.

In December Polk reenunciated Monroe's noncolonization principle. He also asked Congress to abrogate the stopgap agreement with England on Oregon and to extend American laws to that territory, and he recommended a military buildup, though his budget called for a reduction in military spending. War seemed close, closer than war with Mexico. Yet, as Polk well knew, Whigs and dissident Democrats, led by Calhoun and Benton, controlled the Senate. Over the opposition of Allen and his kind, they were able to attach a moderate preamble, inviting negotiation, to the resolution repudiating the 1818 arrangement and to delay final passage until April 1846.

Polk had long since allowed word to reach the British government that almost any offer from London would be laid before the Senate, in other words that "he was . . . prepared to use the 'advice and consent' of the Senate as a means of withdrawing from the extreme demand and accepting compromise."[15] In due course, Foreign Minister Aberdeen, who had been seeking a settlement since before Polk's election, suggested extending the 49-degree line as far as the Straits of Georgia, beyond which it would follow the water to the sea, leaving Vancouver Island to the British. Polk had often pronounced this detail unacceptable. Nevertheless, to pass the buck, he asked the Senate's advice, piously adding that his own position remained as it always had been. Thanks in part to White House lobbying, the Senate voted to accept the British offer. The administration then framed a treaty, which the Senate approved in June. Among the fourteen opponents was "Foghorn Bill" Allen, who resigned as chairman of the Foreign Relations Committee in protest against the president's treachery.

Thus the Americans freed themselves to concentrate on the war with Mexico, which had just begun. "We can now thrash Mexico into decency at our leisure," the *New York Herald* observed. The United States gained almost all the territory at issue, now the western half of the state of Washington, including valuable seaports, but not "the whole of the Territory of Oregon." This was no hollow triumph, but it owed little to Polk. By the end of 1845 Aberdeen had converted Sir Robert Peel, his chief, to his position. The rest of the cabinet came along as soon as it seemed politically safe. Aberdeen's success owed much to British concern about the noisy nationalism during the 1844 campaign and to fears that a deadlock would further strengthen it. Polk's acrobatics, which never fooled Aberdeen, had been only incidental to the conversion of other figures.

The president's greatest skill had been in deluding those who, trusting him, rallied to 54 degrees, 40 minutes. Menace, intrigue, negotiations — all of these he had handled much less well. At the end, "when negotiations finally took place, Polk managed to end a war crisis that was largely of his own creation and secured terms

15 Ibid.

which he might have had earlier by more sophisticated diplomacy."[16]

Britain and the American Civil War

In subsequent years, the spasms of American expansionism and, for most of the period, the presence in the Foreign Office of a congenital jingo, Lord Palmerston, produced a running quarrel over Central America. However, both parties in effect recognized that their interests were too insubstantial to justify real risks. The Clayton-Bulwer Treaty of 1850, by which they agreed neither to fortify nor to exercise exclusive control over an interoceanic canal, when one should be built, glossed over other issues and rivalries in the area. By 1861, largely because even Palmerston sensed danger, the noisy disputes had cooled. They would in any case have been overwhelmed by new issues arising from the Civil War.

Shortly after Abraham Lincoln's election in November 1860, Southern states began to secede from the union. In February 1861, they formed the Confederate States of America. Armed clashes soon followed, and in June, in the first pitched battle of the war, the Confederates won a notable victory at Bull Run, on the very outskirts of Washington. The struggle lasted until the spring of 1865, by far the bloodiest conflict in American history and far more costly, too, than any European war between Waterloo and 1914. In the end, of course, the North ground the Confederacy into submission, but for several years the outcome was in doubt. Had European powers aided the South, in any one of a number of possible ways, the result, as the defeated Southern president, Jefferson Davis, later claimed, might well have been different. His government worked hard to procure intervention. Lincoln's worked equally hard, and much more successfully, to prevent it.

Britain's policy was far more important to Washington and Richmond than that of any other power. Napoleon III disliked the North, and he feared criticism that he was doing little to relieve the plight of France's textile industry, which was crippled by the loss of

16 David M. Pletcher, *The Diplomacy of Annexation* (Columbia, Mo., 1973), 592.

cotton imports from the South. For much of the war he toyed with various schemes that would have benefited the Confederates, but after the Union victory at Gettysburg in 1863 he pulled in his horns. Reflecting the new tilt, his government took steps to prevent delivery of six warships ordered by Confederate agents; in the end, only one was delivered, and it arrived in North America thirty days after Lee's surrender. Even before this shift, however, the emperor, who had a wary respect for American power, was unwilling to proceed without British cooperation. Moreover, neither he nor the London government really trusted one another. European politics were, the son of the American minister to England contentedly observed, in a "delicious state of tangle."

Most British politicians and editors welcomed Lincoln's election. Even the *Times* of London, later one of his most savage critics, did so: "We are glad to think that the march of Slavery, and the domineering tone which its advocates were beginning to assume over Freedom, has been at length arrested and silenced." When, a few weeks after the election, South Carolina became the first state to secede, the *Times* opined that it "had as much right to secede from the . . . United States as Lancashire from England." As late as June 1861 the American minister's son, Henry Adams, wrote, "The English are really on our side."[17]

When Lincoln stressed preservation of the union, not antislavery, many Britons began to have second thoughts. To them, "the struggle between the sections seemed devoid of principle or moral purpose."[18] In a speech delivered in October 1861, Lord John Russell, the foreign minister, told his listeners that South and North were not fighting over slavery but rather were "contending, as so many States of the Old World have contended, the one for empire and the other for power." Moreover, the low-tariff policies of the South were

---

17 This by no means suggested respect for Lincoln personally. He was regarded, until his death, as a nearly illiterate politician. "It would have been impossible," a London magazine commented, "for him, or any of his Cabinet, to have emerged, under British institutions, from the mediocrity to which nature had condemned them."

18 Frank J. Merli, *Great Britain and the Confederate Navy* (Bloomington, Ind., 1970), 21.

far more congenial to Britons than the protectionism Washington espoused. The Morrill tariff of November 1861 "undercut the arguments of those who insisted that the Civil War was a fight against Southern slavery. To many a British freetrader, there was little difference morally between slave-holding and protectionism."[19] Lincoln's conversion to a policy of emancipation in 1862 did not at first change things. Many concluded that, since it applied only to slaves behind enemy lines, it was primarily an invitation to "servile insurrection" in the South. Then, too, many in England came to wonder if a divided continental republic, rather than a unified one, might pose a lesser menace to British interests.

Faced with demands for an extension of the British franchise, conservatives could only welcome the travail and apparently impending dissolution of a republican nation. "I see in America the trial of Democracy and its failure," one peer happily commented. Moreover, at least part of the aristocracy viewed Southerners as very much akin to themselves. "The North will never be our friends. Of the South you can make friends," its leading supporter, John A. Roebuck, told the House of Commons in 1862. "They are Englishmen; they are not the refuse of Europe." One American journalist summed up all of these threads: "Our democracy is disliked by their aristocracy; our manufactures rival theirs; our commerce threatens at many points to supplant theirs. We are in dangerous proximity to some of their best colonies." In fact, British opinion was far from unanimous – the North continued to have many friends. Still, the summary fairly captured the feelings of many influential Englishmen, perhaps even of the governing class as a whole.[20]

However, in England as in France the primary factor conditioning policy was the conviction that restoration of the union was impossible. By the spring of 1861, and especially after Bull Run, "The

19 Norman B. Ferris, *Desperate Diplomacy* (Knoxville, 1976), 182.
20 Historians have long debated the sympathies of the laboring classes, particularly the Lancashire workers who suffered massive unemployment when the Union blockade cut off cotton, forcing many textile mills to reduce output or even close. Some argue, and others deny, that the republican spirit of the workers made them continue to support the Northern cause. Whatever the fact of the matter, their political influence was minimal.

'calamity of disruption' was . . . assumed to be almost inevitable."[21] Because Britain would have to live in the same world as the
Confederacy, many argued, it made little sense to alienate it. It was
truly charitable, as well as good for British trade, to help the North
come to recognize the inevitable, to end the carnage. Even Richard
Cobden, a Radical devoted to the Northern cause, sometimes expressed this view. The people of the North, Chancellor of the Ex-
chequer William E. Gladstone publicly lamented in 1862, "have
not yet drunk the cup . . . which all the rest of the world see they
must nevertheless drink of." Gladstone's speech, though it roused a
furor in the United States, where such sentiments were considered
pro-Confederate, merely expressed what most informed Englishmen
believed.

Whatever their analysis, most Britons, even most of those who
sympathized with the South, were loth to invite trouble by forcing
their views on the North. Among other things, Canada was too
vulnerable; the diversion of a small fraction of the Union Army
would suffice for its conquest. Nothing came of Confederate hopes
that England would be forced to act to secure supplies for the textile
industry, which employed one-sixth of the labor force and produced
one-third of British exports. To create pressure on London, the
Confederates held back cotton exports in 1861, a tactic that won
them no friends without achieving its purpose. Because of the size of
reserve stocks, the cutoff of cotton was not deeply felt until the end
of 1862, and as time passed the development of alternative sources
and the influx of cotton from areas conquered by the Union forces
relieved the shortages. (New Orleans and other ports were opened as
early as May 1862.) However, even when the distress was worst,
when factories were shut down and two-thirds of the operatives were
out of work, calls for action never became loud enough to force
action by the government. Moreover, textiles aside, the British
economy boomed, helped both by declining American competition
and greater American purchases, of arms, ships, and other goods.

In any event, the Northerners, particularly Secretary of State

---

21 Martin Crawford, *The Anglo-American Crisis of the Mid-Nineteenth Century*
(Athens, Ga., 1987), 92.

William H. Seward, made it clear that intervention would mean war. Seward had a reputation, earned in New York politics, as an Anglophobe and a jingo. He was, in the view of a British cabinet member, "the very impersonation of all that is most violent and arrogant in the American character." On news of Seward's appointment, the British minister in Washington predicted that he "would not be very reluctant to provide excitement for the public mind by raising questions with Foreign Powers." The prediction was soon borne out. In a memorandum for Lincoln fittingly dated on April Fool's Day, Seward proposed to foment a quarrel with Spain and France, perhaps Britain and Russia as well, expecting that the South would then abandon secession and fight under the Stars and Stripes. Lincoln charitably brushed aside this scheme, and during the next few months he more than once toned down the secretary's official correspondence. As time passed, Seward became much more balanced. Indeed, his early bellicosity may have been essentially an act "carefully calculated to play upon British concern for the safety of their all too vulnerable empire in North America and their preoccupation with the balance of power in Europe."[22] Whatever the case, especially since he had made no effort to conceal his early views, he convinced the British that serious interference in America was too dangerous to risk.

The leading figures in her majesty's government were Prime Minister Palmerston; Lord John Russell, at the Foreign Office; and Gladstone. The Americans suspected the Liberal leaders of Confederate sympathies, although both Gladstone and "Pam," who in any case had lost his jingoist vigor (he died in 1865), were strongly antislave. Gladstone even wished it were possible to offer Canada to the United States in return for an end to the futile war for reunion. Russell had what an acquaintance called "meddling proclivities." Like Palmerston and many other Englishmen, he believed that "Americans were bullies – brash, boorish, crafty, pushy, cowardly, and entirely unamenable to logical argument or conciliatory persuasion."[23] Privately, and occasionally publicly, Russell and other min-

22 Jenkins, *Britain and the War for the Union,* 2:2.
23 Ferris, *Desperate Diplomacy,* 198.

isters indulged these feelings. Basically, however, they were pragmatists: "It was a matter of keeping out of trouble and playing safe, balancing immediate neutral interests against long-term . . . interests, preserving face against Yankee bluster but avoiding a 'partisan' interference which would divide the English nation."[24]

Throughout the Civil War, the American minister in London was Charles Francis Adams, the third of his family to hold this post.[25] Delayed by a son's wedding, Adams reached London just after the ministry recognized the belligerent rights of the Confederacy in May 1861, at the same time laying down rules for the proper behavior of British subjects in connection with the war. The new minister complained bitterly. So did Seward, who insisted – this was some time after warfare had begun – that the rebels were only "a discontented domestic faction." Actually, unless it wished to treat the Confederates as pirates, the British had little choice, and the Americans had similarly dealt with Canadian rebels in 1837. As the foreign secretary said to Adams, it was "scarcely possible to avoid speaking [of] a war of two sides, without in any way implying an opinion of its justice." Moreover, he continued, Britain could not "withhold an endeavor . . . to bring the management of it within the rules of modern civilized warfare. That was all that was contemplated in the Queen's proclamation."

Moreover, recognition of belligerent rights fell well short of full relations, a course unsuccessfully urged upon his superiors by Lord Lyons, the British minister to the United States, as it was upon theirs by the French and Russian ministers in Washington. When Southern diplomats came to London, Russell declined to hold more than ostentatiously informal talks – and few of those – with men to whom he referred in correspondence as representatives of the "so-called Confederate States." Downing Street would not permit Confederate commerce raiders to sell their prizes in Britain. It tolerated a blockade of the South, which often did not conform to the requirements of international law, especially as that law had been inter-

24 D. P. Crook, *The North, the South, and the Powers* (New York, 1974), 375.
25 Unlike John Quincy Adams, Charles Francis never served a diplomatic apprenticeship under his father. He was, however, taken to Russia by his father at age two and remained in Europe until John Quincy Adams entered Monroe's cabinet.

preted by the Americans themselves in the past. In his memoirs, Jefferson Davis complained that Britain and the rest of Europe "submitted in almost unbroken silence to all the wrongs the United States chose to inflict on its commerce." Northerners did not see it that way; from the moment the Confederacy gained belligerent rights they were convinced of British malevolence.

By its actions, Lincoln's government turned its back upon American tradition and, some would argue, America's long-term interest. The United States had argued for restrictions on belligerent rights in the past. During the war with Mexico it had been careful to stay within, or at least very close to, the rules it had laid down for others. A historian sympathetic to the South has written, "To gain a doubtful advantage over the Confederacy, [Lincoln] flew in the face of all American precedents, all American permanent interests and doctrines of neutral maritime rights. . . . International law was put back where it was in the days of the orders in council and the Milan decrees. Old Abe sold America's birthright for a mess of pottage."[26] Perhaps so, but military necessity has often made its own rules.

Lincoln proclaimed a blockade of the South in April 1861, six days after the Confederate attack on Fort Sumter. At that time the U.S. Navy had available only 3 steam warships to intercept commerce with nearly two hundred ports along a coastline of 3,500 miles. Although reinforcements were steadily fed in, and the number of available ships reached 150 by the end of 1861, the blockade remained permeable until the end of the war. Major ports were effectively closed, almost no heavy equipment reached the South from Europe and only small amounts of cotton were exported, but hundreds of small blockade-runners slipped past the Union patrols. Many of them were British; as Russell admitted, "if money were to be made by it, [his countrymen would] send supplies even to hell at the risk of burning the sails."

By Jeffersonian or Madisonian standards the Union action was not an effective blockade, hence illegal, rather like Fox's Blockade of 1806. Lincoln's administration defended it, however, arguing that "effective" need not mean air-tight. Although Palmerston at first inclined to challenge the blockade, and although Russell sent to

26 Frank Lawrence Owsley, *King Cotton Diplomacy* (Chicago, 1931), 290–1.

Washington literally hundreds of protests against the way it was implemented in specific cases, the British government never denied the Union contention. To challenge the blockade might well lead to war. Moreover, in the long run it was in Britain's interest to encourage relaxed standards of legality. After all, the *Times* observed, "a blockade is by far the most formidable weapon of offense we possess. Surely we ought not to be overready to blunt its edge or injure its temper?" Palmerston emphatically agreed: Britain's "long-term interests were more likely to be advanced through acquiescence in rather than opposition to the Union's definition of belligerent rights."

Not only did the North abandon traditional American views regarding blockade; it also adopted and even expanded the doctrine of continuous voyage against which it had protested fifty years earlier. Union vessels intercepted ships and cargoes on the first leg of a trip to the South, the best-known instance being the seizure in 1863 of the *Springbok,* en route from England to Nassau with, for the cargo at least, a final destination in the Confederacy. The United States also extended the doctrine of continuous voyage to overland passage, something even the British had not done in the past. In 1863 the British ship *Peterhoff* was seized in the Caribbean, still hundreds of miles short of its destination, Matamoros, a Mexican port on the Rio Grande, because the cargo was intended to be shipped onward by land through Texas. "Unless a firm stand be made," the *Times* expostulated, "there will be no end to the indignities and losses we must endure." The Palmerston ministry, more consistent than the *Times,* accepted that the precedent might be helpful in the future.[27]

The Three Crises of the Civil War

The first of three major confrontations between the North and Great Britain came at the end of 1861. In November, an American war-

[27] The *Springbok* and *Peterhoff* cases ultimately went to the Supreme Court. Its decisions, handed down in 1867, "made apparent that the United ·States government was discarding those rules pertaining to neutral rights for which it had made war in 1812 and which it had upheld since then" (Stuart L. Bernath, *Squall Across the Atlantic* [Berkeley, 1970], 97).

ship commanded by Captain Charles Wilkes stopped the British
vessel *Trent* off Cuba. Wilkes carried off James M. Mason and John
Slidell, who, having slipped through the blockade, were en route to
England to represent the Confederacy. They had so ostentatiously
advertised their trip that some suspect that "the South may have
staged the whole . . . affair in a deliberate attempt to precipitate a
war between the North and Great Britain."[28] One of Seward's corre-
spondents wrote, after the men's families reached London, "The
females of the caged Traitors left the impression that the catching
was voluntary."

A storm of applause rang through the nation. Congress urged
Lincoln to give Wilkes a gold medal. The British public reacted
violently in quite the opposite direction to what was pictured as
little better than kidnapping, and the political pressure and its own
sense of outrage decided the ministry to demand the prisoners' release. As crown lawyers insisted, and as Wilkes's own subordinates
had warned, it was illegal, and rather like impressment, to take the
two men from the *Trent,* although the ship might have been required to go to the United States for trial. Anticipating, or fearing,
that Lincoln would refuse to release the Confederate emissaries,
Palmerston considered sending the Channel Fleet across the Atlantic, and the ministry ordered reinforcements to Canada.[29]

Common sense on both sides, overriding public opinion, prevented war. The British government withheld the formal challenge
of an ultimatum, although its protest was so truculent that the
prince consort intervened to soften it. Russell granted Seward time
to consider the protest and yet directed Lord Lyons, the British
minister in Washington, to make it clear to the secretary of state
that an unfavorable response would lead to a break in relations.

Seward first convinced himself and then the president that Britain's case was undeniable: Wilkes had violated the rights of neutrals,
the freedom of the seas. In a note aimed largely at his countrymen
and therefore soon published, Seward argued that, in repudiating

---

28 Lynn M. Case and Warren F. Spencer, *The United States and France: Civil War
   Diplomacy* (Philadelphia, 1970), 591.

29 When the first troops arrived, the St. Lawrence River was ice-bound. Seward
   generously allowed the Redcoats to disembark in Maine and proceed overland.

Wilkes's action, the United States was "defending and maintaining, not an exclusively British interest, but an old, honored, and cherished American cause. . . . We . . . do to the British nation just what we have always insisted all nations ought to do to us." This was, the British concluded, "a satisfactory, if surly, reply to Lyons's demands."[30]

Mason and Slidell were released to go to Europe, where they accomplished little. Napoleon III, who had supported the British, expressed regrets that the Americans had given way, saying to London's ambassador, "England will never find a more favorable occasion to abase the pride of the Americans or to establish her influence in the New World." The crisis was over. In the sense that it reminded England of Canada's vulnerability and showed that Seward was not as hostile as believed, "the *Trent* operated like a thunderstorm to clear the atmosphere."[31] But most Americans only remembered that Britain had demanded the release of rebel agents.

Another dangerous crisis, this time at London's initiative, threatened in 1862. British leaders considered mediation, a request to the belligerents to discuss terms of peace, with recognition of the Confederacy either to follow or, if Lincoln and Seward would not agree to mediation, to be used as punishment of the North. Napoleon III backed the project because it promised to restore the cotton flow and to confirm the erosion of American power, which might otherwise be directed against his Mexican adventure. Palmerston and Russell agreed "that the time is come for offering mediation to the United States Government, with a view to the recognition of the independence of the Confederates." At a critical time, Napoleon was diverted by a cabinet crisis. Shortly afterward, news that General George McClellan had turned back Lee's invasion of the North at Antietam undermined the conviction that the North could not possibly win, and the prime minister shelved the project.

Gladstone revived it in the famous speech that declared that Jefferson Davis had created a nation and called on the United States

30 Bourne, *Britain and the Balance of Power in North America,* 219.
31 Ephraim Douglass Adams, *Great Britain and the American Civil War,* vol. 1 (New York, 1925), 242.

to "drink the cup." The chancellor's speech probably alarmed as many people as it stimulated; he himself confessed that "the public response . . . suggested a widespread disinclination to extend recognition to the South at this time." It did, however, influence those who were ready to be convinced. Russell resumed support. It might be Britain's duty, he wrote, to ask the American contestants "to agree to a suspension of arms for the purpose of weighing calmly the advantages of peace against the contingent gain of further bloodshed and the protraction of so calamitous a war." Napoleon egged on the British.

Learning of the danger, Seward had Charles Francis Adams warn that an offer of mediation would not only be resented but would be considered a declaration of war. Palmerston then pulled back, writing, "we must continue merely to be lookers-on till the war shall have taken a more decided turn." The cabinet agreed. In mid-November the plan was shelved, nominally on grounds of timing, although, because Southern armies never again gained significant victories, no one later tried to dust it off. The move had never been, especially for Gladstone, pro-Southern, but rather an effort to get the North to accept facts. Still, its implementation would have produced a confrontation of incalculable proportions.

During the last major confrontation of the war, as in the *Trent* and mediation crises, Palmerston's ministry was less hostile than Americans believed. Under international and domestic law, British firms could sell arms to the belligerents. Both North and South took advantage of this, to the great benefit of British industry. Ships were a more difficult problem. The Foreign Enlistment Act of 1819, which drew heavily on the American code, allowed shipbuilding for belligerents only as long as the ships were not armed. English yards built or outfitted the *Alabama* and other vessels that, though designed for war, only took on guns after they left British ports to begin careers as Confederate commerce raiders. British courts construed the law very narrowly, and even when Adams's complaints sank home, Russell and his colleagues could not at first find a solution to the problem. When they did try to move, they were blocked by misfortune: The Queen's Advocate carried key documents off to an insane asylum when he suffered a breakdown. Thus the *Alabama* escaped from Liverpool in July 1862 "just whiskers ahead of a detention order issued by royal officials at Whitehall."[32] Before it was sunk by a Northern warship two years later, it captured or destroyed 58 ships; another raider, the *Florida,* seized 38.

The problem became more pressing in 1863 as the so-called Laird Rams neared completion. These two ships were obviously warships, clearly designed to pierce wooden-hulled ships enforcing the blockade, even if they were to be unarmed when leaving British ports, and Confederate crews were already in Liverpool. Adams bombarded the Foreign Office with protests, finally writing Russell, "It is superfluous in me to point out to your Lordship that this is war." It was indeed superfluous, for Russell had already decided to prevent the rams' departure. Still unable to find evidence of Confederate ownership he was sure the courts would accept, in October Russell and his colleagues invoked an old law allowing the government to buy ships it said were needed for national defense, although the Admiralty actually considered them worthless. The crisis ended by this decision proved to be the last. After the autumn of 1863 the war became, in Henry Adams's phrase, "a bore and a nuisance," no longer a matter of serious British concern.

Neither the American people nor, less excusably, those whose job it was to understand British policy gave Palmerston's ministry any credit for its behavior during the Civil War. They especially resented the proclamation of neutrality and British policy during the *Trent* affair, when they had "yielded to a threat, but disliked being told so, and regarded the threat itself as evidence of British ill-will."[33] They concluded not that London's chief concern had been to minimize present and future trouble but that it had been motivated by pro-Confederate feelings. This false conclusion became for many years a substantive factor in Anglo-American relations. Neither people recognized that, having avoided deeper difficulty during the Civil War, their relations had been put on the road to that great rapprochement which was to be one of the most significant developments in international politics after 1895.

32 Merli, *Great Britain and the Confederate Navy,* 92.
33 Adams, *Great Britain and the American Civil War,* 1:237.

On April 9, 1865, General Lee surrendered. On the seventeenth, Lincoln and his cabinet decided to lift the blockade, though scattered resistance continued in the South. That evening he went to the theater, where an assassin shot him. Within days, thousands of letters of condolence and remorse reached Washington. The Department of State later published a 700-page compilation of letters and editorials from foreign countries, more than forty in all. Among them was a letter from Queen Victoria to Mary Lincoln, from "widow" to "widow," written at the cabinet's suggestion.

9. The Republican Empire

In 1866, an English magazine, the *Spectator,* grudgingly observed, "Nobody doubts any more that the United States is a power of the first class, a nation which it is very dangerous to offend and almost impossible to attack." In the immediate sense, this observation reflected the confirmation of nationhood through Union success in the Civil War. In larger perspective, it reflected an amazing growth of power since the republic's birth ninety years earlier, little more than the lifetime of John Quincy Adams's generation.

At the end of the Civil War, the nation's population exceeded 35 million; Britain and France had fewer people. Although still far behind Great Britain, America's industrial output nearly equaled that of France and exceeded that of other countries. American agriculture was the world's most productive. Territory had swelled from fewer than a million square miles in 1783 to exceed 3 million square miles. The arbitrament of war had confirmed the viability of republican government.

The success of the United States owed much to achievements – some earned, some not – in relations with foreign powers. Otto von Bismarck, Germany's "Iron Chancellor," is supposed to have said that God seemed to have a special place in his heart for drunkards, idiots, and Americans. Good fortune did seem to fall on the young Republic, perhaps most notably in its escape from the consequences of mismanagement by Jefferson and Madison, but also in such things as the fortuitous dominance over British policy by Shelburne and Aberdeen at critical times.

But luck, a cynic may claim, tends to fall upon those who already have an edge. In Samuel Flagg Bemis's familiar apothegm, "Europe's distress" was often America's "advantage."[1] The success of the Amer-

---

1 Samuel Flagg Bemis, *Pinckney's Treaty* (Baltimore, 1926), iii.

ican Revolution, from the European point of view a sideshow in a desperate struggle for power, and the peaceful acquisition of Louisiana are perhaps the best examples. Of course, Europe's distresses could also prove contagious, as they did in 1812, but even then the Americans were able to survive in large part because Britain's resources were at full stretch in the war against Napoleon. And Bemis's word, "distress," does not fully encompass those European factors that helped the Americans. Distractions were enough. Simmering rivalries nearer to home, well short of war, made London, in particular, but other capitals as well, wary of adding controversy with the United States. In differing ways, but persistently, European factors were major contributors to American success.

The Americans were also fortunate, whether through God's favor or not, that they were often pushing on half-open or at least insecurely locked doors. They did not have to mobilize large armies of conquest to ensure their expansion, nor did they require standing armies to defend their empire. For the war against Mexico they mobilized forces one-sixteenth the size of those used by the North alone in the civil conflict fifteen years later. Peacetime armed forces never exceeded twenty thousand before the 1840s, and they were fewer than thirty thousand when the Civil War began. The Spanish in Florida, the Mexicans, the Indians – all were too weak to slam shut the door on housebreakers, and it did not take a military genius of Napoleon's caliber to understand that Louisiana was indefensible in 1803.

Above all, however, the Americans owed their success to their own drive and ambition. Sometimes their methods were brutal. Sometimes their leaders miscalculated. Some of them, particularly in the years before the Treaty of Ghent, worried like other citizens about the future of the republican experiment. But all embodied or at least were driven by the republican nationalism of their fellow citizens. Young America may not have been in all ways attractive, besmirched as the nation was by slavery, by nativism, by egotism and arrogance. Certainly European conservatives did not find it so, as may be seen in such matters as their reaction to the Monroe Doctrine and their attitudes during the Civil War. "Lust of wealth, and trust in it; vulgar faith in magnitude and multitude, instead of nobleness; perpetual self-contemplation in passionate vanity" – so John Ruskin, a major figure in mid-Victorian letters, assessed the United States in 1863, during the trial of republicanism. Ruskin's venom aside, these qualities – economic individualism, a belief in popular sovereignty, and conviction of superiority to other peoples – had made the nation what it was. They had provided policy with its quenchless vigor.

"American exceptionalism" and "the American consensus," two concepts once used as interpretive guideposts by historians, have come under heavy attack in recent years. The exceptionalist interpretation stresses the view that the United States is unique, that its history is to a large degree not comparable with that of other nations. The not unrelated consensus view maintains that, in contrast to others, the American people overwhelmingly, nearly unanimously, agree on the fundamentals of government and policy. Both of these, many now argue, reflect the smug conservatism of the years in which they gained prominence. To claim that America has always been governed by consensus suggests a national homogeneity belied by, among other things, the Civil War, and to stress American uniqueness raises the temptation to assert American superiority.

For the diplomatic historian, however, the concept of consensus, and that of exceptionalism, still have usefulness if properly and cautiously applied. The struggles between Federalists and Republicans early in the nation's history and, some decades later, the opposed views of Democrats and Whigs regarding the tactics and timing of expansion are at the heart of the record of American diplomacy. Such differences must not be allowed to obscure the consensus on national aims shared by policymakers and, when they turned their attention to foreign policy, the people. All Americans wanted and expected the nation to expand, territorially and commercially. All wanted to stay aloof from European politics. All believed in republicanism – as they defined it – and considered America a "beacon of liberty" for the world. At this level, a consensus existed.

No nations are clones of one another, yet America, certainly nineteenth-century America, may properly be described as truly "exceptional." To make such a claim is not to assert America's superiority, moral or otherwise, only to underline the distinctiveness of its beliefs, its opportunities, and its view of its own place in the world. We may leave to the founders and builders of the republican empire the claim that American uniqueness and American superiority were synonymous, but we must recognize that their conviction – their arrogance, perhaps – helped to drive national policy. In 1785, continuing the outpouring of nationalistic poetry he had begun at Yale, Timothy Dwight predicted the future:

> Here Empire's last, and brightest throne shall rise;
> And Peace and Right, and Freedom, greet the skies.

So believed his countrymen, and, so believing, by 1865 they had created a republican empire.

Bibliographic Essay

What historians write and teach is a hopefully constructive synthesis of creative thought, labor in the primary sources, and absorption of and reaction to the work of others. The following comments direct interested readers to a selection of the historical literature that has shaped *The Creation of a Republican Empire*. For a comprehensive list of writings on American diplomacy, though limited to works published before 1981, see Richard Dean Burns, ed., *Guide to American Foreign Policy Since 1700* (Santa Barbara, Calif., 1983).

1. The Canvas and the Prism

John Quincy Adams's career is traced in Samuel Flagg Bemis's magisterial biography *John Quincy Adams and the Foundations of American Foreign Policy* (New York, 1949) and *John Quincy Adams and the Union* (New York, 1956), based very largely on Adams's papers, which Bemis was the first to use. Bemis, whose own physical and intellectual affinity with Adams was often noted, treats his subject sympathetically.

For the development of American views of foreign affairs before independence, emphasizing their imperialist but antimercantilist nature, Max Savelle, *The Origins of American Diplomacy* (New York, 1967), is the key work.

Although American diplomatic historians, like those laboring in other fields, often stress particular themes – economic forces, expansionism, and so forth – few efforts have been made to paint the whole "canvas." Dexter Perkins, *The American Approach to Foreign Policy* (Cambridge, Mass., 1952), though a reflection of its times, is a useful exception. Consequently, even more than most chapters in this book, this one rests upon a wide range of writings, many not specifically directed to problems of diplomatic history.

234

Cultural and ideological forces have drawn the attention of a number of scholars. An impressive recent work is Michael H. Hunt, *Ideology and U.S. Foreign Policy* (New Haven, 1987). Akira Iriye has stressed "Culture and Power: International Relations as Intercultural History," *Diplomatic History* 3 (1979): 115–128, and episodes are examined in Morrell Heald and Lawrence S. Kaplan, *Culture and Diplomacy* (Westport, Conn., 1977). Other useful studies include Merle Curti, *The Roots of American Loyalty* (New York, 1946); David M. Potter, *People of Plenty* (Chicago, 1954); Yehoshua Arieli, *Individualism and Nationalism in American Ideology* (Cambridge, Mass., 1964); Ernest Lee Tuveson, *Redeemer Nation* (Chicago, 1968); and Cushing Strout, *The American Image of the Old World* (New York, 1963). For the most part, as these references suggest, one draws insights and evidence from historical studies of diplomacy in which culture and ideology are not central themes or from studies of culture and ideology that pay little attention to foreign relations.

On the theme of republicanism, see the references for Chapter 4.

For the views of the two great foreign commentators on America, see Alexis de Tocqueville, *Democracy in America,* first published in 1835 and 1840, and James Bryce, *The American Commonwealth,* published in 1888. Both have since appeared in many editions.

2. The Birth of American Diplomacy

Foreign relations during the Revolution are surveyed in Samuel Flagg Bemis, *The Diplomacy of the American Revolution* (New York, 1935; rev. ed., Bloomington, Ind., 1957), and a new study, Jonathan R. Dull, *A Diplomatic History of the American Revolution* (New Haven, 1985). Dull avoids the extreme nationalism of Bemis's work, and he also stresses that the war in America was only a part – a relatively small one, he maintains – of a larger conflict between European states. This latter point is also made abundantly clear in Orville T. Murphy, *Charles Gravier, Comte de Vergennes* (Albany, 1982). Still, Bemis's book remains a classic. The first chapters of Lawrence S. Kaplan, *Colonies into Nation* (New York, 1972), are also useful here, and Kaplan has edited a fine selection of essays on

Revolutionary diplomacy, *The American Revolution and "A Candid World"* (Kent, Ohio, 1977).

In *To the Farewell Address* (Princeton, 1961), Felix Gilbert argues that American diplomacy, with its emphasis on trade and internationalism, broke sharply with contemporary European practices. James H. Hutson, "Intellectual Foundations of Early American Diplomacy," *Diplomatic History* 1 (1977): 1–19, takes Gilbert vigorously to task, and Hutson's highly critical biographical work, *John Adams and the Diplomacy of the American Revolution* (Lexington, Ky., 1980), among other things repeats this argument. Hutson tends to ignore the qualifications in Gilbert's work, but his basic argument is not unjustified.

Jonathan R. Dull, *The French Navy and American Independence* (Princeton, 1975), is by far the best treatment of the calculations that led France to enter the war in 1778. William C. Stinchcombe, *The American Revolution and the French Alliance* (Syracuse, 1969), similarly stands alone in its discussion, from an American vantage point, of how the alliance actually worked.

The most comprehensive treatment of the war-ending negotiations at Paris is Richard B. Morris, *The Peacemakers* (New York, 1965), based on extraordinarily broad research. Morris's treatment is not unmarked by xenophobia, however, and more dispassionate accounts of aspects of the negotiations may be found in Ronald Hoffman and Peter J. Albert, eds., *Peace and the Peacemakers* (Charlottesville, Va., 1986). On Franklin, see Gerald Stourzh, *Benjamin Franklin and American Foreign Policy* (Chicago, 1954). Vincent T. Harlow, *The Founding of the Second British Empire,* vol. 1 (London, 1952), traces the policy of Britain, especially of Lord Shelburne, during the negotiations; at present a necessary reliance, it deserves to be replaced. H. M. Scott, *British Foreign Policy in the Age of the American Revolution* (Oxford, 1990), although saying remarkably little about Anglo-American relations, provides a fine picture of Britain's European diplomacy and offers insights into Shelburne.

Kossuth's visit is well described in Donald S. Spencer, *Louis Kossuth and Young America* (Columbia, Mo., 1977).

3. The Constitution

Frederick W. Marks III, *Independence on Trial* (Baton Rouge, 1973), recounts the diplomatic problems of the 1780s and the work of the Constitutional Convention, stressing the importance of the former in the campaign for a new government. In *Aftermath of Revolution* (Dallas, 1969), Charles R. Ritcheson describes in detail American problems with Britain, and in *Struggle for the American Mediterranean* (Athens, Ga., 1976), Lester D. Langley examines the piracy problem.

Recent disputes have stimulated study of the Founding Fathers' intentions regarding the control of foreign policy. See, for example, Walter LaFeber, "The Constitution and United States Foreign Policy," *Journal of American History* 74 (1987–8): 693–717; Leonard W. Levy, *Original Intent and the Framers' Constitution* (New York, 1988); and Charles A. Lofgren, *Government from Reflection and Choice* (New York, 1986).

The treaty-making power is considered in Arthur Bestor, "Respective Roles of Senate and President in the Making and Abrogation of Treaties – the Original Intent of the Framers Historically Reviewed," *Washington Law Review* 55 (1979): 4–135, and Jack N. Rakove, "Solving a Constitutional Puzzle: The Treatymaking Clause as a Case Study," *Perspectives in American History,* n.s., 1 (1984): 233–81. W. Stull Holt, *Treaties Defeated by the Senate* (Baltimore, 1933), is a broader consideration of that body's role than the title suggests.

David Gray Adler, "The President's War-Making Power," in Thomas E. Cronin, ed., *Inventing the American Presidency* (Lawrence, Kan., 1989), 119–53, argues that the Founding Fathers' intentions have been subverted, a claim also made in Francis D. Wormuth and Edwin Firmage, *To Chain the Dogs of War* (Dallas, 1986). Broader treatments of the establishment and use of presidential authority include Abraham D. Sofaer, *War, Foreign Affairs and Constitutional Power: The Origins* (Cambridge, Mass., 1976), and Arthur M. Schlesinger, Jr., *The Imperial Presidency* (Boston, 1973).

4. Federalist Diplomacy

Literature on the theme of republicanism is vast and disputative. A useful introduction, though now somewhat dated, is Robert E. Shalhope, "Toward a Republican Synthesis," *William & Mary Quarterly,* 3 ser., 29 (1972): 49–80. Two especially useful works are Drew R. McCoy, *The Elusive Republic* (Chapel Hill, 1980), and Lance Banning, *The Jeffersonian Persuasion* (Ithaca, 1978). Patrice Higonnet explores the relationship between American and French republicanism in *Sister Republics* (Cambridge, Mass., 1988). See also David Brion Davis, "American Equality and Foreign Revolutions," *Journal of American History* 76 (1988–9): 729–52.

Frank T. Reuter, *Trials and Triumphs* (Fort Worth, Tex., 1983), describes developments during the Washington administrations. Harry Ammon recounts one of the "trials" in *The Genet Mission* (New York, 1973), and Albert H. Bowman organizes a discussion of diplomacy in these years around his theme, *The Struggle for Neutrality* (Knoxville, 1974).

Samuel Flagg Bemis, *Jay's Treaty,* 2d ed. (New Haven, 1962), first published in 1923 and long standard, now shares place with Jerald A. Combs, *The Jay Treaty* (Berkeley, 1970). See also the closing chapters of Ritcheson, *Aftermath of Revolution* (Dallas, 1969). Bradford Perkins, *The First Rapprochement* (Philadelphia, 1955), picks up the story of Anglo-American relations at 1795 and carries it beyond the end of the Federalist era, to 1805.

Alexander DeConde's *Entangling Alliance* (Durham, N.C., 1958) and *The Quasi-War* (New York, 1966) are the indispensable works on relations with France. Samuel Flagg Bemis, *Pinckney's Treaty* (Baltimore, 1926), is the standard authority.

Julian P. Boyd, *Number 7* (Princeton, 1964), explores Hamilton's "treachery."

5. Jefferson and Madison

Jefferson's presidency is traced in great detail in two volumes of Dumas Malone's very sympathetic biography, *Jefferson the President, First Term* (Boston, 1970) and *Jefferson the President, Second Term* (Boston, 1974). More analytic treatments include Robert M. Johnstone, *Jefferson and the Presidency* (Ithaca, 1978); Burton Spivak, *Jefferson's English Crisis* (Charlottesville, Va., 1979); and Lawrence S. Kaplan, *Entangling Alliances with None* (Kent, Ohio, 1987), the last-named also including essays on other subjects. Irving Brant, *James Madison, Secretary of State* (Indianapolis, 1953) and *James Madison, the President* (Indianapolis, 1956), volumes similar to Malone's, are even more annalistic and pietistic.

Alexander DeConde, *This Affair of Louisiana* (New York, 1976), is now the standard treatment, but for a vigorous defense of Jefferson, see Robert W. Tucker and David C. Hendrickson, *Empire of Liberty* (New York, 1990). For later developments in Franco-American relations, see Clifford L. Egan, *Neither Peace Nor War* (Baton Rouge, 1983), a work that fills a long-apparent void.

Bradford Perkins, *Prologue to War* (Berkeley, 1961), very critical of the Republican leaders, examines Anglo-American relations from 1805 to 1812. Among other things, Perkins challenges the argument that expansionism fueled the drive for war, a thesis most forcefully expressed in Julius W. Pratt, *Expansionists of 1812* (New York, 1925). Also critical of Pratt's argument are J. C. A. Stagg, *Mr. Madison's War* (Princeton, 1983), and Reginald C. Stuart, *United States Expansionism and British North America* (Chapel Hill, 1988).

Roger H. Brown, *The Republic in Peril* (New York, 1964), and Steven Watts, *The Republic Reborn* (Baltimore, 1987), link the coming of the war to the republican theme. The war Congress is perhaps best treated in Ronald L. Hatzenbuehler and Robert L. Ivie, *Congress Declares War* (Kent, Ohio, 1983).

The war and its management are discussed in Stagg, *Mr. Madison's War,* mentioned previously, and Donald R. Hickey, *The War of 1812* (Urbana, Ill., 1989). Bradford Perkins, *Castlereagh and Adams* (Berkeley, 1964), contains the only extended modern treatment of the negotiations at Ghent.

6. To the Monroe Doctrine

Harry Ammon, *James Monroe* (New York, 1971), is a highly readable, sensitive biography. For his chief lieutenant, the principal guide is Bemis, *John Quincy Adams and the Foundations of American Foreign Policy*, mentioned previously.

Although there has been substantial recent scholarship on aspects of the problems with which they deal, Philip C. Brooks, *Diplomacy and the Borderlands* (Berkeley, 1939) (on the Adams-Onís Treaty), Charles C. Griffin, *The United States and the Disruption of the Spanish Empire* (New York, 1937), and Arthur Preston Whitaker, *The United States and the Independence of Latin America* (Baltimore, 1941), continue to be the best introductions to their respective subjects. However, new insights are presented in John A. Johnson, *A Hemisphere Apart* (Baltimore, 1990).

Dexter Perkins, *The Monroe Doctrine, 1823–1826* (Cambridge, Mass., 1927), likewise remains the first reliance, although many more general works explore the genesis of the message of 1823. Ernest R. May, *The Making of the Monroe Doctrine* (Cambridge, Mass., 1975), opens up new lines of thought, stressing the importance of domestic political calculations. For an unspoken corollary to the doctrine, see John A. Logan, *No Transfer: An American Security Principle* (New Haven, 1961).

7. Manifest Destiny

The most recent treatment of its subject is Paul H. Bergeron, *The Presidency of James K. Polk* (Lawrence, Kan., 1987), generally quite sympathetic. Charles Sellers, *James K. Polk: Continentalist* (Princeton, 1966), is an able, thorough work, but Sellers's treatment does not extend beyond the summer of 1846. The president's revival of the Monroe Doctrine is explored in Frederick Merk, *The Monroe Doctrine and American Expansionism* (New York, 1966).

The expansionism of the 1840s is most comprehensively treated in David M. Pletcher, *The Diplomacy of Annexation* (Columbia, Mo., 1973), a fine work. The ideology of the movement is the subject of sarcastic treatment in Albert K. Weinberg, *Manifest Destiny* (1935; repr., Chicago, 1963), and more thoughtful consideration in Thomas R. Hietala, *Manifest Design* (Ithaca, 1985), a work that also examines political developments. Very hostile to Manifest Destiny is Frederick Merk, *Manifest Destiny and Mission in American History*

(New York, 1963). Frederick Merk, *Slavery and the Annexation of Texas* (New York, 1972), and Reginald Horsman, *Race and Manifest Destiny* (Cambridge, Mass., 1981), explore the impact of the slavery issue.

Norman Graebner, *Empire on the Pacific* (New York, 1955), argues that ports, more than territory, were the objectives of at least some Americans. Shomer S. Zwelling, *Expansion and Imperialism* (Chicago, 1970), is an explicit challenge to that idea, stronger on logic than evidence.

John H. Schroeder, *Mr. Polk's War* (Madison, 1973), is a fine, brisk treatment. Also helpful is Robert W. Johannsen, *To the Halls of the Montezumas* (New York, 1985).

The opposition of Calhoun and his allies to large-scale territorial expansion is the subject of Ernest McPherson Lander, Jr., *Reluctant Imperialists* (Baton Rouge, 1980). Southern aggressiveness in the 1850s is explored in Robert E. May, *The Southern Dream of a Caribbean Empire* (Baton Rouge, 1973), and Charles H. Brown, *Agents of Manifest Destiny* (Chapel Hill, 1980).

Howard I. Kushner, *Conflict on the Northwest Coast* (Westport, Conn., 1975), and Nikolai N. Bolkhovitinov, *Russian-American Relations and the Sale of Alaska* (in Russian; Moscow, 1990), describe the last American continental expansion.

8. Britain, Canada, and the United States

The limits of governmental support for overseas commerce are made clear in recent studies: Kinley J. Brauer, "Economics and the Diplomacy of American Expansion," in William H. Becker and Samuel F. Wells, eds., *Economics and World Power* (New York, 1984), 55–118; Kinley J. Brauer, "The United States and British Imperial Expansion, 1815–1860," *Diplomatic History* 12 (1988): 19–37; John H. Schroeder, *Shaping a Maritime Empire* (Westport, Conn., 1985); and, on China, Michael H. Hunt, *The Making of a Special Relationship* (New York, 1983). The West Indian settlement and the quarrel over claims against France are recounted in John M. Belohlavek, *"Let the Eagle Soar"* (Lincoln, Neb., 1985).

For Anglo-American relations during the years from the Treaty of

Ghent to 1825, see Bradford Perkins, *Castlereagh and Adams* (Berkeley, 1964).

England's military weakness is the theme of Kenneth Bourne, *Britain and the Balance of Power in North America* (Berkeley, 1967), and also made evident in Reginald C. Stuart, *United States Expansionism and British North America* (Chapel Hill, 1988), which however emphasizes the feebleness of American territorial ambition. Also useful is Donald F. Warner, *The Idea of Continental Union* (Lexington, Ky., 1960).

Howard Jones, *To the Webster-Ashburton Treaty* (Chapel Hill, 1977), describes that important settlement, and Wilbur Devereux Jones, *The American Problem in British Diplomacy* (Athens, Ga., 1974), begins with the negotiations of 1842 and carries the story forward to 1861. Martin Crawford, *The Anglo-American Crisis of the Mid-Nineteenth Century* (Athens, Ga., 1987), uses the *Times* of London as a vehicle to explore British attitudes toward the United States.

Frederick Merk, *The Oregon Question* (Cambridge, Mass., 1967), brings together a lifetime of work on the subject. But see, also, the books by Bergeron, Graebner, Pletcher, and Sellers mentioned earlier.

Civil War diplomacy has attracted a great deal of scholarly attention. D. P. Crook, *The North, the South, and the Powers* (New York, 1974), is a fine overview of the subject. In *The United States and France: Civil War Diplomacy* (Philadelphia, 1970), Lynn M. Case and Warren F. Spencer seek to show, on the basis of massive research, that the French role was critical.

Most historians, however, continue to follow along the path blazed by Ephraim Douglass Adams, *Great Britain and the American Civil War,* 2 vols. (New York, 1925), making Britain by far the more important factor. Adams's is one of those remarkable works that have stood the test of time, not impervious to attack but essentially above it. Brian Jenkins, *Britain and the War for the Union,* 2 vols. (Montreal, 1974–80), for example, is self-consciously revisionist, but Jenkins's most convincing arguments do not seriously undermine Adams's predominance. Adams's basic conclusions are underscored in three capable works: Gordon H. Warren, *Fountain of*

Discontent (Boston, 1981), on the *Trent* affair; Stuart L. Bernath, *Squall Across the Atlantic* (Berkeley, 1970), concerning maritime problems; and Frank J. Merli, *Great Britain and the Confederate Navy* (Bloomington, Ind., 1970), a work much broader than its title.

Glyndon G. Van Deusen, *William Henry Seward* (New York, 1967), is authoritative. Norman B. Ferris, *Desperate Diplomacy* (Knoxville, 1976), is an intriguing account of Seward's apparent eccentricities during the first year of the Civil War. Frank Lawrence Owsley, *King Cotton Diplomacy* (Chicago, 1931), states the Southern position.

Index